INDIA'S RELATIONS
with
RUSSIA AND CHINA

INDIA'S RELATIONS with RUSSIA AND CHINA

By
M. Rasgotra
V. D. Chopra

GYAN

ISBN : 978-81-212-0559-7

Published, 2018

Published by

Gyan Publishing House
5, Ansari Road
Daryaganj, New Delhi-110002
Phone: 011-47034999, 9811692060
www.gyanbooks.com
E-mail: books@gyanbooks.com

GYAN

Printed at: G. Print Process, Delhi.

Contents

List of Contributors

M. RASGOTRA	Chairman, International Institute of Asia-Pacific Studies, Vice-Chairman, Rajiv Gandhi Foundation and Former Foreign Secretary of India.
V.D. CHOPRA	Vice-Chairman, International Institute of Asia-Pacific Studies, specialises in politics and economy of the Asia-Pacific Region.
T.N. KAUL	Former Secretary, General Ministry of External Affairs of India, a leading expert on international affairs, particularly of Russia and China and a well-known author.
DEVENDRA KAUSHIK	Professor, Centre for Soviet Area and East European Studies, Jawaharlal Nehru University and an outstanding expert on Central Asian Republics.
P.M. GREGORIOS	He was a leading expert on international affairs and fighter for peace, anti-nuclear movements and principal Orthodox Theological Seminary.
R.R. SHARMA	Vice-Chancellor, Jammu University (Jammu & Kashmir), Former Professor of Russian, East European Studies, School of International Studies, Jawaharlal Nehru University.
S.K. JHA	He is an Associate Professor of the Centre for Soviet and East European Studies, School of International Studies, Jawaharlal Nehru University, New Delhi. He specialises in political processes and foreign policies of Russia and East European countries.

O.N. MEHROTRA	He is a Research Associate of Institute of Defence Studies and Analyses, New Delhi. An outstanding expert on international affairs with main focus on the erstwhile USSR.
RAVI M. BAKAYA	He taught Russian at the IIT Bombay and in Jawaharlal Nehru University. Apart from writing books and articles on Russian languages, he has translated many books and written widely on Soviet and Russian affairs. He is a close watcher of the developments in Russia.
C.V. RANGANATHAN	Retired from the Indian Foreign Service in 1993. His last few posts were in Hong Kong, Addis Ababa, Moscow, Beijing and Paris. He is now a consultant to business, advising on South-East and East Asia.
SUJIT DUTTA	He is a Senior Fellow at the Institute for Defence Studies and Analyses and a leading expert on China.
SHRI PRAKASH	Director, Academy of Third World Studies, Jamia Millia Islamia. He is one of the leading experts on economic history and economic development.
ARVIND VYAS	He teaches economics in School of International Studies, Jawaharlal Nehru University. He is a specialist on Planning and now working on problems of transformation from state socialism to market economy.
R.L. VARSHNEY	Former deputy director general Indian Institute of Foreign Trade. At present he is a visiting professor to various management institutions.
GULJIT K. ARORA	He is a leading economist and teaches in Zakir Hussain College, University of Delhi.

सत्यमेव जयते

विदेश मंत्री, भारत

MINISTER OF EXTERNAL AFFAIRS, INDIA

Foreword

India enjoys a relationship of traditional friendship with Russia based on continuity, trust and confidence. There is recognition in both countries of the importance of good relations between India and Russia. This recognition cuts across the political spectrums in both countries and is not subject to political vicissitudes.

Transitional difficulties in Indo-Russian relations in the immediate post-Cold War phase are now well behind us. Our relations are multifaceted and encompass different sectors including political consultations in areas of mutual interest, trade and economy, science and technology, culture, defence and core sectors including power, coal, oil and metallurgy. The momentum of bilateral interaction has been provided constant sustenance through the tradition of regular and intensive high level exchanges.

There is recognition in both countries of the strategic dimension to our relations. We share similar perceptions on many international issues. New opportunities for further strengthening of our relations with Russia have arisen out of the changes taking place in both countries and those at the regional and international level. We look forward to ever closer and mutually beneficial cooperation in the years ahead.

China is India's largest neighbour. We have coexisted and interacted with China over centuries. We have had our share of ups and downs in our relationship. It is now time to view our relationship with China in the context of the new realities of a rapidly changing world. China has emerged as one of the most vibrant centres of economic growth in Asia. Having set ambitious goals for itself and having achieved rapid economic growth and development over the past decade and a half, it is poised to enter the ranks of the largest economies of the world. We in India, have also embarked on a very active programme of economic liberalisation, and we have also made considerable progress in the task of integrating our economy with that of the rest of the world. As the two largest developing countries in Asia, it stands to reason that India and China should seek to develop their relations in the future on a more secure foundation, with mutually beneficial economic cooperation as one of the main underpinnings.

In recent years India-China relations have acquired maturity and substance. While continuing to address outstanding issues including the boundary question, we have sought to expand mutually beneficial cooperation in various areas, including in the promotion of culture, expansion of economic, scientific and technological cooperation, protection of the environment, etc. India and China have a common interest in promoting cooperation in regional and international fora. The future of India-China relations will depend on how we resolve the outstanding issues and how we cooperate on issues of common concern.

The present volume covers a broad canvas of issues concerning India's relations with Russia and China after the end of the Cold War. I am confident that this book will be received well not only by experts and policy makers but also by the general reader interested in international affairs.

(I.K.Gujral)

The main merit of this study is that it has attempted to critically examine India's relations with Russia and China on the basis of concrete evidence as it emerged till the end of 1996. With the shifting of gravity of world power from Europe to the Asia-Pacific region and emergence of new economic and military power centres, marked improvement in the bilateral relations between India and Russia, India and China, and China and Russia cannot be wished away nor does it mean that relations of these three countries with the United States and Japan have no relevance. It is a complex process and its complexities need to be objectively assessed. This is precisely what has been attempted in this study and that too after frank and thorough discussions. This study, therefore, is yet another contribution by the International Institute of Asia-Pacific Studies to the theory of international relations. We hope both the Indian and foreign experts on international relations will critically examine the conclusions of this study.

We are grateful to the various scholars who have made their valuable contribution in this volume and that too without expecting any monetary compensation to cover their costs. We must also compliment the senior members of the staff of the Gyan Publishing House for their cooperation and the speed at which they have brought out this book. The publication of the book has been delayed for reasons beyond our control, though we have made this book up-to-date.

M. Rasgotra
V.D. Chopra

New Delhi
January 1, 1997

Preface

In the post cold war period significant geopolitical, geostrategic and geoeconomic trends have begun to unfold themselves. These changes encompass the entire societal and systematic structures of all the countries in this region. These changes in turn have begun to change the bilateral and multilateral relations of the countries in this region. Though at the present stage with the collapse of bipolar world, a multipolar world has yet to emerge, the old period of domination by most powerful states is coming to an end because new powerful states, militarily and economically have begun to emerge. That being the situation, the bilateral and multilateral relations among the various states, big and small are in a process of transition. The old parameters of evaluating these relations within the framework of 'superpower' rivalry have become irrelevant. It is premature to generalise the models of bilateral and multilateral relations of the various states. All the states are engaged in restructuring their relations with other states on the basis of their own interests and experience. In this sense a new concept of building relations on the basis of 'balance of interests' and 'commonality of perception' has begun to emerge. Therefore, no nation can impose its concept of the new world order and its model of restructuring of social, economic and political models on other countries.

It is in the context of this complex scenario, that India's relations with Russia and China are being restructured. This is the broad conclusion which emerged at a two-day national seminar organised by the International Institute of Asia-Pacific Studies. The various studies included in this volume graphically illustrate this point.

India-Russia-China: Changing Equations

V.D. Chopra

India's relations both with Russia and China have begun to unfold a new pattern in more than one sense. This clearly stands out in the various studies compiled in this book. At the first instance Indo-Russian relations are undergoing certain basic changes and they no longer stand on the same footing as they were before the disintegration of the Soviet Union. India-China relations of the 50s had a different flavour. These relations are now developing in a zig-zag manner, primarily because of the internal and external policies of both these countries are characterised by new shifts and turns. In a bipolar world for instance, the developing countries, India in particular were considered to be the 'natural allies' by the former Soviet Union. That premises no longer holds good. Russia's policy after the disintegration of the Soviet Union took a marked pro-Western turn. The Soviet Union's policy towards third world countries came under heavy fire by the outstanding Russian scholars, including by some of those who at one stage were strong exponents of theory of 'natural allies'. However, in the recent past both due to internal and external compulsions, Russia's policy towards third world countries with India especially has begun to show an upward trend. India-China relations are also undergoing important changes as has been pointed out by Mr. C.V. Ranganathan, former Ambassador to China and Mr. Sujit Dutta, two leading experts on China.

A critical examination of these new trends in India-Russia and

India-China relations should not be made in isolation from the shifts which are taking place in the international developments, in the Asia and the Pacific region in particular. The centre of gravity of world power is shifting steadily but inexorably from Europe to the Asia-Pacific. Four countries (USA, China, Japan and Russia) out of possibly about six (plus the European Union or Germany and France) current major global powers are located here. Out of seven nations or state systems that may emerge as major players in the world by the year 2020, six are likely to be from this region (USA, China, Japan, Russia, ASEAN or South-East Asia and India and the EU).

The rise of the Asia-Pacific is presently measured mainly in economic terms, in which East Asia has indeed been transformed dramatically. Gross Domestic Product (GDP) growth rates here are on an average already twice that of other regions, as shown in the following Table. By all reckoning this trend is likely to continue for at least a decade and more. At this rate, by early in the next century quite probably five of the six largest economies in the world may be in the wider Asia-Pacific region (Greater China, USA, Japan, ASEAN and India, excluding the EU).[1]

GDP Growth Rates

(in percentages)

Region	*1989*	*1990*	*1991*	*1992*	*1993*
Asia-Pacific	5.3	3.2	2.7	3.3	3.8
Asia-Pacific excluding USA and Japan	5.8	4.5	3.9	4.9	5.8
EU	3.5	3.0	0.7	1.0	-0.3
India	5.6	4.9	0.9	4.3	4.3 (Apr. to Mar.)
World	3.4	2.2	0.7	1.8	2.3

This study conceals more than what it reveals. Nevertheless, one thing is certain that three countries of this region with their area, natural resources, manpower and potentialities of economic growth will mould the future global economic structures in a significant manner. To say this does not mean that one should ignore the economy of Japan and the United States at the present stage. Let us look at the problem from another angle.

China in another 15 years could become the largest economy in Asia replacing Japan, according to a study by Birla Economic Research Foundation (BERF). China's real GDP growth rates since 1990 exceeds those of other Asian countries like Singapore, Malaysia, Thailand and South Korea, and are much higher than that of industrial countries. As compared to India, China has a consistently high rate of domestic saving supplemented by substantial inflows of foreign direct investment funds which together enable it relatively high levels of investment especially in infrastructure and industry, the study points out.

A notable feature of China's economy has been its external account strength with a steady and substantial build up of foreign exchange reserves to a level nearly 90 billion US dollars that is five times that of India.

The study notes how a nation that is India possessing the second largest pool of talent in the world next to the United States remains so poor.[2]

Economic Potential

As far as Russia is concerned, compared to other countries of the world is exceptionally rich in mineral resources. Even by the most conservative projected figures, it has 13 per cent of the planet's oil reserves, 35 per cent of gas and 12 per cent of coal. Equally considerable is its share of iron ores, non-ferrous and rare metals, i.e., gold, platinum and diamond. Indeed Russia today, produces annually not less than 330-350 million tons of oil and 650-700 billion cubic metres of gas. The world's most unique field with 305 billion tons of oil in commercial reserve, today is in a critical state. Above all, Russian technical cadres are highly skilled and match in their creative work with the most industrialised countries of the world, particularly in space, engineering, etc.

This economic growth of China, its weightage in the world economy after the unification of Hong Kong and possibly of Taiwan at a later stage, the economic potential of India and Russia inevitably lead one to the conclusion that the focus of the world economy in the next century will shift to these three countries—China, India and

Russia. But this alone does not explain the whole situation for a critical examination of the relations among these three countries.

Some time early in the 21st century, on a Friday afternoon after the stock market has closed, the US Department of Commerce will announce the latest trade statistics. For the 100th month in a row, Japan, South Korea and China will all have sold out more goods to the United States than they have bought from it. To stop a run on the dollar and retain Asian capital needed to finance America's 500 billion deficit, the Federal Reserve Board will announce yet another hike in interest rates. A young, ambitious presidential candidate will blame the FRB for caving in to pressures from the Bank of Japan. All that Japan's financiers are interested in, he will charge, is the profit margins of institutions like Nippon Life—which hold so much American debt that they virtually own the US government.

However, not long ago, the idea that the world could look like this in the next century seemed unthinkable. Americans, protected for two centuries by vast oceans, enriched by natural resources and a risk taking spirit, have never taken easily to changes beyond their control. Vietnam drove home the bitter lesson that the United States was no longer a hegemonic, power, and the oil shocks of the 1970s showed its resources were not sufficient enough to insulate it from economic problems.

But during the recent past Americans are striving to roll back the clock and for a time they have succeeded in making the world believe that they had. The cold war did end by the victory of one side and in the defeat of the other. This has changed the balance of forces, which in turn is shaping the developments. The Asia-Pacific region is no exception to this.

Rise of Japan

As the 20th century draws to a close, the world is in the midst of a profound geopolitical shift. Moving to the force today for instance is a nation that just 50 years ago was extricated from the wreckage of war by its conqueror. Now Japan is arguably the world's most powerful economic factor ready to assume leadership in an era of rising Asian power, a period that experts have already dubbed as the

Pacific Century. "If things continue as they are now" predicts Richard Rosecrance, Professor of International Affairs at Cornell University, "it won't be much beyond 2010 before Japan becomes the leading power in world politics". Reinforcing the Asia-Pacific's rising economic influence till recently were the so-called 'four tigers' the newly industrialised countries (NIC's) of South Korea, Taiwan, Singapore and Hong Kong. And stirring ever more energetically after decades of economic idleness is China, perhaps a future superpower. India with its policy of economic liberalisation too is a carving out its place in the world. With Asia coming on so strong, says William Overholt, a Bankers Trust economist in Hong Kong, the United States in the next hundred years could "become a giant Australia". This assessment may look simplistic. Nevertheless, the economic indicators show that in the Asia-Pacific region basic changes in the processes of economic regeneration of economy have begun to shape the international economic relations, though all the tendencies have yet to surface and firm up.

While the Asia-Pacific region is rapidly expanding its global economic influence, the United States has gradually shifted its global interests from Western Europe to the East. The readjustment of US economic strategy will have far-reaching influence.

After World War II, the United States emboldened by its greatly increased economic and military strength declared that its interests spread over the whole globe. It then began to consolidate these interests by expanding its economic influence. US economic interests were focussed on Latin America and Canada from the early post-war years to the 1950s. In the 1960s Western Europe became the focuses of US economic activities. And since the mid-1970s the United States has gradually shifted its emphasis to Asia and the Pacific. Since then also great changes have taken place in US foreign trade patterns, capital export and sources of important raw materials.

Asia and the Pacific have become the largest market for US foreign trade. From the end of World War II to 1975, Western Europe had held that position. In 1970, for example, 31.5 per cent of US foreign trade was with Western Europe, and 26.1 per cent with Asia and the Pacific. But by 1982, 25.7 per cent of US trade was with

Western Europe, while its Asian and Pacific trade rose to 34.8 per cent.

US economic involvement with the Asia-Pacific is substantial and growing. The total trade with the region amounted to US dollars 434 billion in 1994 or 37 per cent of total US trade. This was more than double that with the European Union which was 17 per cent. US exports to the Asia-Pacific were US dollars 156 billion in the same year or 30 per cent of the total. This sustains some three million jobs at home.

This new thrust in the economic policy of the United States has to be examined in the context of recession in its economy and growing unemployment. Therefore, the huge market in the Asia-Pacific region particularly in these three countries has a direct bearing on the American economy. Let us not make any bones about it.

This shows that one billion Asian population, which perhaps will be a little less than the entire population of North America, South America and the European community today will have purchasing power, which will enable them to buy some household goods as colour televisions, refrigerators and motorbikes. Perhaps 400 million of these consumers, three times more than now will have disposable income at least equal to the rich-world average today. They will be spending money on houses, cars, enjoyment of holidays, health care and education. And if all this consumer spending is to take place, immense investment in infrastructure will be needed to make it possible to build power plants, roads and airports among other things. The rocket-like growth and absolute size of Asia's middle class should therefore create some of the biggest business and financial opportunities in history. This will have a direct bearing on the economics of the developed countries.

United States: Geoeconomic Interests

It is in this context that the present trend of increasing US investment in the Asia-Pacific region should be seen. The rate of US investment for instance is growing much faster in the Asia-Pacific region than in Europe. From 1975 to 1982 the gross volume of US direct private investment in the Asia-Pacific region rose from US dollars 5.95 billion to US dollars 28.5 billion, while the investment volume in Western Europe rose from US dollars 49.5 billion to US dollars 99.8 billion a far less dramatic increase. In 1982 the net volume of US investment in the Asia-Pacific region reached US dollars 1.32 billion, almost equal to the net investment in Western Europe and that is not including US Investment in China. US investors are clearly looking to the East.

One obvious reason is that Asian and Pacific countries have much of the raw materials the United States must import to feed its booming electronics and aeronautics industries. Of the 11 minerals the United States imported in large quantities in 1978, eight came from Asia and the Pacific. Titanium from the East accounted for 97 per cent of the gross volume of US titanium imports, alongwith 82 per cent of tin, 80 per cent of mica, 42 per cent of tantanium and 27 per cent of aluminium. The Asia-Pacific region also supplies the United States with 88 per cent of its imported natural rubber, 99 per cent of its palm oil and 95 per cent of its coconut oil. The US interests in oil rich Gulf area are too well known and need not be recaptulated. The US Interests in the Central Asian Republics have assumed a new dimension in the post-cold war period. War for Kuwait in 1991 and recent conflict with Iraq should be seen in this context.

Japan has long been the biggest trade partner of the United States in its growing business with the East. In recent years, the United States has also been strengthening its economic ties with members of the Association of South-East Asian Nations (ASEAN) and rapidly expanding its business with South Korea, Taiwan and Hong Kong. In fact, the shifting emphasis of US economic interests is far more economically, politically and strategically complex than just the presence of raw materials. The United States has become a major partner in Indian trade.

The Asia-Pacific region's economic boom is and enormous attraction to American monopoly corporations. Since the 1970s the unprecedented economic development of Asia-Pacific has increased its influence in the world economy. Japan led the way in 1971 when it emerged as the third economic power after the United States and the Soviet Union. From 1970 to 1980 the average annual increase of

Japan's Gross National Product (GNP) was 4.9 per cent compared with 3.3 per cent in other developed countries.

Take another example, Indo-Japanese economic relations have already undergone a basic change. Japanese investments in India grew from 50 million rupees in 1990 to a little over 4 billion rupees in 1994. Between 1991 and September 1995, Japan was the third largest investor in India on cumulative basis following the United States and United Kingdom.

These economic trends are the main driving force of the new alignment and realignment of forces, relationship, bilateral and multilateral relations among the various states in the Asia-Pacific region and thereof the bilateral relations between India and Russia and India and China. However, it will be naive to come to the conclusion that a new triangle of relationship among these three biggest nations, i.e., India, China and Russia, has already begun to emerge or is likely to take the shape of an alliance. At the same time, it goes without saying that relations among these three countries, have entered a new phase, though at the present stage the relations between Russia and China and India and Russia stand on a higher footing as compared to the relations between India and China. This aspect clearly stands out in the various studies compiled in this book.

Nearly five decades ago when India and later China became sovereign and independent states, its significance was perhaps realized neither in these two countries nor abroad. Out of the biggest colonial and semi-colonial possessions of the biggest empires of the time emerged two sovereign states. It marked that disintegration of the imperialist system and ushered a new era. In the course of the last five decades country after country in the continents of Asia and Africa threw off the shackles of imperialist bondage. Notwithstanding the fact that the erstwhile Soviet Union has disintegrated, the upward trend in the relations among these three countries is of far reaching significance for the global politics in general and of the Asia-Pacific in particular.

Strategically, today's United States and Japan, the two biggest economic powers are not World War Second's political powerhouses surrounded by weak links, including economically senile China and

India. China and India are not the countries of yesteryears, and other East Asian countries are all stronger than ever before, economically and otherwise.

The choice is with the United States and Japan. But China, India the Koreas and all other East and South-East Asian countries and Russia need to be united and ever vigilant.

In the context of the new changes in the Asia-Pacific region, especially the shifting geopolitical and economic power balance, it would be pertinent to give a look to the American policy in this region. The reality is that after the disintegration of the Soviet Union, the American stake in Asia has tremendously increased. There are obvious reasons for this including continuing geoeconomic importance of West Asia and the American thrust for US trade and investment relations with the countries of the region. In fact the American relations with the countries of this region should not be examined in the old framework of bipolar words. The American relations with the countries of the region are broadly speaking three dimensional—strategic, political and economic. The mix of these basic elements varies from country to country and region to region. Therefore, the American policy in this region has various layers. This is best illustrated by close study of certain countries.

In West Asia, the United States has been able to strike new security arrangements with several countries, such as Saudi Arabia, Kuwait, Bahrain, UAE and Oman in the aftermath of the defeat of Iraq in the Gulf War. In this area, the United States has become a dominant power though it again and again comes into confrontation with Iraq and has sharp contradictions with Iran.

As against this American relations with China and Japan represent a different model. While the US-Japanese strategic relations can no longer remain the same, the Chinese-US security ties have already begun to change. There are many speculations that the US-China relations would be marred by the issues, such as the alleged human rights violations in China and the arms sale policy of the Chinese government. The growing Chinese military power alongwith its rapid economic growth clearly explain why the so-called human rights issue has failed to come between the rising US-China economic ties.

Again US-Japan relations too are undergoing certain changes. Strategic distance between the United States and Japan is no longer a taboo in the strategic analysis community. The American and Japanese economic interest in this region has begun to clash. Today several Americans see Japan "in unfriendly terms—not as a key ally but as a country whose unfair trading practices threaten their economic welfare." As a response to this, now a new concept of "American-Japanese leadership" in the Asia-Pacific has been spelt out.

This shows that in the evolution of India-Russia and India-China relations and for that matter Chinese-Russian relations, American factor should not be ignored. Nevertheless during the last decade of the present century, American ambitions to establish its hegemony in the Asia-Pacific region is being challenged by China, India and Russia in varying degrees within the framework of new relationship which these countries are building with the United States in the post-cold war period. Therefore, in evaluating this trend both these aspects should be kept in the forefront to make an objective study.

"NATO expansion runs counter to Russia's interests and this statement reflects the agreement of Russian society, its Foreign Ministry and virtually all factions in the Russian Parliament. NATO expansion will complicate the geopolitical situation for Russia, which does not suit us militarily, as this implies the movement of the infrastructure of a powerful military alliance towards our borders. And this does not suit us psychologically; we find it difficult to accept this possibility".[3]

This candid statement by Russian Foreign Minister speaks for itself. This shows that even the present political dispensation in Russia has begun to evolve and independent policy in its national interests. This does not coincide with the assessment of the North Atlantic Treaty Organization (NATO) experts.

In the assessment of the American experts, Russia's "conversion to democracy is still marked by so many fits and starts: its actions in the Caucasus and Chechanya are so contrary to the commitments under the Geneva Conventions on human rights, which claim to a right to influence the policies and perhaps the independence what it calls the near abroad and to use force to protect some 20 billion

Russians of its Diaspora; uncertainties or the future direction of its foreign policy and, in particular, the announcement that it would not implement the reduction in conventional forces agreed as part of the CFE Treaty signed in Paris on 19th November, 1990, and further more, its nuclear dealing with their own. All these facts justify a different approach to resolving the problems in America's relations with Russia."[4]

Relations between China and the United States since the end of the cold war have been punctuated with one crisis after another. In May 1995, the United States granted Taiwan's Lee Teng-Hui a visa to visit the country, bringing the relationship to the brink of collapse. Aggravating the animosity, a number of prominent US politicians and media organisations are making a big fuss over a so-called 'China threat' and calling for the 'containment' of China.

From the end of World War Second until the early 1990s US global strategy was shaped around the concept of containment of the Soviet Union. After the drastic changes in the Soviet Union and Eastern Europe, however, that foundation ceased to exist. To fill the void, some Americans who are still nostalgic about the cold war now designate China as the arch rival of the United States and a target of containment, whether potent or patent.[5]

This is how China now looks at its relations with the United States. Taiwan has always been the most controversial issue influencing the course of China-US relations. Apart from Taiwan, Washington and Beijing have also repeatedly differed on a wide variety of issues from arms control to trade but none of these issues have been as sensitive as the issue of Taiwan's independence. Accordingly, when the United States decided to allow Lee Teng-Hui to visit New York, even in the face of repeated protests and warning from the Chinese leadership, these consequences were expected. What was probably not gauged correctly by Clinton's advisors was the possible response to this visit. The China-US relations had never plummeted to such a low ever since the United States decided to shift its recognition from Taipei to Beijing in 1979, not even following the June 1989 Tiananmen Square incident which is generally seen as having brought a sudden end to the flourishing China-US relationship.

This shows how both Russia and China will not compromise on the unity and integrity of their countries, Russia on the 'independence' of Chechnya and China on the unification of Taiwan.

In this context, it is pertinent to recall India's stand on the so-called right of self-determination for people of Jammu and Kashmir. American stand to blow up the developments in Punjab and Jammu and Kashmir are too well known to be recapitulated.

This leads one to the conclusion that these three multinational, multicultural, multireligious and multiethnic countries have a commonality of problem, though their experiences of national unity vary from each other differ. But there is something more to it than meets the eye.

Muslim Factor

All these three countries are faced with the problem of religious fundamentalism. In the erstwhile Soviet Union, nearly 12 per cent of the population was of Muslims. The number of Muslim population in Russia is not known. But the fact is that rise of Muslim fundamentalism in the Central Asian Republics has a direct bearing on the unity and security of Russia. In China in 1979, out of total population of 96 crore, the Muslim population was 11.50 crore.[6]

The Muslim population in China is 12 per cent of the total population. The highest concentration of the Muslim population in China is in Sinkiang (80 per cent); Kansu (65 per cent); Tsinghai (99 per cent); three Eastern Provinces (29 per cent); Saiyuan (19 per cent); Shensi (40 per cent) and Yunnam (38 per cent).[7]

This shows that along with economic regeneration of the societies, political structures of these three nations have also begun to change. Though the process of these changes is multidimensional, the main focus is on the rise of religious revivalism, ethnic conflicts and territorial disputes. As these nation-states are coming out of their economic backwardness and moving out of the tribal, feudal and semi-feudal structures, they are confronted with new problems, which are partly rooted in their past and are being encouraged and promoted by external factors, including by certain states in the region such as Pakistan and Saudi Arabia. This coincides with the geo-political interests of certain big powers. In India, this problem has become very acute, particularly after the rise of Hindu revivalism. In Russian Federation, it has assumed a serious dimension as the developments in Chechnya have underlined. In China at the moment the problem on the surface does not appear to be very acute.

Unfortunately for mankind, integrative forces are weaker than forces of disintegration in the world. Of the nearly 196 nations in the international system today, more than 60 have populations less than one million, more than half of them being states with populations less than 20 million. Such a disintegration process has led to increased vulnerabilities of developing nations. However, China, India and Russia stand on a different footing because of their size, population, economic resources, military strength and historical tradition. To say this does not mean that attempts to disintegrate them are not being made.

Black Clouds of War

After the end of the Second World War in September 1945 there have been more than 150 instances of major inter and intra-state violence; 140 of them took place in the developing world. Thus while the industrialised countries spend well over 80 per cent of the world's military expenditure and produce 95 per cent of all weapons, most of the violence is witnessed in the developing world. But here there is no paradox. In two-thirds of the conflicts the developed nations intervened, directly or indirectly. Many of them being inter-state wars, a number of them caused by religious tribal and secessionist factors.

This fact is being mentioned to highlight the common threat which these three nations are facing in their struggle to become modern nation state.

Such turbulence and violence at a time when nation-states are being formed is not unusual. Nation-state as a concept emerged only in the 16th century, and have four centuries of history of evolution of national states, mostly in Europe and for the last one and a half century in the Western hemisphere as well. That period of history was marked by extraordinary violence, such as the 30 years war,

Napoleonic wars, the Balkan wars, the first and second world wars, the American civil war, the decimation of the Red Indian Population, the French revolution, the Bolshevik revolution, etc. Countries which are today known for their commitment to peace such as Sweden and Switzerland had their full share of violence. Religious intolerance, genocide, ethnic conflicts and oppression marked this period.

The developing world has started on this process only since the end of the Second World War and the dawn of the era of decolonisation. For the developed world to preach to the developing world about human rights, provision of minimum needs, keeping peace in the international community, virtues of religious tolerance, etc., is very much like for an adult to preach the adult virtues to a growing child or an adolescent youngster. No doubt this is the direction in which the developing nations have to move.

There is yet another important question which should be examined with an open mind. The specifies of the East today cannot be understood unless the religious factor is taken into account.

The religious systems of the East—Hinduism, Buddhism, Confucianism, Islam, and the teachings of countless different religious sects are, of course, diverse, but they do have something in common. None of these religions, which to this day constitute a major unit linking the entire superstructural sphere, has ever experienced a profound reformation like European Christianity has. Not one of them could provide such a powerful spiritual justification for the political and socio-economic activities of society and the individual as European Christianity did at one time, and especially Protestantism under the protection of which capitalism developed faster and which put the European peasantry and urban population in the foreground of the struggle for a democratic system. The religious beliefs of the East, like in the West, too, in the past, do not include just adoration of a deity, but also a 'consecrated' way of life and thinking of both society and the individual. There is no doubt that the social structure of the East would have been very different if the envelope of ideas surrounding its material existence had taken some other shape or if it had experienced its own Renaissance. The religious systems of the Western world, especially from the 14th and 15th centuries onwards, did much more to promote its socio-economic development than the corresponding system did in the East. It is certainly no chance that the Christian countries of the West, and certainly not the Islamic and Buddhist ones, became the cradle of capitalism.

There is one more aspect to the problem. It is said that for 200 to 300 years, the supremacy of Europe and the United States over their Asian and African colonies consisted in a more advanced mode of production. This is correct, but not an exhaustive explanation. A hundred backward Eastern countries remaining basically peasant ones, with predominantly pre-capitalist economies whole level of development of production science and technology was incomparable with that achieved in the Western countries. However, it has to be admitted that India, China and other Asian states are passing through an unprecedented political, economic, strategic and cultural ferment, which has no parallel in human history. The basic elements of all the revolutions—the French, the American, the Russian, the industrial and scientific—are present in this ferment. We are to close to the developments in this region and therefore cannot draw a firm conclusions, particularly when the processes of change have a multidimensional character and invariably are contradictory. A traditional society is changing and at times skipping over one stage of social evolution either in parts or as a whole. This process comes into conflict with the geoeconomic interests of the developed countries including the United States.

Characteristic of Asia

The specific feature of the Asian societies was and perhaps continues to be that at the one end, these societies had a most self-contained village economics and at the other, highly centralised authority. It is this two-tier social order which is breaking down, though slowly but surely. In this process, a host of problems are being thrown up, some old and some new.

That being the position the developed and industrialised nations cannot impose their models on them, though subtle and not so subtle attempts are being made in this direction. This turn is throwing up new strategic problems, and brings countries like India, China and Russia into conflict with them.

The basic shift in geoeconomic, geopolitical and geostrategic situation in the Asia-Pacific region too needs to be taken into account in any critical examination of India's relations with China and Russia. These shifts have led to a new military build up by some of the countries, especially those which have close strategic relations with the United States.

Firstly, many countries, including those in Asia, have received military weapons and equipment on subsidised rates, lease, or outright grants. The United States, for example, provided 3.2 billion US dollars military and security-related economic assistance to Pakistan in 1981-86, followed by a second package of 4.2 billion US dollars in 1987. Saudi Arabia was reported to have paid for the F-16s acquired by Pakistan, while the US provided eight Brooke-Garcia class frigates in 1987. Pakistan's arms acquisitions from Western sources alone were worth 3.7 billion US dollars between 1987-91. The United States transferred 2,809 tanks, armoured combat vehicles, and artillery to five NATO partners under the Excess Defence Articles (EDA) programme. These arms were supplied on a price discounted down to 5.50 per cent of the original price to Israel, Egypt, Turkey, Oman, and Pakistan among others. Some idea of the extent of such transfers may be obtained from the transfers to Israel, Turkey, and Oman during 1989-91, when arms worth more than 1,084 million US dollars were sold for 120 million US dollars to these countries under Section 516 authority.[8]

Secondly, East Asia is the only region in the world that has witnessed a rise in defence spending in constant US dollars from 1985-93. South Asian countries are converting their armed forces to make them capable of dealing with conventional war. These states are acquiring sophisticated weapons.

Thirdly, after the end of the cold war, US troop level have remained steady at about one lakh soldiers for the last three years in this region. Compared to this, its military strength in Europe has decreased by about 20 per cent annually in the same period.

India cannot remain indifferent to these developments nor can

China and Russia.

From whatever angle you look at the situation, India-Russia and India-China relations have already begun to unfold new trends. The area of their cooperation is expanding though one should not ignore their differences and conflicting perceptions on certain sensitive areas such as nuclear proliferation. Above all China's supply of arms to Pakistan.

The last quarter of 1996 witnessed certain major developments in India's relations with China and Russia. If these developments are pieced together, it becomes clear that in the forseeable future, these relations will be further strengthened, though one should not be euphoric about it.

India-China: Joining Hands

During the three-day visit of Chinese President Jiang Zemin to India beginning in November 28, 1996 important agreements were signed between the two countries.

India and China have pledged themselves not to attack each other or cross the line of actual control (LAC) and reduce troops and armaments along the common border under an agreement. With this objective the agreement outlines a series of confidence building measures in the military field to ensure a peaceful border.

The 12 article, 10-page agreement stipulates that "neither side shall use its military capability against the other side."

Three other agreements were also signed by the two countries. These were maintenance of India's Consulate General in Hong Kong after it comes under Chinese control in July 1, 1997 cooperation in curbing drug trafficking and on maritime transport.

Prime Minister H.D. Deva Gowda described the confidence building measure agreement as a major step forward. He said that it was built on the foundation of the 1993 agreement on maintenance of peace and tranquillity on the border.

Significantly, the agreement on confidence building measures reiterated the determination of the two sides to seek a "fair, reasonable and mutually acceptable settlement of the boundary question and to respect the line of actual control until then."

It says "no armed forces deployed by either side in the border areas along the LAC as part of their respective military strength shall be used to attack the other side or engage in military activity that threaten the other side or undermine peace, tranquillity and stability in the India-China border areas." The agreement stipulates that the two countries will reduce or limit their respective military forces within mutually agreed geographical zone along the LAC.

The two sides also agreed to reduce the number of field army, border defence forces, paramilitary forces and any other mutually agreed category of armed force deployed.

The major categories of armaments to be reduced are: Combat tanks, infantry combat vehicles, guns including Howitzers with 70 mm or bigger calibre, mortars with 120 mm or bigger calibre, surface-to-surface missiles and any other weapon system.

The two sides will exchange data on the military forces and armaments to be reduced and to be kept within the agreed zones.

It was also agreed to avoid holding large scale military exercises involving more than one division (approximately 5,000 troops) in close proximity of the LAC, prior notification should be given to the other side.

The agreement provides that the two sides will take adequate measures to prevent any air intrusions along the LAC.

It lays down that combat aircraft, including fighter, bomber, reconnaissance, military trainer, armed helicopter and other armed aircraft would not fly within 10 kilometres of the LAC.

In case, such flights are to be operated, advance information should be given.

The agreement stipulates that unarmed aircraft, surveyor aircraft and helicopters will be permitted to fly upto the LAC but no military aircraft will be allowed to fly across the LAC except with prior permission.

The agreement will remain valid until either side decides to terminate it after giving six months notice in writing.

The preamble of the agreement says that the five principles of peaceful coexistence serve the interests of the people of India and China to foster a long-term good neighbourly relationship. The principles are: Mutual respect for sovereignty and territorial integrity, mutual non-aggression, mutual non-interference in each other's internal affairs, equality and mutual benefit and peaceful coexistence.

The two sides agreed to exchange data on the military forces and armament to be reduced or limited and decided on ceiling on the military forces. It shall be determined in conformity with the requirement of the principle of mutual and equal security.

The agreement states that both sides will avoid holding large scale military exercises involving more than one division in close proximity of the LAC. However, if such exercises are to be conducted, the strategic direction of the main force involved shall not be towards the other side.

Each side would give prior notification with regard to type level and planned duration of the military exercises along with type of units and formations participating in these exercises.

The two countries could take adequate measures to ensure that air intrusion across the LAC do not take place.

If either side is required to undertake flights of combat aircraft within 10 kilometres from the LAC, it shall give advance information on area of operation and types and number of combat aircraft.

The agreement states that neither side shall open fire, cause bio-degradation, use hazardous chemicals, conduct blast operations or hunt with guns or explosives within two kilometres from the LAC.

In order to strengthen cooperation between their military personnel and establishments in the border areas, it was suggested to expand the regime of schedule and flag meetings between the border representatives.

The two sides shall maintain and expand telecommunication links between their border meeting points.

The two sides agreed to provide each other information pertaining to natural disasters and epidemic disease in contiguous border areas which might affect the other side.

The two sides would exchange maps indicating their respective perceptions of the entire alignment of the LAC as soon as possible.[9]

This agreement is high water mark of India-China relations in the post-cold war period. The main significance of the agreement is that there would be improvement in the climate of peace on the India-China border accompanied by the cooperation and increasing understanding of each other's sensitivities.

If there was greater appreciation of Chinese concern with the activities of Dalai Lama in India, the Chinese leaders did assure the Indian leaders that their relations with Pakistan were not directed against India. May be China had its own compulsions. Perhaps they had in mind the Muslim population in China, though this was not expressed in the discussions.

What is of significance in this connection is that Chinese spokespersons stressed that China would not supply "nuclear delivery system to any country of South Asian region that will affect India or any third country." This assurance is being interpreted by certain experts on China that India need not entertain any apprehension about China's nuclear aims.

Before President Jiang's visit the two countries were not too sure of each other's motives in the absence of any settlement on the important border question which had soured relations in the past. However, after this agreement it has become clear that the two countries had agreed to pull out offensive and dangerous weapons facing each other on the borders in order to enlarge their area of cooperation and understanding in other spheres.

Although the talks did not result in reassurance that missile technology would not be available to Pakistan; there is a great deal to derive comfort from the 12 articles of the agreement. For instance, with the pull out of dangerous weapons by either side from the LAC. There will be less tension on the borders. India would have less to worry on this side of the border than was the case earlier.

The significance of this agreement has to be seen in the context of the fact that this easing of pressure on over 4000 mile long border in the country's north-east would help New Delhi to devote greater attention to problems on borders with neighbours which continue to remain hostile.

On the other hand China too will politically, strategically and economically gain from this agreement. With peace and tranquillity on the border with India and with the reassurance from Indian Government that Tibet is part of China and also that Dalai Lama would not be permitted to indulge in political activities in this country. Beijing will be more confident about Indian policy. In this sense President Jiang's visit would not have been more fruitful from Beijing's point of view.

This is a clear manifestation of evolution of India-China relations on a new footing, though India still has its reservations about China's Pakistan policy.

Let us examine, the deepening of India's relations with Russia in 1996. This has been analysed in some of the studies included in this book. However, one important development needs to be highlighted in the context of changing geopolitical balance of forces in this entire region.

Almost simultaneously after India-China agreement was signed on easing of the tension on the borders of the two countries, India signed in November 30, 1996, rupees 6,142 crore defence deal with Russia. This deal enables India to purchase 40 Sukhoi-30 MK-I multirole fighter war plane for the Indian Air Force to give the much-needed punch to the country's air cover. This agreement includes the supply of ground handling equipment, and also know-how for extending the maintenance of and overhaul infrastructure. There is something more to it.

This agreement stipulates that Russia would transfer technology for production of these warplanes under licence by the Hindustan Aeronautics Limited in India to meet the future requirements of the IAF. Under this agreement, there will be collaboration between Indian and Russian agencies for joint development of certain electronic equipment to ensure that commonality could be established with the indigenous Light Combat Aircraft.

This and the move to enlarge the area of cooperation to strengthen Indian Navy by purchasing Air Craft Carrier, submarines and more frigates indeed are significant developments for strengthening of Indian defence.

These two developments in the end of 1996, India-China agreement on maintenance of peace on the LAC and further expansion of Indo-Russian cooperation in defence undoubtedly confirm that India's relations with these two countries are being restructured on a new footing to face new challenges in the post-cold war period.

References

This article is based on the presentations made by the author on two International Seminars on Japan in September 1996 on Globalism, Regionalism and Nationalism: Asia in search of its role in the 21st century.

1. Major Gen. Dipankar Banerjee, *Strategic Analysis*, November 1955.
2. UNI report, *National Herald*, November 14, 1996.
3. Russian Foreign Minister Mr. Yevgeny Primakov, in an interview to Stanislav Kondrashov, of RIA NovostiIzvestia, *The Hindustan Times*, March 11, 1996.
4. *NATO Review*, July 1995.
5. Wang Jisi: *Beijing Review*, October 21-27, 1996.
6. King Abdulaziz University, Jeddah (Saudi Arabia); Institute of Muslim Minority Affairs, p. 79.
7. Ibid., p. 80.
8. Air Cdr. Jasjit Singh; *Asian Strategic Review*, 1994-95, p. 51.
9. *National Herald*, New Delhi, November 30, 1996.

SECTION I

INDIA-RUSSIA:

Friendly Relations

1

India's Relations with Russia and China: In the Post Cold War Period

T.N. Kaul

Relations between any two countries, specially those which are of considerable size and population, and have an ancient culture and history with links spread almost all over the world, are not usually susceptable to sudden changes, for better or for worse, unless they are directly involved in a clash or congruence of their respective national interests. The cold war period from 1945 to 1995 was a difficult stage in the development of independent democratic secular non-aligned India's relations with other great powers of the world. The two rival ideological and military power blocs were trying to suck the newly independent countries within their respective orbits. India, with its past history and tradition of maintaining friendly relations with all countries of the world, adopted a policy of non-alignment and refused to join the military and political alliances of either bloc.

In the beginning, this policy of India was misunderstood by both the rival blocs as they believed that those who were not with them were against them. They had been used to dealing with allies or client states and had not yet learnt to deal with independent countries that were neither allies nor client states but still wanted to be friendly with both the blocs. Independent India tried to be friendly with America and her allies in the West but almost drew a blank from them as she refused to join their military alliances. India was equally a suspect in the eyes of the Communist bloc led by Russia and China who believed in the beginning that India's policy of non-alignment was a mere cloak to cover her subservience to the Anglo-American bloc. Their academicians and theologues went to the extreme of describing India's leaders such as Mahatma Gandhi and Jawaharlal Nehru as "bourgeois reformers" and even as "running dogs of Anglo-American imperialism".

NAM: A Pace Setter

However, this did not deter India from steadfastly pursuing her independent policy of non-alignment which won respect and adherence from most of the newly independent countries that emerged into freedom from colonialism.

The so-called Communist bloc realised that independent India was not a country to be triffled with, dictated to or dominated as a client state. As their relations with the Western bloc deteriorated and the cold war grew sharper, they began to respect India's policy of non-alignment because it at least did not bring India and like-minded countries under the domination of the anti-Communist bloc. Even though the non-aligned group of countries refused to be part of the Communist bloc, India's policy of non-alignment won respect for her in the world and her impartial judgement based on the merits of each case as it affected her national interests and the larger interest of international peace and security was appreciated. Thus non-aligned India was able to play a positive and constructive role in helping to bring about peace in Korea, Indo-China, the Suez crises, the Congo, etc.

This policy suffered a severe shock from the China-India conflict of 1962 but it did not result in India giving up her policy and joining the Anglo-American bloc. One of the reasons for this was India's firm belief that by joining either bloc she would only become a pawn on the chessboard of military and political rivalry of the two power blocs in the cold war. Another fact that helped India to maintain its policy of non-alignment was the direct and indirect support she received from the Soviet Union both in the political and in the defence fields as well as moral sympathy, though not military support from the Western bloc.

Yet another shock that India's policy of non-alignment had to face was the open attempt by the U.S. Administration and the Western bloc to give military and political support to Pakistan in her differences and conflicts with India. However, India's own inherent strength and the military and political support she received from the Soviet Union helped her to meet this challenge successfully. India thus secured a signal victory over Pakistan in the conflict in 1971 when Bangladesh emerged as a sovereign and independent country and severed itself from West Pakistan. China had adopted a pro-Pakistan and anti-Indian attitude both during the 1965 and the 1971 Indo-Pak wars as indeed had the West. However, Mrs Indira Gandhi's determined leadership and the inherent strength of India as well as the political and military support that was symbolised by the Indo-Soviet Treaty of Peace and Friendship signed on the August 9, 1971, enabled India to hold on its own.

It is important to bear this brief description of India's policy from 1947 to 1991 in mind, in order to judge as to what effect the so-called end of the cold war between the two power blocs has already had, can and will have on India's relations with Russia and China. The following factors are important to bear in mind in this regard:

The cold war may have ended on paper but in fact has not ye ended. The Soviet Union may have broken up into a number o independent states but Russia still remains a superpower with grea military and economic potential. It was bad enough to live in a bi polar world but a unipolar world, with USA dominating and dictatin to the rest of the world, will be even worse. This is not and cannot b acceptable either to the Western allies of America or independer countries like China, India, Russia and even Japan. The world i therefore, likely to move from a bipolar to a multipolar world and nc to a unipolar world. In this new configuration of world forces, centre of military, political and cultural power will emerge not only in Nort America but also in South America and Western Europe, in Easte Europe, in South Africa, West Asia and the Arab world and last b not the least, in India, China and Japan. In this new configuration of world forces India can play a pivotal role as a kind of bridge of communication and understanding, friendship and cooperation between the countries of Asia and Europe and between the North and the South. However, India cannot, need not and should not plough a lonely furrow but try to act in concert and cooperation with other countries of the developing world and in particular with China and Russia who can influence events both in the Asia-Pacific region as well as in Africa and Europe. It is important to examine and analyse the policy of India in this regard with all its neighbours and specially with Russia and China. With Russia, the apparent cooling of relations with India immediately after the 1991 coup was a temporary aberration dictated by the uncertainty of events in Russia. It has now settled down to a new kind of relationship partly based on the old friendship and partly on the new situation existing between Russia and the Western world on the one hand, Russia and the Central Asian states and Russia and China on the other.

India is friendly to all these countries and her tradition of friendly and cooperative relations with the erstwhile Soviet Union can help her in further developing friendly relations with these new States. There is no basic conflict of national interests between India and Russia or with the Commonwealth of Independent States (CIS); on the contrary there is much that draws them closer in the political, economic and strategic spheres.

As for China, the situation is somewhat different because of the differences that arose particularly after 1962 and the anti-Indian and pro-Pakistani policy followed by China thereafter. However, there seems to be a serious attempt by both India and China to put their border differences and difficulties on the back burner and try to develop relations in various fields—economic, political, cultural, communication, science and technology. Some progress has been made in this direction and this policy could make further progress if both the sides so desire, which seems to be the case at present. The recent treaty signed by China with Russia, Kazakhstan, Tajikistan, and Kyrgyzstan is a significant pointer towards the possibility of not allowing border differences to interfere with the development of relations in other fields. It is, therefore, likely and in fact possible, for India and China to develop closer relations in various fields, keeping the border question in the background for future discussions and decisions through mutual negotiations. This would be in the interest of both India and China as well as the Asia-Pacific region specially in view of the attempts by the so-called sole surviving superpower, i.e. America, to dominate and dictate to the rest of the world, and which is not acceptable to either China, Russia, India or other leading countries.

Japan is an important country in this region and her continued association with and subordination to the strategic and other policies of the USA are likely to hamper the cooperation of Japan with other countries of Asia and Russia for some time. However, Japan's own economic, political and strategic interests will compel her to adopt, sooner than later, a policy of closer cooperation with her important Asian countries and Russia rather than become a mere client state of the USA.

In this brief description of the larger background of international relations in the Asia-Pacific region, it is possible and indeed probable that economic, political and strategic interests of India, China and Russia are likely to result in closer cooperation among these three countries to the advantage of each and not to the detriment of any.

This will not amount to a military or political alliance but an attempt to bring about greater understanding, friendship and cooperation among them in the larger interests of international peace and security and in the respective interests of each country and its neighbours. It would be well for America and its allies to appreciate this possibility and not do anything to hamper it as that may prove counter-productive.

The time is fast coming when all countries of the world and, in particular, the so-called great powers and important developing countries like India, as well as important developed countries like Japan and Germany, should cooperate with one another in bringing about a greater peace and cooperation between the East and the West, the North and the South to the mutual advantage of each and all.

2

India's Relations with Russia and China: An Overview

DEVENDRA KAUSHIK

The recent Chinese-American military confrontation in the Formosan strait was somewhat reminiscent of the crisis created by China's shelling of offshore islands during the cold war period in the late fifties as is the proposed expansion of the NATO despite the collapse of the USSR—once the communist superpower. But they have raised serious doubts about the much-publicized end of the cold war. Even Russian President Boris Yeltsin, an ardent champion of partnership on strategic alliance with the United States, was forced to describe at, not so long ago held the European Summit in Budapest, the present international situation as the 'cold peace'. So far as India is concerned, the new world alignment of forces has by no means led to the establishment of a more just and equitable new international order favourable to it or other the Third World countries. Nor has the supposed end of the cold war helped India to resolve its regional conflict with neighbouring Pakistan over Kashmir. Instead of two rival power blocs contending for supremacy in the cold war era, a new alliance directed against the Third World is shaping itself up.

This alliance, as originally conceived, was to comprise of both the East and the West and Japan. Militarily the United States is the only superpower left now in the international arena, though in the economic sphere. Europe, dominated by Germany, and the Pacific dominated by Japan, are posing a challenge to the economic power of the United States which is controlling the economies of North and South America. Germany and Japan, while economically compete with the United States, they depend on it for their defence security. The post-communist Russia too is eager to join this U.S.-led new alliance, notwithstanding repeated snubs and cold-shouldering it has received from Washington and the NATO. Communist China has also been reluctant to challenge this alliance, and is, in fact, striving for an accommodation with it.

Impact of Globalization

The modern technological revolution embracing such fields as microelectronics, informatics and robotics, communication, biotechnology and space and new material sciences has given rise to globalization of production, consumption and distribution. It has strengthened the interdependence of nations. Yet under the new dispensation this interdependence has remained lopsides and asymmetrical as it is the industrialized North which is calling the shots. Globalization has consequently only marginalized the developing South. New regional markets and economic groupings, like the European Economic Area — an extension of the European Community and European Free Trade Association (EFTA), the North American Free Trade Association (NAFTA), the Asia and Pacific Economic Cooperation (APEC) and the movement of the ASEAN towards a free trade area, forming a part of the wider Asia-Pacific framework for economic cooperation, have left a vast majority of the Asian and the African countries in isolation. India, Russia and China are the three great powers which have yet to find a place in any of these new regional economic groupings.

Multilateralism under the United Nations has not been allowed to grow by the new alliance of the North, an expanded version of the 19th century concept of Europe. Vital economic issues like development strategies, trade international debt, money and finance have not found a place on the agenda of the United Nations and has got transferred to the International Monetary Fund (IMF), World Bank and the General Agreement on Trade and Tariff (GATT). The discriminatory arrangements like the Australian Club, the COCOM Arrangements and the MTCR have an adverse impact on the technological advance of the developing countries. The new alliance of the North has frequently tried to intervene in other countries in the name of human rights, good governance and self-determination, thus undermining the principle of national sovereignty. The outside encouragement and help to secessionist movements has been a cause for anxiety to countries like India, Russia and China. In short, the post-cold war international environment has been far from conducive to economic development and political stability of most of the nations. The mounting pressure of the alliance of the advanced North on the countries of the poor South under conditions of unipolarity and the growing isolation of Russia and China has, however, extended the prospects of Russia and China joining these countries ultimately in their prospective struggle for a just and equitable international order to replace the 'Pax Americana' type new world order.

Gorbachev's Perestroika

One can only lament the failure of the policy-making elite in India as also of the Left, in general, to understand properly and timely the historical developments leading to the emergence of a unipolar world as a result of the collapse of the communist regimes in East Europe and disintegration of the Soviet Union. The wrong perceptions of the 'Perestroika' of Mikhail Gorbachev and his novel concepts of the 'new political thinking', based on primacy of common interests of the mankind and advocated by him as ideas cast in the Gandhian mould, and sharing the non-aligned approach, tended to ignore the fact that the futility of the cold war confrontationist approach was not realized by the other superpower, the USA. It was wrongly attributed to universal recognition of the global problems posing threat to survival of humanity. The Delhi Declaration with its acceptance of non-violence made us euphoric about prospects of ushering in a new millennium of peace and prosperity for all nations as a result of the new policies initiated by Gorbachev.

It is unfortunate that Gorbachev's book *Perestroika New Thinking for Our Country and the World*, published in 1987, was not carefully read as the collaboration offered against the Third World by him to the West was not given the attention it deserved. Gorbachev wrote: "I have explained on many occasions that we do not pursue goals inimical to Western interests. We know how important the Middle East, Latin America, other Third World regions and South Africa are for American and West European economies. To cut these links is the last thing we want to do and we have no desire to provoke ruptures in historically formed economic ties."[1] It was not for nothing that American publicist, Jerry Hough, praised Gorbachev's thesis on a 'Common European Home' as aimed against the threat posed by China and India in the 21st century. Thus an alliance of the North against the South was already underway through collusion between the two superpowers, though the second superpower under the Gorbachev regime of the Soviet Union era had reconciled itself to the role of a junior partner.

The genesis of a unipolar world can be traced not to the crisis of the communist world due to its incapability to face the tasks of the post-industrial society but to the growth of a global crisis produced by the current stage of development threatening human civilization with self-destruction. This crisis arose due to failure of the existing international economic mechanism to cope with the increasing rate of consumption of non-renewable natural resources and environmental degradation and social stratification. The path of development availed by one billion people of the affluent West was not available to the teeming billions of the developing world. Such a situation was fraught with risks and compelled the West, led by the US, to work out a strategy which would change the power balance by eliminating the socialist USSR.

The key link in this strategy was provided by removal of the Soviet Union from the world stage and the consequent destruction of a historically formed geopolitical equilibrium. This action proved to be unique and unprecedented in history. For the first time in contemporary history a powerful state forced the collapse of another powerful state, which was enjoying military parity with it, without an armed conflict. Russian Communist Party leader G. Zyuganov has rightly observed: "Some ten years back a full scale world war would have been needed but instead it was achieved through ideological cave of the adversary by means of skilful use on its territory of social technique of a slowly moving catastrophy and low intensity civil war."[2] This fact is now increasingly being realised by several non-communist Russian intellectuals and military leaders. Thus Alexei Pushkov, a leading Russian commentator, and Nikolai Sokov, a prominent Russian diplomat, have taken strong exception to the over-bearing American treatment of Russia as a power defeated in the cold war to merit imposition of an occupation regime to extract guarantees of future responsible behaviour as in the case of Germany and Japan following their defeat in World War II. They assert that the Soviet Union 'lost' the cold war only because it chose to abandon its confrontationist approach in response to pressures generated within the country. Similarly, Admiral E. Baltin, who was recently sacked by Russian President Boris Yeltsin as Commander of the Black Sea fleet, in his article entitled 'The Third World...?' wrote about the ongoing Third World war which he termed as the 'velvet' war. This war is supposed to have commenced in 1989 with the demolition of the Berlin Wall. According to him, it has not stopped with the dissolution of the USSR and is now aimed at disarming Russia as a nuclear power and destabilising it through ethnic conflicts.

The pronouncedly pro-Atlanticist posture in the Russian foreign policy lasted for just five years, i.e., 1992. The Russian honeymoon with America, like all honeymoons, ended soon. Among its dubious achievements one might recall the 14 applause which President Yeltsin received during his address on the joint session of both houses of the American Congress followed by promise of an economic aid package of 43.5 million dollars by the West. It was, however, later made clear that the West had only the desire to extend financial assistance but had really not enough money for it. The American policy-making elite, including Brzezinski and Kissinger, began to encourage centrifugal forces in the post-Soviet space under the cover of supporting 'geopolitical pluralism'. To add insult to injury, Kissinger dubbed the talk of 'partnership' with Russia as premature and declared that

Russia being an Asian power had nothing to do with Europe. No strong domestic constituency emerged in Russia in favour of western assistance because an overwhelming majority of Russians could see little tangible benefits coming to their way in their daily lives.

Faced with hostile criticism of their pro-West policies in the Russian Parliament by 1993, President Yeltsin and then Foreign Minister Kozyrev adopted a tougher tone to explain and defend the Russian policies. Having come under attack for alleged subservience to the West and failure to defend Russia's national interests, they just adopted a more militant rhetoric aimed at convincing the people that they were defending the country's interests. Thus pointing to his state visits to South Korea, China and India, President Yeltsin claimed in January 1993 that these visits were indicative of the fact that we are moving away from Western emphasis in their policy. His tone became more apologetic in the face of continued hostility of the new Duma (Russian Parliament) after the December 1993 elections. In February 24, 1994, President Yeltsin acknowledged in the Duma the past shortcomings in government's foreign policy in which he declared that "the main task of our foreign policy is consistent advancement of Russia's national interests". The Russian policy acquired a new assertiveness in matters related to peace-keeping in Moldova, Georgia, Tajikistan and Azerbaijan. It also became more active in favour of Yugoslavia. The February 1994 agreement with Serbia to send Russian peace keeping forces around Sarajevo and agreement to sell cryogenic engines to India and atomic reactors to Iran represented the high watermark of this new-found assertiveness. But Moscow did not carry out its threat to veto sanctions against Libya and Iraq and espoused the case for lifting embargo against these states in the Security Council only in a guarded way. Similarly despite its loud-mouthed opposition to the expansion of NATO to Central and East Europe, it did not hesitate to join the 'Partnership for Peace Programme' of the NATO.

The trend towards new Eurasianism, which became prominent during 1993 on account of growing opposition to the concept of strategic alliance with America in the Supreme Soviet and subsequently in the Duma during 1994 and 1995, is bound to gain further strength following the victory of the communists and the ultra-nationalists in the recent elections to the Duma. The newly appointed Russian Foreign Minister Y. Primakov, who replaced the pro-West previous Foreign Minister A. Kozyrev, in his recent interview with Russian journalist S. Kondrashov, clearly stated that NATO expansion ran counter to Russia's interests. He indicated his preference for an 'equitable partnership' with the West in place of the 'strategic alliance' — a favourite theme of his predecessor.[3] It would, however, be too much to expect that Primakov, as President Yeltsin's Foreign Minister, will make a sharp departure from the general line of pro-Atlanticism. Surprisingly, in his above interview cited, Primakov did not choose to make any reference to the course of new Eurasianism favoured by the opposition. The parameters of change envisaged by him is confined to the general statement that Russian foreign policy should "uphold national interests more energetically than before" and "yet prevent the slide back to confrontation and the cold war relations".[4] Even while declaring that relations with the CIS are a priority for Russia, he admitted that integration processes underway in these countries indirectly affected Russia's relations with the USA. In order not to offend the USA, Primakov stated that integration process would be confined to "Belarus, possibly Kazakhstan and Kyrgyzstan", thus leaving the Baltic and Transcaucasian states, Ukraine, Uzbekistan, Turkmenistan and Tajikistan outside the pale of CIS integration. There is no mention of closer relations with China, Iran and even India which he visited soon after. One can only hope Primakov has not forgotten what he wrote after Gorbachev's 1986 visit to India. In his article, published in *Pravda*, once mouthpiece of the Communist Party of the USSR era, Primakov had observed that "be it Morarji Desai, Indira Gandhi or Rajiv Gandhi in power, our relations have acquired a new stability or a momentum of their own on account of lack of geopolitical incompatibility of interests".

The disabling factor of political instability and its declining economic power apart, Russia's geostrategic location on the Eurasian landscape, its highly advanced nuclear and space technological capabilities, its vast human and natural resources make it difficult for that country to reconcile itself for long to the status of a mere regional power. It is quite natural for Moscow to perceive its interests covering a vast area extending from Central and Northern Europe to Asia Minor, the Middle East and the Pacific region. Being the core of the Eurasian landmass, it cannot put up with its exclusion from either Europe or Asia. Interestingly, noted British geographer Halford Macinder called the Eurasian empire of Russia a unique institution representing a "remarkable correlation between natural environment and political organization... unlikely to be altered by any possible social revolution". The Vostochniki (Oriental) philosophers, poets and historians in the pre-Soviet period viewed Eurasia as a geopolitical entity brought about by a cultural process of "genetic mutation" and not by conquest and coercion. Thus wrote Russian historian Vernadsky: "The Russian state is a Eurasian State and all separate nationalities of Eurasia must feel and recognize that it is their state". In a way, Vernadsky was pleading for Russian-Muslim cultural cooperation that was also suggested by leading Tartar educationist and modernist reformer, Ismail Bey Gasprinsky. Lenin too underlined the Eurasian character of Russia. He visualised the unity of the peoples of Russia, China and India for the triumph of the cause of the world proletarian revolution.

Central Asian Republics Geopolitics

Historically speaking there has existed a certain convergence of Russian and Indian geopolitical interests in peace and stability of the Central Asian region forming the southern part of the Eurasian landmass separated from the subcontinent by the Pamirs and the Hindukush chain of mountains. Developments in this part of the world have shaped the destiny of our two peoples more than once in the past and continue to be of great interest to them even after the disintegration of the Soviet Union. While under the changed conditions rejection by Moscow of the earlier active Soviet globalism, characterised by unremitting opposition to the West, has heightened the need to administer the necessary correctives in the old Indo-Soviet strategic alliance. It has to be done without impairment to the high level of relationship already attained. Both Moscow and New Delhi have by now realised that the situation calls for a certain transitional period during which conditions must be created for a painless movement towards a new structure of Indo-Russian cooperation, preserving the essential elements of the old strategic partnership of the two great Asian powers. Rejection of the Soviet globalism does not mean vanishing of serious common geopolitical interests dictating long-term mutual active cooperation.

The growing Islamic factor is increasingly assuming an aggressive fundamentalist character in the former Soviet Republics of Central Asia and fuelling secessionist movement in the Chechen Autonomous Republic of Russia with the active encouragement and assistance from the neighbouring Islamic states. The increasing threat of inter-ethnic conflicts in the Muslim republics of the CIS, particularly in the wake of advent of Mujahidin power in Afghanistan, also impinge on the situation in India where a secessionist movement in Kashmir is being sustained through transborder terrorism. Besides the common threat of Islamic Fundamentalism to their territorial integrity, the China factor has also placed some common tasks before India and Russia. The increasing role of China in the region and the world as a whole under conditions of changed correlation of forces following the disintegration of the Soviet Union also calls for active strategic cooperation between India and Russia. Cooperation among these three great powers — India, Russia and China — is an essential condition for checkmating the new alliance of the North. Indo-Russian strategic alliance within a trilateral framework of cooperation is likely to prevent a chauvinist China from going wayward. Formation of an economic grouping by these three countries will end their growing isolation in the global economy and help them in facing the challenge of globalisation.

The strong criticism of a blindly pro-US policy by the national patriotic opposition has resulted in a somewhat sobering reassessment based on recent experience of conducting relations with the West. Much before President Yeltsin's India visit in December 1992, policy-makers in Moscow had begun to realize the need for modifying the course of exclusive dependence on the United States advocated by the then Foreign Minister Kozyrev. Notwithstanding President Yeltsin's assertion in his address to the Indian businesspersons not to make 'unjustified unilateral concessions' and his declaration on Russia's conduct of its relations with India in a deideologized manner so as to prevent their being directed against a 'third party' (world imperialism and Chinese hegemonism), a breakthrough was achieved in the Indo-Russian relations. President Yeltsin's denunciation of the ideologized course in the past was more in the nature of a populist compulsion to project Russia's new foreign policy as a total break from the Soviet past. The Russian President talked about an "Asian tilt" in Russian foreign policy and the Russia-China-India axis for peace in Asia. A new Treaty of Friendship and Cooperation was signed in place of the 1971 Treaty of Peace, Friendship and Cooperation. President Yeltsin denied that the change in the name of the treaty indicated any reduction in the importance of strategic security and referred to the agreement on defence cooperation with India.

The Inter-Governmental Protocol of the Russian-Indian Consultation, he explained, had only replaced the obligation to enter into mutual consultation contained in the 1971 Treaty. President Yeltsin declared unequivocal Russian support for 'settlement in Kashmir', according to the Indian version. The vexed rupee-rouble parity issue for re-estimating the size of the past Soviet credits was satisfactorily solved during the visit, thus removing a major irritant in the way of resumption of trade relations. An understanding was reached to ensure smooth supply of defence spares. The cryogenic engines supply agreement was essentially implemented in spite of the US opposition and a mutually acceptable solution was found. Former Prime Minister P. V. Narasimha Rao's visit to Moscow in June 1994 further underscored the strategic aspect of the Indo-Russian relations, though the problem of utilisation of the rupee reserves of Russia in India for boosting their trade relations and the supply of defence spares still continued to elude a satisfactory solution. The Moscow Declaration signed by the two leaders is a historic document of great importance as if highlights the commitment of the two countries to support the territorial integrity of the multireligious, multiethnic pluralistic states. The Moscow Declaration is an indication of the growing realisation of both the countries to raise anew their relationship to a strategic long-term level as demanded by the changed context.

It is obvious that the "infantile pro-Americanism" that persisted as a predominant strain in Moscow's foreign policy until quite recently is gradually giving place to a great diversification by upgrading relations with countries like India to a strategic level. The collapse of the shock-therapy free market reforms for want of adequate logistical support from the United States resulted in Moscow's disillusionment with Washington as a dependable ally and partner. The relationship has been further soured by Washington's failure to take Moscow into confidence over the expansion of the NATO to include the former East European allies of Russia, as also over the NATO air strikes in Bosnia. At the Budapest European summit President Yeltsin described the proposed extension of the NATO to Russia's borders as an act, plunging Europe into 'cold peace'. The Duma's Foreign Affairs Committee Chairman Vladimir Lukin termed Eastern Europe and the CIS as Russia's natural area of interest claiming a leading role for his country. Moscow is insisting on its right to police the peace-keeping operations in Tajikistan and Georgia and is demanding that the CSCE should take over from the NATO as guarantor of European frontiers. Russian Prime Minister Viktor Chernomyrdin's visit to India in December 1995 marked a distinct move in the direction of restoring the strategic character of the relationship with New Delhi. His statement that Russia was not supplying any military equipment to Pakistan and it had no intention of doing so in the future put an end to speculations about Moscow's offer to sell sophisticated military hardware to Pakistan. Among the several agreements signed by Chernomyrdin in New Delhi, the agreement on military and technical cooperation till the year 2000 is of great importance. Going by recent press reports on impending Indo-Russian deal for purchase of SU-30 fighters and advanced submarines there is reason to think that Russia's relations with India are further acquiring a strategic character. The strategic ties of Russia are also expanding with China through sales of sophisticated military hardware. It is hoped that formation of an economic grouping by India, China and Russia would be a correct step in the direction of challenging a unipolar world dominated by the United States.

The India-Russia-China triangle is an important prerequisite for undoing the unholy alliance of the North against the South. Making a critical evaluation of the scope and limitations of forming this triple entente, one is likely to conclude that it is not just a pipedream but has a strong objective basis for its materialization. The three countries are close neighbours and have ancient civilizational roots and linkages to bind them together. Barring controversy over border common to many neighbouring states and some short armed conflicts on their partly undemarcated frontier, there has been no prolonged adversary relationships or wars between them. Russia and China are Pacific states and India is an Indian Ocean country, but they have a common geopolitical relationship with the landlocked Central Asia. These three powers by virtue of their vast human and natural resources are fully capable of cooperating in the interest of mutual prosperity and peace and stability in the world. All the three are nuclear and space powers (India in the non-military field) and possess the material and scientific capability to achieve the post-industrial development. The internal stability, territorial integrity and border security of Russia, India and China, as Russian Duma, former Speaker Ivan Rybkin told the *Hindu* in his interview, faced a common threat from aggressive Islamic fundamentalism.[5] Besides, they have also a common problem of foreign supported secessionist movements threatening their territorial integrity. Zyuganov's observations during his visit to India for participation in the 15th Party Congress of the Communist Party of India (Marxist) on his Party's world view in which India, China and Russia occupy notable position and are perceived as ensuring stability in the Euro-Asian hemisphere are not without significance. The Russian Communist leader, a Presidential hopeful in the previous Presidential poll, accepted the Chinese Party delegation's invitation to visit Beijing in route to Moscow. The Chinese-Russian relations, which have been continuously improving since 1986, are thus poised for further upswing as a result of this dialogue.

The China-India detente, initiated nearly a decade ago with Rajiv Gandhi's meeting with Deng Xiaoping in Beijing, has succeeded in maintaining peace and tranquillity along the LAC on the border. The agreement on disengagement in the Sumdorong Chu Valley of India achieved by the Joint Working Group in August 1995, is indicative of some movement in the otherwise stagnant situation on the border since the conclusion of the Agreement on Peace and Tranquillity along the LAC during Narasimha Rao's China visit in 1993. Bilateral trade has since increased 300 per cent. However, the irritants over China's cooperation with Pakistan in the field of missiles and atomic weapons and non-recognition of Sikkim's accession to India are yet to be overcome. There has been a distinct change in China's attitude on Kashmir and the Chinese supply of enriched uranium for the Tarapur plant has given a new momentum to China-India bilateral relations.

While China never accepted the International Monetary Fund—World Bank conditionalities for foreign investment and economic cooperation with the West, Russia had, in the wake of the Duma elections of December 1995, moved away from the shock therapy reforms of the monetarists, notwithstanding ritualistic pronouncements of President Yeltsin on continuation of the market economy course. In India too the ruling classes had been forced to renege on their commitments to liberal economic reforms on account of the political constraints on the eve of the Parliamentary elections. India has a foreign policy agenda (evolved albeit in a piecemeal manner) to face the challenge of a unipolar world which needs to be pursued firmly in a systematic way. It has questioned the US approach to ecological security, unilateral demands with regard to non-proliferation, unilateral interpretation of human rights, unilateral conditionalities, supervision and verification regimes, trends of protectionism, restrictions and threats of penalties against the developing countries. Instead of supplicating for membership of the American sponsored economic groupings, it must strive for creation of a new regional economic bloc with China and Russia. The so-called post-communist reform era in East Europe and Russia is likely to end in 1996 and there are unmistakable signs of the impending breakdown of the present bloated world financial and monetary system dominated by speculative capital largely derived from narcotic trade and engaged not in physical economy but in trade in derivatives.

References

1. See p. 185, Russian language edition published from Moscow. The Collins edition in English published from London distorted the transition by changing it to "We have no desire to provoke ruptures in historically formed mutual economic interests", p. 178.
2. G.A. Zyuganov, *Za Gorizontom*, Moscow, 1995, pp. 86-87.
3. *The Hindustan Times*, 11 March 1996, p. 12.
4. Ibid.
5. *The Hindu*, 4 November 1995.

3

Indo-Russian-Chinese Relations: Towards Opening A New Chapter

PAULOS MAR GREGORIOS

History always makes new demands on the foreign policy of every nation, and India or China or Russia can in no way be the exceptions, especially in the last decade of this millennium. All the three nations are in the process of formulating their new foreign policies.

Russia, as of March 1, 1996, has been accepted as a member of the Council of Europe — a development hailed by Russian Foreign Minister Yevgeni Primakov as a 'truly great event'. Primakov also stated, in February 28 in Strasbourg, that "both the domestic and foreign policy of Russia is now undergoing certain new adjustments, in addition to the protection of its national interests".

NATO and Russia

It should interest us in India to know what is the general orientation of these adjustments, while formulating our own policy towards Russia and China. Two factors are clearly noticeable: first, Russia regards herself more and more as a European nation, without abandoning her interest in Asia where lies the seven-tenths of her territory. At the same time she has no reason to trust Europe completely, particularly in view of the NATO's obvious Eastward expansion efforts. Russia has already reacted negatively to NATO's attempts which look like wanting to encircle Russia militarily, geopolitically, as well as psychologically, through engulfing more and more Central and Eastern European countries into the NATO membership.

Russia is obviously anxious that such negative reactions do not amount to any thing like military confrontation or hostility. However, the protection of Russia's national interests demands both increasing her military strength and keeping herself on a guard against NATO for the foreseeable future. Warren Christopher's visit to Moscow might not have made all that difference in allaying Russia's fears of encirclement.

It requires special skill for Russia to remain a member of the Council of Europe and at the same time firmly resist the NATO attempts to encircle her. Wooing of the ex-socialist nations of Central and Eastern Europe thus gains a high priority for Russia at this moment to check the Eastward expansion of the NATO. This cannot, however, be at the expense of Russia's giving up the promotion of Russia's geopolitical, military-strategic and trade-related interests in the Asia-Pacific region.

With the international arms exhibition, held in Delhi in March 1996, exhibiting the Russian military technology, the weapons connection between India and Russia became evident. Ever since the signing of the Indo-Soviet agreement in 1960, India has become increasingly dependent on the Soviet military technology, and 8000 of our defence personnel have been trained in the USSR, now Russia. There was a rupture with the collapse of the Soviet Union in 1991. But today Indo-Russian military cooperation is at a higher level than in 1991. There is a joint programme for military-technological cooperation between India and Russia up to the year 2000 and new agreements were signed in 1993 and thereafter.

Russia's Asia policy will come up for general discussion in the next Asia-Europe summit in London in 1998, where beside Thailand, the host, India and Pakistan as well as Russia, among others have applied for participation. By that time many things will have to be sorted out among ourselves, particularly relations among the India-Pakistan-Russia trio. China will also be there which has her own geopolitical interests.

At this juncture we in India have to take into account several factors:

1. There have been some avoidable tensions and unnecessary bickerings in the Russia-India weapons trade. Russia is understandably more commercial minded than was the former Soviet Union. The terms of trade between the two countries will have to be looked into again in an ambiance less dominated by commercial concerns but more oriented towards mutual interests.

2. One hopeful sign is that Yevgeny Primakov is a much more seasoned and mature statesman than President Yeltsin, who visited us in 1993, or Prime Minister Victor Chernomyrdin, who was at the time of his visit to India in 1994 Chairman of the Government of the Russian Federation. Primakov's visit to India, which was the first for a Russian (as distinct from Soviet) Foreign Minister, conceivably opened a new chapter in Indo-Russian relations. Primakov chose India as the first country to visit, rather than USA or other Western countries. It is not without significance that Primakov, as a Foreign Minister, has now been empowered by a Presidential decree to formulate the foreign policy for Russia. India should make a full use of this new opportunity.

3. Primakov is fully aware of the potentiality of the great influence that a Russia-India-China collaboration can have, not only for the economic benefit of the three countries, but also in democratising the present one-sided power equation in the international decision making. There is a lot of bilateral—India-China and China-Russia—rancour generated by events of the last half century. The Mao-Stalin quarrels need not permanently affect the relations between China and Russia. Nor need the territorial disputes between China and India defy peaceful settlement. The ethnic prejudices generated largely by these quarrels and disputes can also eventually be overcome with some effort and goodwill on the part of all concerned.

People more competent and better informed than I can ever hope to be have time and again discussed the six large areas of possible fruitful cooperation between India and Russia, which are: (1) trade and trade-related services; (2) energy generation, including oil prospecting; (3) science-technology (including metallurgy and military and rocket technology); (4) higher education; (5) computer software development and marketing; and (6) cultural exchange. With China our priorities may be slightly different. But I have no doubt in my mind that we should work for a three-sided cooperation in all these six areas as well as in working towards democratic, peaceful and just societies everywhere in the world.

China-India-Russia Cooperation

I would add only one other point. In the days of the Soviet Union, there was a great emphasis on people to people cooperation. In India there was some struggle between the ruling party and some Left parties to gain control of this people to people cooperation and to use it for narrow party-political ends. Times have changed, and Indo-Russian peoples' friendship is no longer as useful to the political parties as it used to be. Consequently, interest in and support for peoples' friendship societies have noticeably waned. I believe the time has already come to form a China-India-Russia Friendship group, not under the aegis of any particular political party, nor with any narrow political ends in sight, but in the interest of the greater democratisation of international power-politics and of greater international socio-cultural and economic justice. Both these things are absolutely essential for a world of peace with justice and a healthy life-environment in the Third Millennium.

Of course, the Presidential elections in Russia did have its own effect on these-power relationships. India under her Minister of External Affairs Mr. I.K. Gujral's seasoned leadership seems all set to flex a few muscles without getting into a direct confrontation with the USA, for instance, refusal to sign the Comprehensive Test Ban Treaty (CTBT) despite tremendous pressure, including from Russia, the India-China-Russia accord on specific topics could have some effect in making America more accountable to the world community.

Yeltsin's visit to Beijing at the end of April 1996 gave further support to our main argument. Russia and China have definitely, though rather cautiously, begun to resolve their fences. The Japanese newspaper *Sankei Shimbun* has reported that Russia now exports 5.2

billion dollars worth of arms annually to China—mostly SU-27 bombers and diesel submarines. Negotiations are now in process to build an atomic power station in China's Liaoning province as a joint Russian-Chinese project. Yeltsin has expressed the hope that Russian-Chinese bilateral trade will soon rise to 20 billion dollars a year. They have now succeeded in settling their border disputes and making their huge boundaries most transparent to both sides by withdrawing most of their troops from the border.

Chinese President Jiang Zemin has welcomed both the Russian friendship and Russia's full participation in the development of the Asia-Pacific region. Both have also prepared the ground for signing a mutual non-aggression pact, and are committed to mutual co-operation in the military-technological and nuclear fields. These are indeed momentous developments which should make India radically rethink her relationships with both China and Russia.

The beginning has, however, to be made by developing relations with China on the same lines as we now have with Russia in the six areas listed above. The Deve Gowda Government, if it lasts for a while, needs a little push in this direction. When Yevgeni Primakov came, the Narasimha Rao Government gave the Russian Foreign Minister a somewhat cool reception, though some progress was made towards mutual relations. The time has now come to think of our relations with China and Russia as a major plank of our foreign policy.

4

Indo-Russian Relations in the Emerging Context

R.R. Sharma

The former Soviet Union always claimed that it was both a European as well as an Asian power. Being the core of the Eurasian landmass, it would not agree to its exclusion from either Europe or Asia. In the aftermath of the Soviet dissolution, Russia, which emerged as the successor state, was more than inclined to underplay its geostrategic location on the Eurasian landscape. It revised its priorities, which created the erroneous impression that it was a mere regional power. However, gradually the perception changed. It gave way to the old and natural perception that the Russian interests cover a vast area extending from the central and the northern Europe to Asia Minor, the Middle East and the Pacific Region. The renewed emphasis on this is a remarkable endorsement of the views held by such diverse personalities as Macinder and Lenin.

Macinder, for example, regarded Russia as a unique Eurasian power, and its empire as a 'unique institution', which, for him, represented a 'remarkable correlation between natural environment and political organisation'.

Lenin, likewise, took pains to underline the Eurasian Character of Russia. In fact, in his analysis, the Asian dimension was so overwhelmingly projected that it sought to create a unity of peoples of Russia, India and China. In between these two extremes, the academics also emphasised that the 'Russian State' was a 'Eurasian State', and all separate nationalities of Eurasia 'must feel and recognise that it is their state'. The reemergence of this perception has several and serious implications for the Russian foreign policy. From the Indian standpoint, this means that the two countries have put behind a cool period in their relations.

Shift in Russian Policy

The cool period of 1992-93 was characterised by a visible credibility gap in Indo-Russian ties. The source of the credibility gap may be located, largely, in the Russian government's views regarding the future of Indo-Russian relations. The scope of Indo-Russian relations was defined on the eve of President Boris Yeltsin's visit to India. There was a wide ranging discussions both in the Russian Duma (Parliament), as well as in the governing board of the Russian Foreign Ministry. The dominant view, put forth by Mr. Kozyrov and his team, was that there was no need to preserve the 'special relationship' with India which existed in the Soviet era. The Soviet Union was not only very friendly to India, but was also its largest trading partner, and key supplier of sophisticated military hardware. The new argument, invented by Mr. Kozyrov and his team, was that a special relationship with India is likely to undermine Russia's interaction with other countries in South Asia, and more particularly Pakistan. Obviously, for them the era of 'special relationships' should come to an end. In the Parliamentary (Duma's) hearings on relations with India, Deputy Foreign Minister Georgy Kunadze freely articulated these views.

In fact, this was only a continuation of the policy projections made in the working paper on the Russia's foreign policy adopted in late 1992. The 58-page document devoted large space to relations with the United States of America. It stated that Russia looked towards the US for support in carrying out the complex economic and strategic tasks in its foreign policy. Therefore, it was necessary that Russia should strive to achieve 'stable' relationship with the US on the basis of 'strategic partnership'. It also envisaged a long term perspective of a 'union'.

Mr. Kozyrov, and his close associates, held a strong view that, basically, the West, was a non-military centre for collective regulation of the global economy and international relations. The paper regarded the so called 'Third World' as the 'chief source of conflicts' in the future. This does not imply that there was a consensus on Russia's new foreign policy course. Mr. Kozyrov, in his early statements, went on to assert that Russia had 'no enemy', and, therefore, there was no threat to its security. Of course, this infantile view was not shared by many others in the Russian Foreign Ministry and elsewhere. These people on the other side contended that Russia faced a series of serious problems with a host of countries on its borders. Such threats included from the Islamic resurgence in the Central Asia, tensions in Transcaucasia, and between Russia and Ukraine, Russian-Japanese differences over territory. Some observers, like the Russian Duma's Foreign Affairs Committee former Chairman Lukin, noted that the West, including U.S., were trying to take advantage of Russia's immediate weakness to realise their economic, political and military objectives. He also reminded all concerned about the West having established large number of military bases around Russia.

It is important to note that the so-called 'working paper' made pointed and critical comments on India's stand on international issues and problems, primarily on nuclear non-proliferation. It pleaded that this should be taken note of while developing military and technical ties with India.

Of course, this was not the sole point of view regarding the scope of the Indo-Russian relations. In political circles, and in the academic community, there also existed an entirely different perspective regarding the course of these relations. It was argued on this side that the Russian relations with a major country like India could not be, and should not be, reduced to the level of other countries of the South Asian region. The important members of the Russian Duma, such as Ambartsumov and Pudovkin, openly articulated the view that 'India was, is and should remain, Russia's first priority'. The leader of the

Communist party in a lengthy article, published in *Pravda*, went on to forcefully argue that India has 'a great strategic potential' in global affairs, and this will be 'felt more and more as the years pass'. It was, therefore, in the 'vital interest of Russia' to preserve its closer relationship, which inherited from the Soviet period, with countries like India. These views were shared by quite a few other well-known political actors like Zhirinovsky, Burbolous and Lukianov, who were earlier Chairmen of the Duma's Group on India.

Indo-Russian Strategic Partnership

Thanks to the efforts of these, and the Russian Diplomatic mission in Delhi, President Yeltsin, during his visit to India in December 1992, boldly declared that India must continue to be a 'strategic partner of Russia', which was strongly in favour of 'bilateral equal relations between countries, confirming to the interests of each other'. Of course, he also emphasised that Russia would like to develop its ties with India 'in a deideologised manner' so as to minimize the possibility of these being directed against a 'third party'. He also endorsed India's stand on the Kashmir issue, and assured that Russia would refrain from selling arms to Pakistan. The complicated Rupee-Rouble issue, for reestimating the size of the past Soviet credits, too was satisfactorily solved. This removed a major irritant in the way of resumption of trade relations. An understanding was also reached to ensure smooth supply of defence spares. Likewise, a mutually acceptable solution was found with regard to the issue of supply of cryogenic engines.

It is, therefore, legitimate to infer that the visit of President Yeltsin marked a breakthrough in the Indo-Russian relations. One cannot but take note of the fact that he openly talked about an 'Asian tilt' in the foreign policy of Russia. He also spoke of 'Russia-China-India axis' for building durable peace in Asia. During this visit, a new 'Treaty of Peace, Friendship and Cooperation' was signed between the two countries. The new Treaty replaced 1971 Soviet era Treaty of Peace, Friendship and Cooperation. The credibility gap, thus, in Indo-Russian ties was considerably reduced.

Former Prime Minister P. V. Narasimha Rao visited Moscow in

June 1994. This visit further underscored the strategic aspect of the Indo-Russian relations. The so-called 'Moscow Declaration', signed by President Yeltsin and Prime Minister Rao, was indeed a historic document of paramount importance. It tried to pinpoint the commitment of the two countries to their territorial integrity. At a conceptual level, the Declaration highlighted the fact that the two countries were variegated, multicultural, multiethnic pluralistic states. As such, they faced a variety of common challenges to their territorial integrity. The Moscow Declaration gave a clear indication of the growing mutual understanding between the two countries, besides a realisation to raise afresh their relationship to a strategic long-term level in the changed context.

Russian Prime Minister Chernomyrdin was in Delhi in December, 1994. His visit came at a most appropriate time as reports, emanating from ITAR-TASS, had indicated that Russia was making serious efforts to push up its arms exports, and that it prefered cash sales, which Pakistan was in a position to offer. In fact, the press reports had gone to extent of claiming that a Russian military delegation had visited Pakistan to negotiate the sale of arms, and Su-27. These reports were, however, denied by Russian Deputy Foreign Minister Alexander Panov. Such reports had, in fact, given a setback to the mental drawings of mutual relationship which had been drawn up in the recent past, as they appeared to be falling apart.

Mr. Chenomyrdin's visit, however, went a long way in clearing the emerging doubts. He categorically declared that Russia was neither supplying any military equipment to Pakistan, nor it intended to do so in the future. This put an end to all speculations which spoke about Russia's interest in selling its sophisticated military hardware to Pakistan. He castigated Pakistan for lending its support to the rebels in Chechnya. He disclosed that mercenaries from Pakistan had been captured in Chechnya along with others. During his visit, a number of vital agreements, concerning cooperation in Defence, space research, and so on, were signed. Likewise, issues pertaining to merchant shipping, promotion of air traffic were discussed, and agreed upon.

Convergence of Interests

Historically, there has always existed a certain convergence of mutual geopolitical interests in peace and stability of the Central Asian region. This region forms the southern flank of the Eurasian landmass, which is separated from the Indian subcontinent by the Pamirs and the Hindukush chain of mountains. This area is of great interest to both India and Russia. During the Soviet period there was a clear perception of this interest, which was made subservient to the old Indo-Soviet strategic alliance. Of course, Russia, as a successor state, rejected the idea of earlier Soviet policy of active globalism. However, this rejection does not imply that Russia has no wider geo-political interests. In fact, Russia appears to be quite aware of the common Indo-Russian geopolitical interests, which demand a long-term mutual active cooperation. Both the countries feel that the situation in this region is in a transitional period, during which conditions must be created for a painless movement towards structuring a new Indo-Russia cooperation, preserving the essential elements of the old strategic partnership of the two great Asian powers.

Though there is no aggressive and active Islamic fundamentalism so far, yet Islamic factor is seeking a larger role in the Central Asia. Additionally, the secessionist movement in the Chechen autonomous republic of Russia has been receiving active assistance, as well as encouragement, from some of the neighbouring Islamic states. There is also a potentially greater threat of interethnic conflicts in the Muslim republics of CIS. In India, similarly, the secessionist movement in Kashmir is being sustained through trans-border terrorism. Until both, Russia and India, arrive at a common long-term understanding, China factor has to be taken into strategic considerations. Obviously, this calls for active strategic cooperation between India and Russia. In the final analysis, Indo-Russian cooperation and the formation of economic grouping by Russia, India and China will bring to an end their growing isolation in the world economy, and would help them to face the new challenge of globalisation. It will not be out of place to specifically mention that India, Russia and China are the three great powers which are yet to find a place in any of the new regional economic groupings.

It is necessary to point out at this juncture that the continued relevance of a strong and healthy Indo-Russian relationship in the changed global environment was a point of dispute among a section of influential public opinion in India also. There is no dearth of skeptics who doubt the wisdom of reenergizing the Indian ties with Russia in view of the present economic and military weakness of Russia. They also invariably point to the political instability prevailing there. The argument is that India's requirements of economic and technological restructuring can be met out only by the U.S. and Europe. These skeptics forget that Russia's geostrategic location on the Eurasian landscape, its advanced nuclear and human resources make it difficult for that country to reconcile itself for a long to the status of a mere regional power. It is bound to regain its stature as a powerful player in the international politics.

New Russian Perception

It has become increasingly obvious that Russia's foreign policy is undergoing a major face lift. The earlier tilt towards the U.S. has gradually yielded place to diversification. There is an open effort to upgrade its relations with countries like India to a strategic level. The new Russian Foreign Minister Yevgeni Primakov asserts that "Russian foreign policy today should uphold national interests more energetically than before". Obviously, the Russian diplomacy now has a well-defined foreign policy concept. Some years ago, it was often pointed out in the Russian academic circles that Russia continues to be lost in its "search for a true place between the East and the West, the North and the South".

Soon after taking over as the Foreign Minister, Mr. Primakov spelled out the parameters of the Russian foreign policy in the new context. He at once agreed that Russia's foreign policy suffered from 'imbalances', which, he said, must be 'overcome'. He admitted that the "development of relations with the U.S. as a state, having considerable weight and influence in the world", was only one among the priority tasks of the Russian foreign policy. He repeatedly underlined the need to diversify—the word 'diversify' figured several times in his exposition—Russia's international ties. "Of great importance for us is the development of relations with the European Community as a whole, as well as China, India, Japan, the near and the Middle East countries, and the Asia Pacific countries," he emphasized. In his tongue in cheek remark, he suggested that the idea of "normalising relations with our former cold war opponents" was "overdone too strongly." He stressed the imperative need to "counter balance" those negative trends that could be discerned in the international affairs. This, he added, was so because "not all power centres of the multipolar would have been formed".

Apparently, Russia is paying a lot of more attention to CIS countries, particularly those which are located in Central Asia. In fact, Mr. Primakov has hinted that the process of "closest integration with Belarus, Kazakhstan and Kyrgyzstan" is fast developing. He visualises that this could 'effect' Russia's relations 'with the West'. If the projected integration gradually becomes, as Mr. Primakov says, "an irritant in Russia's relations with the USA and some Western countries", then it opens up new possibilities for developing closer ties between India and Russia. Both countries cannot but take into consideration the new geopolitical realities. Russia has a point when it says that its relations with the CIS, and particularly with Central Asia, are of 'prime importance' for a variety of reasons. Foremost among them is, as Primakov points out, that it is a "way for Russia to become aware of itself as a great power". The CIS integration is now an established Russian policy, and nobody seems to be against it. Of course, it is not intended to restore the Soviet state.

Likewise, India too has a deep strategic interest in the Central Asia. It may be argued that these interests do not exclude each other in any major way. The projected 'strategic partnership' between Russia and India has this, and several other causes, to serve, and benefit from. From historical standpoint, there has always been a certain convergence of the Russian and the Indian interests in peace and stability of the Eurasian landmass separated from India by a chain of mountains. It is useful from the standpoint of India that Russia cogently redefines its priorities, foreign policy goals and its national interests. India apparently figures high up in these new projections.

The new strain in Moscow's foreign policy basically stems from the growing realisation—also in India—to elevate anew its relationship with India to a strategic long-term level. Their so-called 'strategic partnership' has the necessary potential to counterbalance all those negative trends which may be perceived in the current international politics. It is also necessary to come to understand that we have serious common geopolitical interests dictating long-term mutual active cooperation, particularly in the Central Asia. Moreover, this relationship can go a long way in perfecting the process of formation of different power centres of the emerging multipolar world, though they may take quite some time to crystalise.

Lastly, one of the major problems is to overcome the snags in the implementation of various agreements. Invariably, there hangs this perennial question as to what extent various accords and agreements are likely to be fulfilled? Obviously, there is a crying need to activize the bureaucracy, as also devise a mechanism for better coordination between the concerned bodies and establishments.

5

Indo-Russian Relations: In the Light of New Realities

SHASHI KANT JHA

The disintegration of the Soviet Union and the end of the cold war brought about a fundamental transformation in the geopolitical map of the world. The most prominent among the successor states of the Soviet Union, Russia, in spite of inheriting the formidable military might of its predecessor, suddenly found itself reduced to the position of a second ranking or regional power. Its predicament was further compounded by economic chaos and political uncertainty at the domestic level. The new leaders of Russia, besieged by domestic constraints, were not immediately in a position to clearly define the foreign policy goals of their state and ascertain its position in the emerging post cold war international order. With the ideology having been jettisoned, the new Russian foreign policy elite, in its attempt to carve out a new international role for Russia, found itself suffering from a priority cleavage. It was clearly pulled between a declining nostalgia for past relations with countries like India and growing proclivity towards cultivating relations with the West.

For India the consequences of the Soviet collapse and the new priorities of the Russian foreign policy were shattering. Though 'complicated' and 'unusual', there had been a highly beneficial trade relationship between the two countries. The Soviet Union was India's largest supplier of arms and a major market for its exports. But much more than that India was damaged by the loss of a strategic partner. The Soviet Union could always be relied on to provide political support at multilateral fora, particularly at the U.N. on issues like the one related to Kashmir. It is difficult now to imagine about such support from Russia.[1]

The first couple of years of India's relations with post-Soviet Russia were marked by a good deal of uncertainty, inconsistency, lack of clarity and even 'unreliability' from India's point of view. 'Learning to live with the uncertainties of the new era', India did take early steps to 'protect its own interests', though without making any significant headway. The two-track approach that India adopted was on the one hand, aimed at resurrecting the vital elements of its economic and military relations with Russia and, on the other, searching out alternatives in the West. On both these counts, however, India's efforts were rewarded to a limited extent. India's difficulties were compounded both by the magnitude of her dependence on Russia and the political-economic uncertainty faced by the latter. It meant that it often had to 'wait and see' what Russia would do and how this would affect the relationship of the two countries.[2] However, Russia seems to be shedding its initial hesitation, inconsistency and unclarity. The contours of new Russia's foreign policy are becoming clearer. It is now giving all the indications of its ability and intentions of redefining its foreign policy goals, priorities and international role. With India the objectives and character of its relations are being defined with a measure of clarity. The national goals of two countries are being looked upon in the light of new international realities. The two countries have once again begun to rediscover the mutual importance but with a qualitative difference, which commensurates with the realities of the post cold war era

An attempt is being made in this study to present an analytical survey of the pattern of India's relations with Russia in the post cold war period.

How do Russia and India visualize and place each other in the new global context? Free from the constraints of the ideological strait-jacket foreign policy, Russia has been trying to define its goals, priorities and international role in accordance with its post Soviet domestic compulsions and needs. Its search for new friends in the international arena led to a good deal of shift of emphasis from what used to be the characteristic features of the old Soviet foreign policy. The new approach has made Russia to look upon the erstwhile adversaries like the United States, Western Europe, China and Japan as friends and partners. The compulsions of enhancing economic cooperation with former adversaries were considered too great to be ignored the basic aim being to attract much needed economic aid and advanced technology.

Yeltsin's Policy

It was natural that this shift of emphasis in Russia's foreign policy goals was to considerably modify her attitude towards India and affect the larger gamut of Indo-Russian relations. The whole Russian outlook was expressed through a concept called 'deideologization' which Russian President Boris Yeltsin, during his visit to India in January 1993, claimed was permeating 'all spheres' of Russian life, including its foreign policy.[3] This was a clever way of conveying to India that in the post cold war era Russia did not consider any country as its enemy and was, therefore, in no need to support one state against the other. This approach also ignored much of the pragmatic commonality of strategic and diplomatic interests between India and the former Soviet Union, though it could still be of quite relevance to both India and Russia.

For India the larger implications of the new Russian foreign policy assertions can be identified in two ways. First, from Russia's point of view, the special relationship between India and the former Soviet Union was motivated by the need for a balance against the West and China as well as shared security and geopolitical concerns The new Indo-Russian relationship would have to be based primarily on common business interests and balance of power and coloured only marginally by geopolitics and security. This attitude was reflected by Russia expressing its satisfaction about India's efforts to improve her relations with China. Indeed Russia herself has signifi cantly improved her relations with China. In either case such improvement of relations was not viewed as targetted against the third country. Furthermore, this was specifically emphasized that the post-Soviet Russia had a desire for good relations with all countries serving its interests and needs. "We do not at present regard anyone in Asia even as a potential adversary of ours", declared President Yeltsin, adding "we see only partners".[4]

Second, though Russia and India renewed the Indo-Soviet Treaty of 1971, they transformed its fundamental character. The new treaty does not contain any clauses, viz., requiring military consultations in the event of a threat to Russia's or India's security; prohibiting the parties from joining military alliances directed against each other; and forbidding each party from providing assistance to a third party engaged in armed conflict against the other. Instead, it calls vaguely for regular consultations on all matters and for coordination in dealing with any developing threats to peace. But both parties undertake to refrain from actions that might damage each other's security.[5] "We are against axes, triangles, polygons, and in general, any blocs",[6] said Yeltsin. Russia sought what it called 'mutually advantageous' relations with India.

In search of 'mutually advantageous' relations between the two countries the Indian and Russian leaders have been confronting some harsh realities.

First, India clearly recognises that for its role in international environment, the end of bipolarism has created some definite adverse consequences. In a bipolar international environment India's policy of non-alignment was the symbol of its sovereignty, independent foreign policy, ability to judge issues on merits and also an instrument of maximizing its diplomatic options. This may not be the case any longer.[7]

Second, it is also recognized by India that in view of serious economic difficulties faced by Russia it cannot be the source of aid in the sense the former Soviet Union was. Russia could at best provide 'cooperation' and 'partnership' based on mutual interest. As the economic development is the most pressing need for both the countries, they look for the diversification of the sources of aid. For India, among such new sources of aid, investment, technology and economic cooperation are North America, the European Union and the Asia-Pacific region in general, and the USA, Germany and Japan in particular. During the past few years India's efforts in this direction have made reasonable headway.

Third, India's place in Russia's new world view needs to be seen in the light of the latter's search for a new identity and international role. The uniqueness of Russian geopolitical situation as both a European and Asian power has enabled it to present certain baffling instances. It was Mikhail Gorbachev who first made major efforts for the Soviet Union's greater identification with the West. The policy of 'common European home' being the conceptual articulation of such a drive. The post-Soviet Russian leaders during the initial few years tried to maintain the momentum of this Euro-centric drive which was greeted with no less optimism in the West. However, the honeymoon of East-West relations did not last long. Within just two years, it became apparent that the initial optimism had been misplaced. The support for close cooperation with the West declined within Russia as its foreign policy became more assertive and it clashed with the interests of the West on a number of important issues.[8] The factors which compelled Russia to make a change in its stance consisted of broad spectrum of issues ranging from economic to political and military.

However, as the Euro-centric drive in its foreign policy started losing its momentum Russia began to specifically emphasize its Asian connection and commitment. While in India, in January 1993, President Yeltsin underlined the Eurasian identity of Russia by pointing out that most of its territory—10 million out of 17 million square kms—lay in Asia and that most Russian citizens lived in the Asian part of Russia.[9] This assertion was further reiterated during former Indian Prime Minister P. V. Narasimha Rao's visit to Russia in July 1994.[10] One possible objective of such assertions was to reassure India and also the internal Russian critics that Russia would not cultivate its relations with the West at the cost of Asia. In reality, however, Russia herself began looking for partners in Asia, after its disappointment was growing stronger with the Western policy and attitude towards it.

But which Asian partners was it looking for? And what was India's position among them? The post-Soviet Russia has accorded higher priority to the Asia-Pacific region than South and West Asia. India does not find a very high place in Russia's list of priorities — it is ranked seventh on its ten-point priority list.[11] The Asia-Pacific region includes countries like China with whom Russia shares 'the longest border in the world' and which is becoming a major trading partner, next only to Germany, Japan and South Korea, which are considered as potential developers of Russia's Far East. China, particularly, has become not only a renewed focus of Russian policy attention in Asia as a direct neighbour, but also as a possible counter-balance to the West.[12]

China-Russia Friendship

The Chinese-Russian relations are on the upswing indeed. In just over three years there have been three summits between the two countries and two visits by Russian President Yeltsin to China, the latest was undertaken in the last week of April 1996. During this visit of the Russian President to China the two countries signed as many as fourteen major agreements. Among them was a three billion dollar 10-year accord on the peaceful uses of nuclear energy under which Russia will build a nuclear power plant and a uranium—enriching facility in China. Also a project on the joint development of a pipeline to bring Siberian gas to China, and there were other project proposals covering cooperation in machine building, space research, transport and high technology.[13]

Besides the fourteen accords signed between the two countries, there was a political declaration defining the format of Chinese-Russian relations, which was called 'constructive partnership'. Another important international dimension of the visit was a pact the Russian President signed in Shanghai with the leaders of China, Kazakhstan, Tazikistan and Kyrgyzstan on confidence-building measures along their common border. The Yeltsin side hailed this accord as a path finder to a 'new system of inter-state relations in Central Asia'. There appears to be an attempt by both the countries to convert their developing bilateral ties into a border cooperation in international affairs. Developing such a cooperation, it is said, is a part of Russia's plan to build a new strategic alignment in Asia with China, Iran and India. It is not without significance that Russian Foreign Minister, Yevgeny Primakov's visit to New Delhi in the first week of April 1996 followed his consultations with the Iranian leadership in Tehran, "which the Iranian capital. Iran appears to be emerging as a surprise global turnaround partner of sorts for Russia". It became evident as Yeltsin's China visit the same month was preceded by Primakov's Tehran consultation. The Consultations, about whose import none of the countries have been forthcoming, have given rise to speculation about a quadrangular strategic understanding on the crucial region of the Central Asia. According to reports, the main objective of Primakov's discussions with the Indian leaders was to identify areas of agreement among these nations.[14]

It was, of course, futile for the Indian Government to provide any definite indication of its position, especially at a juncture when the country was then faced with the coming of the crucial general elections. An additional reason for maintenance of restraint by India was the caution against giving any currency to the impression that it was ready to be a part of the tie up whose principal target possibly could be the United States. It was legitimate for India to calculate that its difference of perspectives and grievances against US policies towards subcontinental relations notwithstanding, a strategic alliance, howsoever dressed up it was, aimed against Washington would not be in her national interest.

The Close-knit Trinity

There are, however, clear signs that Russia, China and Iran have been strengthening their bilateral and trilateral relations in an attempt to stem the increasing American influence in their region. Iran's unceasing efforts to get a foothold in the Central Asia had been initially countered by Russia as it shared the American strategic perspective in the early phase of the Yeltsin regime. With a greater balance in U.S.-Russia relations, new alignments have emerged. The United States now finds that both Russia and Iran are ranged against it in that old game of geopolitics—competition for strategic and commercial interests. In the rush to exploit the natural resources in the Central Asian region, Russia has stood firm in its stand that Caspian reserves should be exploited only with the agreement of all states in the region. America has also staked its claims to a share in the development of the vast gas and oil resources in the Caspian, with the American companies already investing heavily in friendly republics like Kazakhstan. In any case, Russia is no longer an unquestioned ally of America. With perceived humiliations by Washington and disappointment with the West, Russia has now been pursuing a more energetic Asian policy by deepening its relations with both Iran and China. The Iranian government, targeted by America with a relentless zeal, has been ready for the Russian bear hug.[15]

On the other hand, the Chinese leadership finds that its own relations with the United States have not been running smooth either, though the latter has, for vital economic reasons, been reluctant to apply the type of sanctions that it imposed against Iran on China. China, therefore, is keen to use its improving relations with Russia to counter the U.S. pressure. China certainly has reasons to be concerned. The Joint Japan-U.S. Declaration on 'Security Alliance' for the 21st century that was signed between US President Bill Clinton and Japanese Premier Ryutaro Hashimoto in April 17, 1996 has, among others, made it known that a review of the 1978 Defence Cooperation guidelines for military cooperation with the U.S. in a military crisis, not just in case of Japan but for the Asia-Pacific region would be undertaken. It is reasonable to argue that the U.S.-Japan Treaty in its new shape envisions a structure for the containment of China and commits Japan as a means to strengthening this structure. It is not surprising, therefore, that China was first to voiced against such a team playing on the Asia-Pacific turf. The deepening China-Russia relations with a speculation about its larger regional ramifications has assumed significance. Indeed, a delicate situation is emerging but India needs to show utmost restrain.

India-Russia: Convergence of Interests

In spite of these constraints and latest developments, India and Russia are once again in the process of rediscovering their bilateral level common interests which are multidimensional in nature. There is a growing appreciation for each in both the countries as both are multinational, multiethnic and multilinguistic states. The Russian President lauded India as the world's major democratic federal state, and observed that consensus was necessary to transform any society as to avoid conflicts and to adjust to economic, political, technical and military realities of the post cold war era. Russia attaches great importance to India's efforts to balance different interests, linguistic and religious groups. President Yeltsin declared that India's motto of 'unity in diversity' could be an effective formula for solving endemic social and political problems of post-Soviet Russia also.[17]

Both the countries have faced challenges to their territorial integrity and have appreciated each other's efforts in overcoming them. The joint Indo-Russian declaration, issued on the conclusion of the July 1994 visit of the Indian Prime Minister, emphasized on the protection of the interests of multinational states. Russia, accordingly, declared its support for India's stance on Kashmir.[18]

Moreover, India and Russia share an interest in moderating the resurgent fundamentalist challenges which could threaten the secular identity and territorial integrity of both the states. This provides a fresh basis for India and Russia to establish a bridge across the Islamic world in South-West and Central Asia which have the potential of affecting their border regions. Even short of spread of fundamentalism, Russia and India share an interest in stabilising the situation in the interconnected regions of Afghanistan and Central Asia. The border between Afghanistan and Central Asia is porous and the conflicts in the region involve ethnic groups spread across several political frontiers. They also threaten the safety and welfare of large population of Russians left behind in the Central Asian republics after the break up of the Soviet Union.[19] The fact that within months of his becoming the Russia's new Foreign Minister Yevgeny Primakov visited India. Thus it underscores the importance Russia once again has begun to attach to India. In a meeting with the Parliamentary Standing Committee on External Affairs, Primakov sought to convey the message that the imperatives of Indo-Russian friendship and cooperation were enduring as they cut across political divisions, and would remain unaffected by the political fortunes of the ruling parties in the two countries.[20]

It would be interesting to see how these commonalities are reflected in the military and economic aspects of the new Indo-Russian relationship.

The greatest impact of the political changes in Russia was felt in India's defence sector. The Soviet Union had a dominant position among India's major arms suppliers until its demise in 1991. Almost seventy per cent of India's military imports came from the Soviet Union. Practically all the frontline armour and mechanized units of the Indian army have used the Soviet made equipment. The Soviet supplied weaponry have also formed an important part of the artillery and constituted the entire anti-aircraft artillery, including the panoply of surface-to-air missile (SAM) batteries. All but seven of IAF squadrons have used various versions of MiGs. Ilyushins and Miseries set of helicopters. Most of the Navy's submarine destroyers missile boat division has come up on the Soviet equipment.[21]

The Soviet break-up disrupted India's most important source of defence supplies, as it took away a major Indian export market, left it vulnerable to potentially hostile resolutions at the UN, introduced fresh instabilities in its northern neighbourhood and brought new competitors for foreign aid. In terms of India's overall goals, the Soviet connection had proved important for modernisation and indigenisation of its defence forces' equipment in keeping consonance with the country's own assessment of its needs for not only protection of its vital interests against international pressure, but for counterbalancing possible Chinese and American pressures in the fields of economic assistance especially for the public sector. In concrete terms India's reliance on the Soviet defence supplies had three distinct advantages. One, Soviet aircraft, ships and tanks enjoyed significant price advantages over comparable Western equipment. Two, the period between the signing of contract and delivery of weapons was normally a year, in contrast to the two-three years of the U.S. Three, in spite of a wide range and volume of Soviet military sales to India, the bilateral military relationship was of limited association rather than in the nature of an alliance or a protector-client bond.[22]

Thus India had to pay a price with the breaking up of the Soviet Union. It was in the form of delays in the supplies of spares, ammunition and fulfilling maintenance contracts. The question of spares supplies became particularly acute for India's fleet of MiG-29s in early 1992. While India produces some types of MiGs under licence, it lacks the capacity to supply all the required equipment and instruments. A journey by former Indian Defence Minister Sharad Pawar to Moscow in September 1991 to try for the supply of spares was a disappointing experience. Amidst uncertainty about the independent republics' ability and willingness to supply spares for the Indian Air Force, India got an assurance for the supply from Ukraine. Sharad Pawar led a delegation to Ukraine then. India's AN-32 military transport aircraft and TU-142M, patrol driven Anti-Submarine Warfare (ASW) planes had been badly affected by the disruption in Ukrainian supplies of spares. India also showed its interest in buying nuclear or diesel powered submarines from Ukraine. At the end of Pawar's visit it was agreed that Ukraine would supply armaments and spares in return of medicines and cloth and if partial payment was made in hard currency.[23]

The initial confusion notwithstanding, the Russian policy-makers are aware that India is potentially one of Russia's best customers. They see the enormous commercial scope of expanding a modified security and technology relationship with India.

In March 1992 Russia offered India Charlie-class nuclear-powered submarines, MiG-31 aircraft and SU-28 fighter bombers. India's interest in these lay in the wish to counter the acquisition of armada of French Mirage-2000s and the US F-16s by Pakistan. In May 1992, Russian Deputy Prime Minister Gennady Burbulis visited India and assured India of Russia's continued defence and spare supplies. However, it was declared that the new credits would be available at double the existing interest rates plus one-tenth of the payment was required in advance. Under an agreement signed in September 1992, India received a credit line of 830 million dollars to buy special equipment. In June 1994, Russia agreed to offer India credits to buy SU-30 fighters and a production licence for the manufacture of Russian aeroplanes spares too was granted in India's favour.[24]

The Indo-Russian military relations received a degree of stabilization after the defence agreements were signed between the two countries during the then Indian Prime Minister's Moscow visit in July 1994. Russia agreed to help India in the upgradation of its 170 MiG aircraft to keep them combat-worthy well into the next century. The two sides formalised agreements to set up joint ventures in the field of civil and military aviation. Of particular importance is the Indo-Russian Aviation Private Ltd.—a joint venture company set up in India with an equity base of 400 million dollars to manufacture spare parts to upgrade and service military aircraft of Russian origin being operated by India and the third world countries. Such ventures are to be based on purely commercial considerations. Russian Deputy Prime Minister, Yuri Yarov on his Indian journey in the summer of 1994, talked of reviving the Soviet proposal to build a safeguarded 2000 MW nuclear power plant in Tamil Nadu, besides finding ways to continue business in the field of space and nuclear science "without violating international regimes and agreements". Plans to set up engine overhaul plants for MiG-29s and for the upgrading of T-72 tanks were also finalized subsequently. It was also agreed that Malaysian pilots would be trained in India to fly MiG-29 supplies to the Malaysian Air Force under the June 1994 Russia-Malaysia agreement.[25]

The Indo-Russian military ties have of late received greater momentum. According to a recent report, two trends are visible in India's demands for Russian equipment—one is the outright purchase of equipment, and the second is collaboration for upgradation, joint ventures and joint production. As a part of its decades old self-reliance and indigenization drive, India plans to produce 70 per cent of its weaponry within the country by the year 2005. But during the interregnum, it would seek to upgrade existing systems, acquire parts and components and get knowhow besides looking for coproduction proposals. In these areas, India may rediscover Russia as a reliable partner in the coming decade.

Upgradation being of top priority for India, it wants MiG-21, Bis and Kilo class submarines modernised. Russia has also agreed to upgrade the 21 km range BM-21 multiple rocket system that is with India. The Indian side is also negotiating with Russia for a possible lease of aircraft carrier, Admiral Gorshkov. Among the new weapons, the Indian Navy is negotiating for the new Ilga shoulder fired missile with several 'smart' features. The Indian Air Force wants SU-30 planes whose price is being negotiated by the Ministry of Defence.[26]

Roosvorouzhenie, Deputy Director General Stanislav Filin, recently said that the sale of Russian arms to India had continued unhindered and Russia had provided weapons, equipment, accessories and servicing facilities worth 1.5 billion dollars to India in 1995. He emphasized that defence cooperation was developing strictly in accordance with the provisions of the agreements existing between the two countries. Filin clarified that India was being supplied with MiG-20s and MiG-29s, anti-missile complexes, ammunition of various types and other defence equipments. According to him, Russia considered India its important partner in the field of military-technical cooperation.[27]

In spite of these positive developments, India has been trying to find alternative weapon sources and develop defence cooperation with other countries. India thus approached other arms sellers including United States, France, Britain and Israel. Moreover, India has also taken initiative to edge closer to the United States in limited military sectors, which included the conduct of joint exercises with the United States Navy in 1992-93. It included dispatch of a naval contingent to Somalia to assist the multinational effort there.[28]

There have indeed been occasional irritants in Indo-Russian military relationship. Some of them though have been settled, others are lingering on. For example, to India a rude shock and a pointer to the changed equation came in 1993 when under the US pressures, Russia reneged on its old commitment for the supply of technology for the manufacture of cryogenic engines for India's use in ongoing Polar Satellite Launch Vehicle (PSLV) programme. The deal now stands reduced to the supply of some engines without technology transfer. In India's estimation it construed a major sign of Russia's unreliability and susceptability to outside pressures and loss of its international stature.[29] India was also irritated by the reports of Russian offers to Pakistan for sale of armaments on a commercial basis. This unease was, however, removed through President Yeltsin's assurance in India in 1993 that Russia would not supply arms to Pakistan.

Further, India and Russia have also differed on the question of nuclear non-proliferation. The Russian Government has supported the idea of a nuclear-free zone in South Asia which runs counter to India's efforts to prevent such a regionalization of the nuclear issue. In November 1991, Russia caused shock and consternation in India by supporting a joint Pakistani-Bangladeshi NWFZ resolution in the disarmament committee of the UN General Assembly. Yet, shortly before his visit to India in January 1993, President Yeltsin announced on the Russian TV that NPT was not on the agenda of his discussions in India.[30] The disagreement, however, continues. In a report on the NPT problems, prepared in 1995 by Russian Foreign Intelligence Service which then headed by the present Russian Foreign Minister Yergeny Primakov, it was stated that India, Pakistan and Israel were the main sources of nuclear arms proliferation threat as they de facto possessed nuclear weapons but refused to sign the NPT.[31] The two countries are, however, learning to live with these irritants and exploring the areas of wider cooperation.

India's Economic Relation with Russia

Apart from the supply of spares to India's defence sector, there were two crucial issues which had created some friction in the Indo-Russian economic relationship. These were: Outstanding payments for past military purchases by India from the former Soviet Union and part rupee, part dollar payments for fresh supplies of military spares. The central issue was the fixing of a new exchange rate between Rupee and Rouble. The worst problem of all was the debt — a whopping amount of about Rs. 37000 crore standing against India from the former Soviet Union days. Though India was slowly repaying at the rate of Rs. 31 to a Rouble, Russia, as the inheritor the Soviet Union mantle, wanted payment of the entire amount in one go.

Trade between the two countries almost collapsed in 1991-92 because of dispute over the Rupee-Rouble exchange rate. Russia claimed India owed it 16 billion dollars, but India claimed it owed only 12 billion dollars. India was trying to balk at the prospect of shelling out such a large sum on the basis that old currency equation could hardly hold good in a changed financial order. At that time a dollar equated 417 roubles.

The Indian side also maintained that with the entry of Russia into the World Bank and International Monetary Fund fold it must accept international rates of exchange. Russia's point, on the contrary, was that India incurred the debt-predominantly for the purchase of military equipment and spares during a time when it had accepted the superior value of Rouble.

During President Yeltsin's visit to India in January 1993, the two countries agreed that 63 per cent of the debt would be repayed over next 12 years at an interest rate of 2.4 per cent using the exchange rate of one rouble to 19.9 rupees, which existed in January 1, 1990. This gave a net 32 per cent debt reduction advantage to India. The remaining 37 per cent of the principal was agreed to be repaid over a period of 45 years without interest and at the exchange rate of one rouble for 3.1 rupees. The whole repayment was agreed to be made through Indian goods.[32]

Russia in 1994 had shown an inclination to auction part of its accumulated rupee funds. This was seen in India as a way to use the credit to buy the Indian goods cheaply for resale in other markets.[33] Further, in order to boost imports from India, the Russian government announced a six-month deferred payment facility to the Russian importers of the Indian goods besides an interest-free credit. It was also announced that goods imported against debt repayment would be exempted from the value added tax to the extent of 20 per cent and a special tax rebate of 3 per cent. These concessions were to help increase exports from India of such items as tea, tobacco, pharmaceuticals and Soya over next three years and give some predictability to the producers in India. In view of this, the Russian government also called off in September 1994 the proposed auction of the Indian rupee stocks but went back on its six-month interest-free commitment for the Russian importers of the Indian goods. This disrupted the momentum which the Indo-Russian trade would have acquired. In India's estimation, Russia reneged on its promise because it feared that India's debt-burden might get reduced by 40-50 per cent. It obviously dismayed the Indian side and indignation at Russia's erratic behaviour ran high.[34]

Nevertheless, there has been a broad agreement between India and Russia about how to use the rupee funds. While a large proportion is to be used to import Indian consumer goods, some will be spent on joint ventures in Russia and India. Out of the rupee funds Russia agreed to contribute to the equity of joint ventures in India. The areas in which these funds will be utilised are to include setting up of new enterprises, modernization of existing units, and development of infrastructure. Russia is also to help India in building hydro-electric and nuclear power stations.

As far as India is concerned it is taking part in a large construction project to expand the Novorossiisk seaport. There are already more than 30 joint ventures in operation. They cover leather goods, computer hardware and engineering plastic. The State Bank of India and the Exim Bank are collaborating to set up a joint bank. In August 1994, India and Russia in a protocol identified new areas of collaboration, including aluminium, zinc and copper industries, research and development in ferrous metallurgy. Bilateral trade in iron and steel has also increased.[35]

With the settlement of most outstandings between the two countries, the activised Indian exporters have started pushing the government for easier norms of countertrade with Russia. The new exim policy has eased the quantitative restrictions, provided for the opening of escrow accounts in India and entitling trading houses for pre-shipment and post-shipment credit. But procedural delays have often meant losing money and cancellation of contracts. Most Indian companies, therefore, prefer to deal with Russia through third countries such as Singapore or the free trade Gulf kingdoms. The true extent of the export of the Indian goods to Russia is, therefore, difficult to gauge.[36]

This is quite interesting to note that most of the Indian companies operating in Russia do trading only. The serious operators include names like ITC Global, Ranbaxy and Thermax, etc. Among the engineering firms Bharat Forge and Dalal Machine Tools have done well. Phoenix, manufacturer of shoes, has gone in with its own brand name in Russia. This company also runs its three restaurants in the country. On the project side, there is Larson and Toubro, which is currently executing the largest military housing project at Zerongrad for soldiers returning from Germany.

Among the Russian companies with strong links in India is Leningradsky Metalworks which has 9 per cent share in the world market. In the wake of Soviet collapse, this company had stopped supply to India. However, it has now resumed its ties. In mid-1995, this company was in the process of signing a contract with Orissa State Electricity Board for modernising its power stations. Another company, International Consortium Mekor, is a joint venture of 11 Russian pulp and paper industry specialists. This, too, is now focusing on India.[37]

In a meeting of the Indo-Russian Joint Commission held in October 1995, both sides expressed satisfaction over the steadily rising volume of trade between the two countries. It is expected to cross Rs. 5000 crore mark by 1995-96. The comparable figures of 1993-94 were Rs. 2300 crore and Rs. 4000 crore respectively.[38]

The Indo-Russian trade has, however, been facing difficulties, too. India confronts strong competition from more industrialised countries which took early initiatives to take advantage of the new openings in the Russian market. Even in Asia, Japan and China are way ahead of India. Over 2 per cent of the Soviet Union's trade was with India which in the case of Russia's trade with India fell down to 1.04 per cent in 1993. In contrast, in 1993, 17.7 per cent of Russia's trade was with Germany, 10.6 per cent with China, 5.4 per cent with Italy and 5 per cent with Japan and United States. India, indeed, has lost substantial ground in Russia which would not be quite easy to regain.[39]

India and the former Soviet Union had a multifaceted relationship. In the changed situation of the post cold war era there has been a metamorphosis in how Russia and India define their national goals and international role. In the process certain older complementarities as well as differences have disappeared whereas some old common interests have survived, too. What is, however, interesting is the emergence of both new complementarities and some potential areas of clash of redefined interests.

In the immediate aftermath of the Soviet collapse, there was a definite dislocation as to how Russia and India should place each other in international arena. The former Soviet Union, in entering into economic relations with India, had sought to erode Western influence, counterbalance West and China and secure an outlet for its own expanding economy. Additionally, India was considered the centrepiece of the Soviet Asia policy. India was a major country of the Third World and a prominent leader of the Non-Aligned Movement. Even then Russia lost no time in absolving itself with this burden of history. The Yeltsin-Kozyrev combine launched Russia's foreign policy with the pronounced objective of forging closer cooperation with the West. Quite obviously in such a scheme India did not find a significant position for itself. India's position began to assume importance only when Russian foreign policy turned to Asia. But even in the Asian context India came next only to China, Japan and other expanding economies of the Asia-Pacific region.

India, nevertheless, remains a potentially crucial partner for Russia which the latter appears now trying to rediscover. There is an enormous legacy of multifaceted relationship and vast reservoir of goodwill between the two countries which, with necessary modification and restructuring to the mutual satisfaction of both, could be expanded in new areas. India remains a reliable and low-cost supplier of some traditional products as well as a market for some long-established Russian exports. Some protective measures to cushion the Indo-Russian economic relations had been agreed upon in May 1992 and were further underlined in 1993 during the Russian President's visit.

The irritants like supply of defence spares, rupee-rouble exchange rate, repayment of debt, etc., have been resolved to mutual satisfaction. India is aware that its economic strength will play a determining role in shaping the character of its relations with Russia. Since 1993 India's GDP has been growing by more than 5 per cent which cannot be possibly ignored by Russia. A modernized, dynamic and vibrant Indian economy could always prove useful to Russia's interest.

Though there are disagreements on the question of nuclear disarmament between Russia and India, both sides are capable of ignoring them in order to promote vital common interests like respect for the territorial integrity and unity of the two countries, stability and peace in Central Asia among other things of mutual interest. Both have cultivated their relationship with China without trying to adversely affect the interest of the other. But what is extremely important is that the improvement in the China-Russia relations offers India additional strategic manoeuverability, if handled skillfully. China under pressure from the United States may find significant mutuality of strategic interests with India, whereas the enduring Indo-Russian friendship is poised to grow. The undying cold war mindset of the American policy-makers and their overconfidence that they can manipulate the balance of power in Asia may only forge a greater understanding among the major Asian powers to the long-term disadvantage of the United States. Even though Russia and China may have conflicting strategic ambitions, the recent Beijing summit between the two is an indication of the shape of things to come in Asia.

As far as India is concerned any concrete reaction on her part to this new development will depend on how does the Deve Gowda United Front Government look at it. However, it is gratifying for India that Russia continues to support her on the Kashmir question and promises not to give any military aid to Pakistan. The Indo-Russian relations are, thus, assuming realistic character once again.

REFERENCES

1. Shekhar Gupta, "India Redefines its Role", *Adelphi Paper 293*, p. 61.
2. Anita Inder Singh, "India's Relations with Russia and Central Asia", *International Affairs*, vol. 71, no. 1, January 1995, p. 70.
3. Ibid.
4. Ibid.
5. BBC, SWB, SU/1601, A1/1-6, 30 January 1993.
6. Quoted in Anita Inder Singh, n. 2, p. 70.
7. Ibid., p. 71.
8. Paul Marantz, "Neither Adversaries nor Partners: Russia and the West Search for a New Relationship", *International Journal*, vol. XLIX, no. 4, Autumn 1994, pp. 725-50.

9. *FBIS SOV*-93-019, 1 February 1993.
10. *FBIS SOV*-94-127, 1 July 1994.
11. According to a Russian foreign policy report these priorities are the following: (1) the CIS (2) arms control and international security (3) economic reform (4) the United States (5) Europe (6) the Asia-Pacific region (7) East and South Asia (8) the Near East (9) Africa (10) Latin America. See Singh, n. 2, p. 72.
12. Klaus Fritsche, "Russia Refocuses on China", *Aussen Politik*, vol. 46, no. 4, 1995, p. 379.
13. *The Hindu*, 25 April 1996.
14. *The Hindu*, 4 April 1996 and *The Times of India* (New Delhi), 27 April 1996.
15. Ibid.
16. *The Hindu*, 21 April 1996.
17. *FBIS SOV*-93-018, 29 January 1993.
18. See Anita Inder Singh, n. 2, p. 72.
19. Ramesh Thakur, "The Impact of the Soviet Collapse on Military Relations with India", *Europe-Asia Studies*, vol. 45, no. 5, pp. 840-41.
20. *The Hindu* (New Delhi), 3 April 1996.
21. Shekhar Gupta, n. 1, p. 41.
22. Ramesh Thakur, n. 15, pp. 831-32. However, in the wake of 1991 Gulf War and afterwards India had slowly started to realise that there were certain definite difficulties in her defence partnership with Soviet Union and Russia, viz., the previous history of uninterrupted and quick delivery of Soviet arms during a war was no longer an assurance of continued deliveries in future conflicts; it was being perceived that Soviet military doctrines had critical flaws and performance of its weaponry was poor, and the technological gap between Soviet and US weapon systems was widening to dangerous proportions for Indian security. Thus there was an inclination of India's part for the diversification of the sources of arms supply. Ibid., pp. 835-36.
23. Ibid., p. 837.
24. Ibid., Also see Anita Inder Singh, n. 2, p. 74.
25. Anita Inder Singh, ibid., pp. 74-75, and Shekhar Gupta, n. 1, pp. 61-62.
26. *The Hindu*, 10 March 1996.
27. Ibid., 21 April 1996.
28. *Hindu Weekly*, 13 March 1993.
29. Ramesh Thakur, n. 19, pp. 844-45 and Anita Inder Singh, n. 2, pp. 73-74.
30. Ramesh Thakur, ibid., pp. 839-40.
31. *The Hindu*, 24 March 1995.
32. *Far Eastern Economic Review*, 11 February 1993, p. 18.
33. R.G. Gidadhubli, "Auctioning of the Rupee Funds: New Issues in Indo-

Russian Economic Relations", *Economic and Political Weekly*, 31 July 1994, pp. 1994-96.

34. *The Times of India*, 2 July 1994 and *Economic Times*, 23 September 1994.
35. Anita Inder Singh, n. 2, pp. 76-77 and *FBIS SOV*-94-127, 1 July 1994.
36. *Economic Times*, 12 June 1995.
37. Ibid.
38. *National Herald* (New Delhi), 14 October 1995.
39. Anita Inder Singh, n. 2, p. 77 and Fritsche, n. 12, p. 376.

6

Indo-Russian Relations after Disintegration of the USSR

O.N. MEHROTRA

The post-Soviet Russian foreign policy was initially an extension of the policy pursued by Mikhail Gorbachev in the last two years of his leadership. In his efforts to build the 'Common European Home', he advocated the de-ideologization of the Soviet foreign policy, though largely maintained the old economic and military relations with the developing countries. However those relations began to decrease lately and many Third World clients complained about irregular delivery of the Soviet commodities on the eve of disintegration of the Soviet Union.

The original objective of the Russian foreign policy appeared to be an effort to break away from the former Soviet allies, clients and friends and develop close friendly relations with the 'civilized' developed world, especially the United States. In fact the Russian leadership made frantic efforts to establish a new identity for the Russian foreign policy. It was governed by the negative considerations as it was believed that by renouncing the former foreign policy priorities Russia could formulate a new foreign policy which would be appreciated by the West. At times it was unpredictable and was not also based on the long term national interests. Since it largely failed to achieve the desired objective, which was to obtain large economic assistance from the developed world and to retain its independent role in the international affairs, the Russian leadership came under heavy domestic political and military pressure for unshackling its foreign policy from the Washington's stranglehold. But acting Prime Minister Yeogor Gaidar and Foreign Minister Andrei Kozynev continued to follow the 'Atlanticism' or 'Westerntricism'. Perhaps, India's initial response to the 1991 coup in the Soviet Union could have determined the Yeltsin administration's perception of the Indian Government's view on Russia's current political developments based on an uncalled for remark of former Prime Minister P.V. Narasimha Rao that the overthrow of Mikhail Gorbachev was an instructive example of an overenthusiastic reformer. Russian President Boris Yeltsin was himself a self-proclaimed radical reformer.

End of the Cold War

The Indian foreign policy at the same time also came in for a review because of the end of the cold war with the disintegration of the Soviet Union and adoption of liberalised economic policy by the Narasimha Rao Government. In June 1991, when Mr Narasimha Rao assumed the country's leadership, problems were mounting against the Indo-Soviet trade relations because of erratic supply of the Soviet goods. The Soviet oil deliveries to India fell short by 1.5 billion dollars in that year.[1] India had already been facing acute problem of irregular supply of spares for the Soviet supplied weaponry. The problem for India got further aggravated because of the Gulf War which, however, imparted three lessons for the Indian defence policy, though the lessons were inimical to the Delhi-Moscow military relationship. The lessons were: The previous history of uninterrupted delivery of the Soviet arms during a war bore no assurance of continued deliveries in future conflicts; the Soviet war fighting doctrines had critical flaws; and the technological gap between the Soviet and the U.S. weapon systems was widening to the dangerous dimensions for the Indian security.[2] Moreover it was a difficult task for the Indian bureaucracy to identify some 3500 odd militaryware suppliers, who were scattered all around the newly independent countries. And the same was true for the manufacturers of those military hardwares that India required. It was because the central authority that Moscow once wielded over defence industries had vanished.

The international environment too was fast changing and India was left with no option but to adjust itself accordingly. It did make efforts to develop relations with the US defence establishments and even arranged for military exercises with the armed forces of the US and also some other countries. These exercises had political significance more than that of the militarily for they were meant to convey a message to Moscow that Delhi was looking for some other sources to meet its defence needs. According to a Russian commentator, the Moscow-Delhi ties had lost their basis with the end of the cold war and the disintegration of the Soviet Union.[3]

Incidentally, Moscow too was trying to mend its relations with Islamabad as it reportedly offered sale of weapons to Pakistan. No doubt leading Russian political personage like Vice President Alexander Ruskoi, Chairman Ruslan Khasbulatov and Secretary of State Gennady Burbulis as well as a major section of its legislators were advocating for a strong relationship with India. President Yeltsin and his close advisers were, however, not eager to maintain close relations with New Delhi. While relations between Moscow and New Delhi were worsening, no serious political efforts were made to repair them.

Indo-Russian Trade

Understandably New Delhi presumed since Russia was passing through a period of political and economic transition any high-level political visit by an Indian leader would turn out to be an exercise in futility. The Indian leadership thus lost an opportunity to acquaint itself with the Russian political atmosphere and formulate its policy towards Moscow not based on media perceptions. At that juncture Russian Secretary of State Burbulis paid an official visit to New Delhi. The trade differences between the two countries had already surfaced. Russia's Economic Minister Andrei Nechayev had said that

India continued to want bilateral trade in traditional form of the Russian credits, but he maintained that the new credits would be available at double the existing interest rates and one-tenth of the payment would have to be made in advance.[4] It may be recalled that India had closed trading accounts with the Soviet Union in December 28, 1991 immediately of the formal disintegration of the Soviet Union and new accounts were opened in the name of the new CIS.

The Indo-Russian relations were not conducted with the proper understanding and sensitivity that they deserved. The Russian leadership would have appreciated if New Delhi had taken into view the fact that Russia was passing through a difficult phase and needed assistance and sympathy of the friends. Initially India extended humanitarian aid to Russia but suddenly suspended delivery of some essential commodities that were urgently required there. The regular supply of Russian weapons and spare parts was most crucial for India to keep its defence machinery in preparedness. In a most insensitive fashion the then Indian Defence Minister Sharad Pawar announced appointment of a committee to evaluate the British and French advanced air trainers on the very day a high powered Russian delegation landed in New Delhi. Also the Israeli aeronautical industry had also submitted some proposals too were made public. These announcements were apparently made to exert pressure on Moscow to expedite supply of military holdings and their spare parts to India. But it was not a right move for Russia was not interested to meet the Soviet commitments on old terms as it was looking for a more lucrative market wherefrom it could earn much sought after hard-currency. In the circumstances that prevailed any declarations about bilateral trade and military relations by India were mere rhetoric and devoid of ground realities. Though Russian Ambassador to India later announced that Russia was ready to produce frontline aircraft, tanks, armoured cars and other military equipment for use in the Indian use and also for export to third countries.[5] Unfortunately there was no proper implementation mechanism to translate such proposals in a reality.

Be that as it may India could not afford to ignore supply of Russian weapons or their spare parts. Consequently, numerous high-level military cooperation discussions took place. They began with the then Defence Minister Sharad Pawar's visit to Russia in September 1992. He met with Russian Defence Minister Pavel Grachev and Secretary of State Burbulis and was assured of uninterrupted delivery of spare parts to India. Moreover, he was told that India remained "a priority" for Russia. Pawar expressed the Indian keenness to purchase an improved version of the MiG-29 fighter.[6] Though Pawar described his visit to Russia as successful, bilateral relations remained unsatisfactory. Either as a desperate effort to meet the Indian defence needs or to convey the message to Russia that there were other military sources to fulfil the Indian defence requirements, Pawar went flew to Ukraine in October 1992. Ukraine had been lobbying to sell weapons to India since January 1992. Kiev was a major weapons manufacturing centre in the former Soviet Union and had in the past supplied weapons to India under the Indo-Soviet defence contracts. Ukraine agreed to supply armaments and spare parts to India, partly as a barter for medicine and cloth, and partly to obtain payment in hard currency. Immediately Moscow offered variety of military holdings to India. Subsequently Indo-Ukrainian military ties could not be established on a firm footing.

Despite numerous high-level military cooperation agreements and discussions, India kept on complaining about erratic delivery of the Russian commodities, especially those of armaments, spare parts and crude oil. The major hurdles in the implementation of agreements were the disruption of Russian military industrial complex, oil extraction facilities and mutually acceptable terms of payment. In January 1992 India agreed to grant 32 billion Rupee technical credit to Russia to pay for the Indian goods. The credits could be repaid through export of Russian oil, petrochemicals and fertilizers. India also gave a Rs. 150 million humanitarian assistance to Russia. For the first time India and Russia signed a rupee-payment protocol in February 1992 and following May a five-year trade and cooperation accord, based on most favoured-nation treatment principle, too was initialled between them. Yet normal bilateral trade relations could not be established between the two.

For the Yeltsin-Kozyrev combine, first priority was to maintain

Russia's relations with former Soviet republics. The second in priority came development of relations with the West. At the bottom of the priority list was to establish or maintain relations with the Third World.[7] According to another view, Russia's foreign policy had ten priorities wherein the CIS countries were placed at the top and the United States, Europe and South Asia came fourth, fifth and seventh, respectively.[8] The pro-West policy appeared to have come for review by the Kremlin as the Russian leadership began to focus more sharply on the country's Asian neighbours. The change in Russia's foreign policy was described variously "from romanticism to pragmaticism". Initial efforts were made to normalise relations with Japan. But Tokyo was not keen on mending fences with Moscow until territorial dispute between the two were settled.

Yeltsin's Visit: New Horizons

President Yeltsin visited South Korea and China in November and December 1992 respectively. The ostensible purpose of his visit to these countries was to establish economic and military relations with the two countries as both have emerged prominent economic powers in the recent past. Besides, both are members of the Asia Pacific Economic Community. China has also emerged as an important military power of Asia. China is also a permanent member of the United Nations Security Council, thus is an important actor in the international affairs. During his visit to Beijing, President Yeltsin agreed to sell military hardwares to China. Justification given for this move was that Russia wanted to sell weapons and China wanted to purchase, provided payments were made in hard currency. It may be noted that earlier he had declared that weapon producing industries would be allowed to export weapons provided they contribute a certain percentage of their hard currency earnings to the hard currency strapped Russian government.

After establishing trade and military relations with South Korea and China, President Yeltsin paid the much awaited visit to India in the last days of January 1993. In his address to the Indian businesspersons, President Yeltsin justified his foreign policy priorities to establish close relations with the United States for, he then claimed, achieving reduction in strategic nuclear armaments and establishing a stable world peace. After accomplishment of the objective, he added, Russia, being a powerful Eurasian state, attached great importance to the Asia Pacific region. It was with consequently this aim in mind that he had visited South Korea, China and finally India, he had stressed. He did make it explicit that the Indo-Russian relations would be developed on the "mutually beneficial, friendly cooperation, good neighbourliness" principles. "We do not like any 'axes', 'triangles', 'polygons' or any other blocs. Nor do we want to participate in any such bloc. We want to build our foreign relations, including those with India, on bilateral basis, not directed against any third party."[9] President Yeltsin's statement sharply separated the Indo-Soviet relations with that of Indo-Russian relations which, he maintained, would stand against the "world imperialism and the so-called Chinese hegemonism."[10] In fact, he called for good relations among Russia, China and India, describing them as "the three biggest nations of Asia" which had a strong, stabilising influence on the international politics.[11]

During President Yeltsin's visit to India, the Indo-Russian Treaty of Friendship and Cooperation, 1993, was signed. As expected, the word 'peace', which was an important characteristic of the Indo-Soviet Treaty of 1971, stood removed. There was no security clause in the 14-Clause 1993 treaty. Numerous defence and economic agreements too were signed during this visit. The new defence cooperation agreement included a clause for mutual consultation for spare parts production. The Russian delegation expressed its keenness on setting up joint ventures for the production of spares and defence equipment. It resumed supply of spares, modernisation of equipment through technology transfer as well as supporting India's military hardware exports.

The most vexed problem in the Indo-Russian trade was the rupee-rouble imbroglio. India was to pay Rs. 36,000 crore to Russia. During President Yeltsin's visit India promised to pay the amount over a period of 12 years through an annual instalment of Rs. 3,000 crore. The sum could be repaid through goods bought by the Russian entrepreneurs, or through investment in Russian projects in India or simply through direct selling of the Indian rupee on Russia's stock exchanges. For sometime the issue appeared to be unsurmountable because of underutilisation of rupees by Russia and also because of Moscow's decision to auction rupee in the open market.

The highlight of President Yeltsin's visit to India was his unequivocal support to India's stand on the Kashmir issue.[12] His support to the Indian position was in total contrast to the Kozyrev-Gaider policy line which had advocated for an equidistance between India and Pakistan.''[13] The another crucial issue was the supply of cryogenic rocket engines and transfer of its technology to India. The visiting Russian leader reaffirmed the implementation of the Indo-Soviet agreement on the cryogenic deal despite Washington having imposed sanctions against the sale or transfer of technology by Russia in May 1992 on the ground that the cryogenic deal with India was not in conformity with the Missile Technical Control Regime (MTCR). But later under the American pressure, and promise to compensate Moscow for reneging on the cryogenic deal with India. Moscow cancelled the cryogenic deal with India in July 1993. Cancellation of the deal especially applied to the transfer of technology clause. Consequently, Russia made an announcement about the sale of seven cryogenic rocket engines alone to India.[14]

So the Indo-Russian relations dipped to a new low. The high sounding declaration of President Yeltsin that "No strong eastern policy is possible without India or without taking into consideration India's interests, its global weight and its authority" was of no relevance. The American move to cancel Russian cryogenic rocket engine deal with India was reportedly motivated by commercial considerations as the US firm General Dynamics had been outbid by the Russian space agency, Glavkosmos.

Inspite of the serious setback it gave to the Indo-Russian relations, scientists from both countries kept on visiting each other's laboratories to exchange information and research in variety of areas. Efforts were made by New Delhi to adjust with the unpredictable Russian policy instead of breaking the bilateral ties. During former Prime Minister Narasimha Rao's visit to Russia in June-July 1994, the bilateral relations got repaired. The outcome of Mr. Narasimha

Rao's visit was aptly summed by Russian Deputy Prime Minister Yuri Yarov. "India and Russia have completed the stage of learning as to how to work in new conditions,"[15] said Mr. Yarov Russian Prime Minister Victor Cheromyrdin's return visit in December 1994 gave new thrust to the Indo-Russian relations.[16]

The military cooperation between the two countries has now been developing steadily. Russia has been helping India to upgrade its 170 MiG-21 fighter to keep them combat-worthy well into the next century. In July 1994, both countries agreed to set up a joint venture company, Indo-Russia Aviation Private Ltd., in India with an equity base of 400 million dollar to manufacture spare parts for military aircraft of the Russian origin. India would be the first country outside Russia to offer maintenance facilities for Russian aircraft on commercial basis. According to a June 1994 agreement between Russia and Malaysia, Malaysian pilots would be trained in India for flying the MiG-29s which were bought by Malaysia from Russia. India and Russia have jointly been working on many other military related projects.

Both have signed an umbrella agreement on space cooperation. Russia also assisted in setting up a nuclear power plant in Tamil Nadu under the International Atomic Energy Agency (IAEA) safeguards, with most of the funding coming out of the debt India owes Russia.[17] The Indo-Russian trade is also on the upswing. In 1990, for instance, the Indo-Soviet trade turn-over was nearly 5.5 billion dollar. In the subsequent years the trade volume got seriously decreased and in 1993 the Indo-Russians trade was reportedly around 1.1 billion dollar. Since 1994, Indo-Russian trade has grown steadily and is expected to be twice the volume registered in 1993.[18]

Indo-Russian Ties

The political links between the two countries too have strengthened in the last three years. Russia reiterated its support to India's position on Kashmir. President Yeltsin also expressed support for India to be a permanent member of the UN Security Council. The commonality of political interests was clearly seen in the Moscow Declaration of 1994. It stressed on protecting the interest of multiethnic, multilingual and multireligious states. Both countries have agreed to fight against terrorism and drug-trafficking. During his New Delhi visit, Russian Premier Chernomyrdin reiterated in no uncertain terms that his country was not supplying any military equipment to Pakistan and had no intention of doing so in the future. He also named Pakistan as one of the countries from where mercenaries were fighting against Russians in Chechnya. Russia has expressed its willingness to launch a joint war with India against fundamentalist-religious and other ethnic movements.

As observed earlier that Andrei Kozyrev was a pro-West Russian Foreign Minister, his replacement by Yevgeny Primakov may be considered as an indication that Yeltsin wants to balance his country's foreign policy. Incidentally Kozyrev avoided to visit India inspite of persistent attempt by Indian and Russian diplomats to persuade him to visit New Delhi. In contrast Primakov decided to visit India on the eve of parliamentary elections in India and Presidential election in Russia. During his visit to India in March 29 to 31, 1996, three agreements were signed, one to establish a hot line telephone connection between the Indian Prime Minister's office and the office of the Russian President, a second one on cultural cooperation and the third on expanding scientific and technological cooperation.

It is expected that Indo-Russian military cooperation will further strengthen with the Indian move to purchase 40 Russian made SU-30 MK combat aircraft. The defence deal, possibly the most expensive for a one-weapon system, will nearly be completed in six-year timeframe up to February 2002. According to a report, Russia intends to sell nearly 8 million dollars worth of weapons to India till the year 2000.[19] Russian official has expressed his country's willingness to sell only defensive weapon systems to Pakistan. Therefore, Moscow has expressed its unhappiness on Ukraine's decision to sign the 550 million dollars deal for supply of 320 of the latest Soviet designed T-80 battle tanks to Pakistan.

Recently differences between Moscow and New Delhi were reported on the proposed text of the CTBT. However, both countries reiterated their commitments to maintain their special bilateral ties inspite of their differences on the CTBT. There are still some irritants persist on bilateral trade and defence dealings but by and large bilateral relations have improved in the last two years.

The post-Soviet Indo-Russian relations have passed through a difficult transition period. The military relations have gradually been strengthened. There is some cause of concern on the growing close military relations between China and Russia. In the recent past China has emerged the second largest trade partner of Russia. Inspite of his busy election campaign, President Yeltsin paid an official visit to China in April 1996 and signed fourteen major agreements. In certain quarters it has widely been talked about that a strategic understanding among Moscow, Beijing and New Delhi should be worked out. It is also argued that Iran should also be associated in this proposed arrangement. Iran has recently developed cordial relations with all the three countries.

In the post cold war period, the United States has been dictating other countries to follow certain policy lines on crucial issues or face punishment for defying American directions. Russia, China and India have encountered such warnings. Iran has already been declared as a 'rogue' state by the United States. It has been proposed that all the four countries should jointly stand against American unreasonable dictates. In the existing international environment, it appears difficult that four countries can join together and formulate a common policy on dealing with American overbearings.

Russia is an important Euroasian country whose foreign policy can play a crucial role in establishing durable peace in Asia. For India, Russia is a close trade, defence and diplomatic partner. It has promised to support India's candidature for a permanent membership of the Security Council of United Nations.

India and Russia have agreed to forge closer military and strategic relations and conduct joint exercises to promote friendly ties between the armed forces of the two countries.

An agreement to this effect in October 19, 1996, in New Delhi by the Defence Minister Mulayam Singh Yadav, and the visiting Russian Defence Minister Mr. Igor Rodionov was signed.

The agreement also paves the way for periodic exchange of views and information on matters of military interest including operational doctrines of military equipment of which there is considerable commonality between the armed forces of the two countries.

This agreement also envisages reciprocal training of service personnel at each other's training institutions, the conduct of joint exercises and the deputation of observers to each other's military exercises.

The agreement also provides for sending on deputation, military specialists in the context of maintenance of weapon systems and equipment of Russian origin. It provides for visits by senior officers of the respective countries, participation in seminars and a symposia and joint sporting and adventure activities.

It is expected that the agreement will bring about closer ties as well as understanding of the functioning of the armed forces of India and Russia.

Great importance is attached to the proposed Sukhoi-30 deal which is billed as one of the biggest aircraft deals between the two countries in decades of defence cooperation.

The fact that this was the third visit by a Russian defence related delegation to India during the course of the current year underlines the continuing nature of the cooperation. The visit of the Russian defence delegation appeared to be in the nature of fully clearing loopholes, if any, before the final seal of approval was put on the deal during Russian President Boris Yeltsin's visit to India expected to take place to India in 1997.

In an apparent reference to recent developments in Afghanistan, India and Russia voiced their opposition to fundamentalist and extremist forces and called upon nations to desist from interfering in the internal affairs of other countries in the region. This identity of views emerged during one-to-one discussions between the Prime Minister Mr. H.D. Deve Gowda and Russian Defence Minister General Rodionov when the two leaders reviewed the regional situation during their meeting.

While no formal official announcement either in New Delhi or in Moscow has been made about the impending deal, a report in a recent issue of the Jane's Defence Weekly said Russia was pushing hard to finalise the deal for the purchase of at least 40 Sukhoi-30 fighters for the Indian Air Force (IAF).

The long-range SU-30 into the IAF can substantially increase its capacity to carry out long-range strikes.

Russian President Boris Yeltsin sent his top adviser on Defence and Foreign Policy Boris N. Kuzyk to New Delhi in August 1996, to settle the SU-30 deal. Kuzyk met Prime Minister H. D. Deve Gowda and delivered a personal message from President Yeltsin expressing hope that Indo-Russian ties in all spheres including in the field of defence would forge ahead.

According to defence experts the SU-30 has many firsts to its credit. If inducted, IAF planes for the first time will be able to intercept targets moving at a speed of 120 km using medium range missiles. As of now no plane in the IAF possesses such an interception range.

The MiG-29 specialising in shooting down encroaching planes and inducted in the IAF to counter the Pakistani F-16 possesses Beyond Visual Range (BVR) missiles, which can strike only at about half the distance.

The SU-30 is said to have some formidable performance statistics. Having a range of 3,000 km with internal fuel with some special provisioning in the rear cockpit the aircraft can be operated as a mini awacs operating in conjunction with up to four other similar fighters automatically controlling them onto targets and via realitimedate links transferring information as to the best possible tactical situation.[21]

Again Russian Deputy Prime Minister Oleg D. Davydov, declared in October 30, 1996 that his country will not supply arms to any country inimical to India. This assurance has its own significance, if seen in the context of earlier indications given by Moscow. Davydov's observations emerged from the discussions he had with Defence Minister, Mulayam Singh Yadav, on bilateral relations in the sphere of defence.

During his one-to-one meeting with Mr. Yadav at the New Delhi, Davydov said "Russia will continue to ensure that it does not enter into an arms supply relationship with any country inimical to India".

Another major outcome of the discussion was that it was decided that a large number of important defence-related projects between the two countries should be implemented.

Davydov, who is also the Russian Minister of Economic Relations, also called on the Prime Minister H. D. Deve Gowda during his visit to India.

The two leaders recalled the traditional relations between Indian and the Russian people. They agreed that concrete steps should be taken to step up Indo-Russian economic cooperation.

During Davydov's five-day visit to India, which concluded in October 30, 1996 the two countries agreed to consider measures to expedite finalisation of the supplement to the agreement of November 1988 on cooperation in construction of a nuclear power station in Kudankulam.

During this visit the two sides considered steps to eliminate the existing bottlenecks in the rupee trade and in technical cooperation. Indian and Russian leaders expressed satisfaction over the 54 per cent growth of bilateral trade during 1995-96 compared to 1994-95. The two sides noted the wide scope of closer cooperation in power and metallurgy items.

They also discussed value addition norms for Indian exports to Russia, export to third countries of the goods exported under the rupee debt repayment fund, guarantee offered by Russian banks for projects in India and widening of the range of goods exported under the rupee debt payment fund.[22]

REFERENCES

1. BBC, Summary of World Broadcast (SWB), part 1, SU/1372, May 5, 1992, p. A3/2.
2. Ramesh Thakur, "Russian Policy Toward India: A Relationship on Hold", in Peter Shearman (ed), *Russian Foreign Policy since 1990*, Westview, Colorado, 1995, pp. 228-29.
3. Dimtry Volsky, *New Times*, October 1992 as quoted by Shanta Nedungandi Varma in "Russia and India: From Hiatus to Resurrection", *Strategic Analysis*, New Delhi, vol. XVIII, no. 4, July 1995, pp. 575-76.
4. SWB, Part 3, FE/1372, May 5, 1992, p. A1/2 and Part 1', SU/WO230, May 15, 1992, p. A/9.

5. *Asian Defence Journal*, August 1992, p. 96.
6. SWB, Part 1, SU/1483, September 11, 1992, p. A1/3 and SU/1484, September 12, 1992, p. C2/5.
7. Peter Shearman, "Russians Three Circles of Interests" in Ramesh Thakur and Carlyle A. Thayer edited *Reshaping Regional Relations: Asia Pacific and the Former Soviet Union*, Westview 1993, pp. 45-64.
8. Anita Inder Singh, "India's Relations with Russia and Central Asia", *International Affairs*, vol. 71, no. 1, 1995, p. 72, a Russian periodical stated Russia's priorities in January 1993 as follows:
   (1) the CIS, (2) arms control and international security, (3) economic reforms, (4) the United States, (5) Europe, (6) the Asia-Pacific region, (7) West and South Asia, (8) the Near East, (9) Africa and (10) Latin America.
9. Speech by Boris Yeltsin at a meeting with Indian businessmen—a Document on Russian President Boris Yeltsin's visit to India, *Strategic Digest* (New Delhi), April 1993, p. 585.
10. Ibid.
11. Speech of Boris Yeltsin, President of the Russian Federation in the Central Hall, Parliament, New Delhi, on January 24, 1993, Ibid, pp. 593-94.
12. Ibid., p. 593.
13. Varma, n. 3, p. 589.
14. Singh, n. 8, p. 74 and Nandan Unnikrishnan, India-Russia Relations, *World Focus*, (New Delhi), vol. 16, no. 4, April 1995, p. 22.
15. G. Sudhakar Nair, New Vistas in Indo-Russian Relations, *PTI Feature*, (Press Trust of India), XIII (98)-94, 9 July, 1994, p. 4.
16. O.N. Mehrotra, Prospects for Indo-Russian Relations, *INFA Features* (India News and Features Alliance), New Delhi, vol. XIII, no. 303, January 2, 1995.
17. Unnikrishnan, n.14, p. 23.
18. Gennady Shcherbakov, *Pioneer*, New Delhi, January 23, 1996. According to another estimate, the current volume of trade is nearly 3.5 dollars to 4 billion dollars and is likely to double in volume in the next four years. See J.N. Dixit, Primakov's visit: Towards Enduring Ties, *Indian Express*, New Delhi, April 9, 1996.
19. *Pioneer*, New Delhi, March 31, 1996.
20. See interview of Russian Ambassador to India Albert S. Tchernishev, *The Times of India*, New Delhi, April 10, 1996.
21. *National Herald*, New Delhi, 21st October 1996.
22. Ibid., New Delhi, 31st October 1996.

7

New Emerging Realities in Russia

RAVI M. BAKAYA

This study was prepared at a time when far reaching changes are taking place both in India and Russia. In our country after the 11th General Elections to the Lok Sabha, a United Front Government has been formed under the Prime Ministership of Mr. H.D. Deve Gowda. In Russia though President Boris Yeltsin has been again elected, the composition of the Duma has changed.

Forty-three political organisations took part in the elections to the State Duma in Russia. (See Appendix for votes gained by each of these groups.)

Yeltsin's Popularity

After the Boris Yeltsin regime had literally shot down the old Russian Parliament in October 1993 and arrested former Vice President Alexander Rutskoi and Speaker Ruslan Khasbulatov (both former Yeltsin nominees for their posts), a new constitution was adopted by a snap referendum in December 1993. This "Yeltsin Constitution" not only gave overwhelming powers to the President but also restricted the term of the first State Duma to just two years, while leaving President Yeltsin to run his full 5-year term until June 1996, notwithstanding the fact that he was elected President in 1991 under the old Soviet Russian constitution. It was expected that having a subservient Duma elected after the forcible dispersal of the old parliament, Yeltsin would succeed in consolidating his rule by the time of the next presidential election which was then still two and a half years away. However, even the first Duma turned out to be very different from what Yeltsin and his entourage had hoped for. The pro-Yeltsin Democratic Choice of Russia party came a poor second with 15.5% of the vote, yielding first place to the ultranationalist neo-fascist Liberal Democratic Party of Russia (LDPR) of Vladimir Zhirinovsky, which bagged 22.9% of the votes. The third place was occupied by the Communist Party of the Russian Federation (CPRF) with 12.4% of the vote, followed by the Women of Russia group (8.1%), Agrarian Party of Russia (8%) and Grigory Yavlinsky's "Yabloko" bloc (7.9%).

In its two years of existence the Duma forced the President to change his policies and personnel to some extent, securing the resignation of acting Premier Yegor Gaidar and his replacement by the pragmatic Viktor Chernomyrdin. Soon after Yeltsin and his Defence Minister Pavel Grachev launched the Chechen adventure at the end of 1994 many of the President's former supporters like Gaidar had left him and formed their own blocs.

At the beginning of 1995 Boris Yeltsin publicly blessed the formation of two new blocs, one led by Prime Minister Viktor Chernomyrdin and the other by Duma Speaker Ivan Rybkin. While formally staying out of any political party, the President wanted to assure himself of the support of these blocs in the election campaign for the new Duma in December 1995, and later in the Presidential contest of June 1996.

The results of the 17th December 1995 elections to the Duma have been widely discussed both in and outside Russia. The electorate's turnout surprised many who had thought that since people were getting disillusioned with politicians of all hues, the turnout would be lower than in 1993. It was feared that the youth would keep away and only the older generation and pensioners, who had lost most of their social security benefits of the Soviet times, would come to exercise their vote, swinging the results in favour of the Communists. In an interview published on 6th November 1995 in *Literaturnaya Gazeta* Yegor Gaidar had warned that if 40% or fewer came to the polling booths on 17th December 1995, "Russia will return to queues and empty shelves". Belying all such forecasts 65% of the electorate turned out to vote (as against 50.62% in December 1993, which had put Gaidar's party in power). This high turnout showed that a majority of the Russians were not indifferent to what kind of parliament was elected before the crucial presidential election in 1996.

Though most impartial observers were agreed that the Communists would improve their position and Zhirinovsky's strength would be somewhat reduced, the final results were not without surprises. The blocs led by some of the "strong men" like Gen. Alexander Lebed and former Vice-President Alexander Rutskoi could not break through the 5% barrier to enter the Duma, nor could Gaidar's party, the Agrarians and the "Women of Russia", all of whom were represented in the old parliament. With 22.31% of the vote the Communists led by Gennady Zyuganov not only occupied the first place in the party list but also did extremely well in the individual constituencies, winning as many as 58 seats in them. Zhirinovsky's LDPR came a poor second with its vote (11.6%) reduced to half of what, it was in 1993. The third place was occupied by Chernomyrdin's "Our Home is Russia" bloc which won 9.89% of the vote, and the fourth by Grigory Yavlinsky's "Yabloko" with 6.93%. No other bloc could cross the crucial 5% mark to be able to enter the Duma, though many prominent leaders did get in through the individual constituencies. (In the Russian Duma there are 450 seats. Half of these are allotted to party lists and half to individual constituencies on the principle of "first past the post". In order to be represented on the party list a party or bloc must poll at least 5% of the vote cast. The votes polled by groups that fail to cross the 5% mark are divided proportionately among those who got more than 5%.)

Summing up the final results, Vladimir Pribylovsky, writing from Moscow for the emigre Russian language weekly *Russkaya Mysl* published in Paris, gives an interesting breakup of the new Russian parliament's profile. He divides the deputies (members of parliament) into seven groups:

1. *Communists and their allies.* The CPRF has 99 + 58 = 157 deputies, plus one from Anpilov's Workers' Russia group, plus 9 from ex-Soviet Prime Minister Ryzhkov's and Sergeo Baburin's groups, plus 20 from the Agrarian Party of Russia, plus one from Women of Russia, plus 23 independents with Left wing affiliations, totalling 211 "Red" deputies.

2. *Zhirinovsky's LDPR* has 50 + 1 = 51 deputies.

3. *Gen. Lebed's Congress of Russian Communities* with its allies (the "moderate imperial opposition") has a total of 9 or 10 deputies.

4. The *Non-progovernment Centrists and Left Centrists*, including those from Arkady Volsky's Soyuz Truda (Union of Labour), Svyatoslav Fyodorov's Party of Workers' Self-Management, two other groups and 6 independents make a total of 10 deputies.

5. The *Party of Power and its allies* have from Chernomyrdin's 'Our Home is Russia' (OHR) 45 + 10 = 55, plus one from Sergei Shakhrai's PRES, plus one from Bloc of 89 regions, plus 27 independents, making a total of 90 deputies.

6. *Gaidar's Democratic Choice of Russia and other Democrats* (excluding Yavlinsk's "Yabloko") has from Gaidar's group 9, plus 3 from B, Fyodorov's "Forward, Russia!", plus 2 from Panfilova-Gurov-Lysenko bloc, plus one from Khakamada's Common Cause, plus one from K. Borovoi's Party of Economic Freedom, plus 11 or 12 independents, making a total of 27 or 28 deputies.

7. *Grigory Yavlinsky's "Yabloko"* has 31 + 14 = 45, plus one independent, totalling 46 deputies.

In addition there are 4 deputies whose political affiliations are not yet clear:

It should be mentioned here that all such groupings are tentative and provide only an approximate picture.

The results of the Duma elections created near panic in anti-communist circles among both the Yeltsin supporters and Democrats like Gaidar, who had parted company with the President. With Yeltsin's plummeting popularity rating and his fragile health, they have been looking frantically but without success for an alternative. According to Moscow Radio no less than 78 individuals had expressed their desire to contest the presidential election. But this number came down drastically as a candidate had to collect a million signatures of support in his favour in order to qualify.

The fact that no alternative charismatic leader to Yeltsin could be found is a great disappointment to the anti-communists of all shades as Gennady Zyuganov is daily improving his position in popularity ratings. According to Dr. Yuri Levada, Director of the All-Russian Public Opinion Centre, Zyuganov was backed by 24% of the voters, while Yeltsin with 11% support came third after Zhirinovsky who had 12% support. Other contenders of some significance included G. Yavlinsky, Gen. A. Lebed and eye surgeon Svyatoslav Fyodorov who might muster 9, 8 and 7 per cent respectively.

Boris Yeltsin announced his intention to contest for a second term on 15th February almost simultaneously with Zyuganov's nomination by a group of communist parties as their unanimous candidate. A day later, Nicholas Burns at the State Department's daily press briefing said: "We believe it would be advantageous and wise for the various reform parties to coalesce around a candidate in these elections. The A. P. report in *The Times of India* of 17th February 1996 that carried Burns' remarks, added "Burns specialised in Soviet affairs as a member of the National Security Council staff under President Bush. His extensive and blunt remarks at the State Department's daily briefing could reflect growing US anxiety that Yeltsin cannot win re-election... Yeltsin's popularity has plummeted, his policies are in disarray and he has heart trouble. Multiple reform candidates could split pro-democracy support. Meanwhile, despite his lead, Zyuganov could not win without attracting non-communist voters."

As if to satisfy the overseas friends and inspire some confidence amongst the Russian doubting Thomases, Moscow Radio announced on 3rd March: "In a significant move Boris Yeltsin was unanimously nominated on Sunday as the common democratic candidate for the coming presidential election to be held on June 16. A conference of 40 different political parties and groups, forming a common platform for the defence of democracy in the country, sponsored Mr. Yeltsin as the common candidate. The parties also founded 'an all-Russian movement' to carry out the election campaign for Mr. Yeltsin."

With the final registration of the presidential candidates the pre-election lineup in Russia became clear. Meanwhile interesting shifts took place amongst the warring sides. The old trick of lumping together the Communists and Zhirinovsky followers and trying to frighten the people by warning them of the "Red-and-Brown" danger no longer seemed to work as both the electorate and the media recognise now that the interests of the Communists and Zhirinovsky were radically different. Writing from Moscow for the Paris weekly *Russkaya Mysl*, Mikhail Gokhman said: "Vladimir Zhirinovsky, having entered into coalition with the government fraction in the parliament has become for state television almost a respectable person. He is more and more being offered broadcasting time, being used as a stick to beat the Communists and 'Yabloko' with." The writer went on to say that in the event of an anti-Communist candidate not making it in the first round, the only way in which the Communists can be prevented from coming to power is through sabotaging the election itself. He wrote:

"If Zhirinovsky and a candidate from the Communists emerge as the two rivals in the final round, then boycott of election is the only way open to the country. In the event of less than 50% of the voters coming to the booths the election would be considered invalid. In that case Yeltsin will remain to carry on, though for a short period. We shall get one more breathing spell."

Strength of Communists

The actual finale was not so dramatic, as the mass of the electorate were frightened by anti-Communist slogans, having lived under Communist rule for seven decades. The Communists themselves have learnt much from their past and for the last three years they have been discussing their strategy. They have no illusions regarding the possibility of a "return to the past" on the morrow of an electoral victory. In their programmatic statements they have made it clear that socialism is a distant goal. Their immediate concerns were highlighted in Zyuganov's replies in a debate with Yavlinsky before the Duma elections, published in the popular weekly *Argumenty i Fakty* (Arguments and Facts). The leader of the CPRF said:

"The CPSU was destroyed by the monopoly of the politbureau on truth. The chief lesson is: no one should have a monopoly on truth...We are for all political parties competing, so that people can decide at the time of elections who is more suited to the times and who can satisfy their aspirations. We have given up militant atheism... No one will privatise an enterprise in the West unless this changed its working qualitatively. In our country they are giving away the Magnitogorsk Plant for a song, a plant that was constructed by the efforts of the entire country. Is this privatisation? But then there is already an existing reality. Taking our cue from the reality, we shall support what has been privatised and is working well. But where there is a hundred percent criminal act, it is not Zyuganov but the law-enforcing authorities that will act..."

When interviewed after the Duma elections, Zyuganov laid down the following three conditions as the minimum programme for cooperation with others in the Duma: (1) they must agree on the territorial integrity of Russia; (2) they must agree on achieving peace, including peace in Chechnya, which should be found by all parties agreeing to negotiate without any preconditions; (3) they must agree that the government should ensure a reasonable standard of living for all, especially for the children and the old people."

Russian Nationalism

Notwithstanding the result of the presidential election, one thing is clear: Russia is moving towards policies—both internally and in the external sphere—that are more acceptable to the majority of its people who have now realised the bankruptcy of blindly imitating the West. After the Duma elections of December 1993 President Yeltsin had to get rid of Yegor Gaidar and appoint Viktor Chernomyrdin Prime Minister. After the Duma elections of December 1995 he had to get rid of the blatantly pro-west Foreign Minister Andrei Kozyrev and First Deputy Prime Minister in charge of economy, the architect of Russia's privatisation, Anatoli Chubais, and appoint in their places Yevgeny Primakov and Vladimir Kadannikov.

India and Russia enjoyed a prolonged period of cooperation in the past, which benefited both countries. They also enjoyed a modicum of understanding and cooperation in the field of foreign policy. Since India's foreign policy has traditionally been a matter of national consensus, the prospect of restoration of old Indo-Russian close ties is not likely to be cardinally affected by the coming to power of a new government in our country.

APPENDIX

Results of Elections to the Duma held on 17 December 1995

Forty-three parties/blocs took part in elections to the State Duma held on 17th December 1995. Only 4 of them were able to cross the 5% barrier for entry into the Duma. These were :

1. Communist Party of Russian Federation (CPRF), leader Gennady Zyuganov—22.31%

2. Liberal Democratic Party of Russia (LDPR), leader Vladimir Zhirinovsky—11.6%

3. Our Home is Russia (OHR), leader Viktor Chernomyrdin—9.89%

4. "Yabloko", leader Grigory Yavlinsky—6.93%

The rest of the parties got no representation in the party list in the Duma, having failed to cross the 5% mark. Their names and the votes they obtained are as follows:

5. Women of Russia—4.60%

6. Communists, Workers' Russia for the Soviet Union, leader V. Anpilov—4.52%

7. Congress of Russian Communities, leader General A. Lebed—4.29%

8. Party of Workers' Self-Management, leader Svyatoslav Fyodorov, famous eye surgeon—4.01%

9. Democratic Choice of Russia, United Democrats, leader Yegor Gaidar—3.90%

10. Agrarian Party of Russia, leader M. Lapshin—3.78%

11. "Derzhava", leader A. Rutskoi—2.59%

12. "Forward, Russia!", leader Boris Fyodorov—1.96%

13. Soyuz Truda (Union of Labour), leader Arkady Volsky—1.63%

14. Power to the People!, leaders Nikolai Ryzhkov, Sergei Baburin—1.61%
15. Panfilova—Gurov—Vladimir Lysenko—1.61%
16. "Kedr"—1.40%
17. Ivan Rybkin's Bloc—1.12%
18. Stanislav Govoryukhin's Bloc—1.00%
19. My Fatherland—0.72%
20. Common Cause—0.68%
21. "Party of Beer-Lovers"—0.65%
22. "Noor"—0.52%
23. Preobrazhenie Otechestva (Transformation of the Fatherland)—0.50%
24. National Republican Party of Russia—0.48%
25. "Partiya Dzhuny"—0.48%.
26. "Party of Unity and Accord (PRES), leader Sergei Shakhrai—0.36%.
27. Association of Advocates of Russia—0.35%.
28. "Za Rodinu!" (For the Motherland!)—0.28%.
29. Christian Democratic Union, Christians of Russia—0.28%.
30. Cause of Peter I—0.21%.
31. Narodny Soyuz (People's Union)—0.21%.
32. Rosszhilkommunsoyuz—0.15%.
33. Tikhonov-Tupolev-Tikhonov—0.15%.
34. Social Democrats—0.13%.
35. Party of Economic Freedom—0.13%.
36. Russian Popular Movement—0.13%.
37. Bloc of Independents—0.12%.
38. Federal-Democratic Movement—0.12%.
39. Russia's Stability—0.12%.
40. Duma-96—0.08%.
41. "Pokolenie Rubezha"—0.06%.
42. Bloc of 89 Regions—0.06%.
43. Mezhnatsionalny Soyuz (Inter-National Union)—0.05%.

Of all those taking part in the poll 2.79% voted against all lists. The total number of voters in Russia was 105,409,443. Valid and invalid votes were 66,613,619; 1,300,958 respectively.

(Source: *Russkaya Mysl*, Paris, No. 4107, 5-10 Jan. 1996)

For the sake of record it may be useful to list here all those who were candidates for the presidentship. The last four in the list are hardly known abroad. Here are the eleven: 1. Boris Yeltsin, 2. Gennady Zyuganov, 3. Grigory Yavlinsky, 4. Vladimir Zhirinovsky, 5. Gen. Alexander Lebed, 6. Svyatoslav Fyodorov, 7. Mikhail Gorbachev, 8. Vladimir Bryntsalov (a billionaire businessman), 9. Yuri Vlasov (former Olympic champion and at present member of Duma), 10. Martin Shakkum (vice-president of the "Reform" fund) and 11. Aman Tuleyev (belongs to the extreme left communist group).

None of these eleven candidates got a clear majority in the first round which was held on 16th June 1996. Therefore, a second round was held on 7th July 1996. To be elected outright a candidate must get at least 50% of the vote of those voting, provided not less than 50% of the electorate turns up to vote.

The entire mass media, especially television and radio, were mobilised to campaign for Yeltsin as the only saviour from the Communists who, allegedly, wanted to restore not only queues outside stores but also concentration camps of Stalinist days.

8

Indo-Russian Relations: Historical Background

V.D. Chopra

The essence of the Indo-Russian relations as they have developed over the years, including the period of the Soviet Union is the mutual recognition of the importance of our two vast aggregates of territory and population and the benefits that our two nations and the world derive if our work for peace and development is corelated and reinforced. In the contemporary world, which is increasingly becoming interdependent and interconnected, Indo-Russian relations have already set a model in the evolution of democratisation of international relations. However, of far reaching importance is the close ties of friendship between these two countries, rooted in their history spread over many centuries. In the present century, the world has produced three outstanding leaders, Gandhi, Lenin and Jawaharlal Nehru who were literally and metaphorically makers of history. In this process, they drew their own lessons from the struggles of the peoples of these two countries. That is why when one talks of Indo-Russian friendship, one cannot forget the fact that Lenin and Jawaharlal Nehru stood at the source of this friendship.

Jawaharlal Nehru in his book *Glimpses of World History* has described Lenin as "the greatest modern exponent of Marxism", who did not consider "Marxism as a dogma" and "was not prepared to accept or apply its details everywhere unthinkingly". On the other hand, Russian scholars in their effort to democratise and humanise their society have begun to study in depth the Indian experience of democratic political set-up and its road to economic development through mixed economy.

Our Glorious Past

Long before most parts of the world had embarked upon the path of civilisation, Indians could already boast of a culture and progress, with millennia of human endeavour behind it. These civilisations very likely flourished in the third millennium before Christ. The mystery of the ancient Indian culture remains a mystery even today because the distinction between 'history' and 'pre-history' is peculiarly elusive in her case. No one has been able so far to fully reconstruct the story of the culture that once thrived in this great country. It is a recognised fact, however, that along with Persia, Mesopotamia and Egypt, India was one of the most important centres of the world where civilisation processes were initiated and had matured.

No wonder that India and its cultural achievements had started shaping the evolution of human thought, even during the unrecorded period of human history, by contacts with foreign countries and people.

Mohenjo-daro and Harappa are two outstanding examples of what once was the Indus Valley Civilisation. That this civilisation ranks with the great civilisations of the Valleys of the Nile, the Tigris and the Euphrates, and had witnessed the rise of the ancient civilisations of Egypt, Assyria and Babylonia are indisputable facts. Its people knew the art of laying out towns and claimed a highly developed culture. Cotton and woollen fabrics were in common use; ornaments were worn both by men and women; polished pottery was produced; the sculptor's technique was fashioned. The carpenter, the mason, the blacksmith, the goldsmith, the jeweller, the stone-cutter and the ivory worker had flourishing trade, and a great religion with its system of rituals prevailed. The Indus Valley Civilisation is believed to be older than the culture of the Vedic Age. While the Aryans were rural, the people of this Valley possessed the amenities of a developed town-life. Some hold that they were the same as the Sumerians, while others opine that they were in fact the Dravidians who at one time inhabited the whole of India, including the modern Punjab, the Sind and Baluchistan and had even migrated to Mesopotamia. The Dravidian language is still spoken by the Brahui people of Baluchistan. But Mohenjo-daro and Harappa maintain a serene silence, like the inscrutable Sphinx, at the labours of the scholars. Darkness envelopes several succeeding countries.

The most remarkable of the epic poems of ancient India are the *Ramayana* and the *Mahabharata* which were written down far later, between the fourth century B.C. and the fourth century A.D. However, the main subject matter of these poems and many of the stories that went into their making undoubtedly originated in the first half of the first millennium B.C. Both these epics are extremely well integrated works, not mosaics comprising a variety of texts, each being a compositional whole. The authorship of the *Mahabharata* is traditionally ascribed to Vyasa and that of the *Ramayana* to Valmiki, but nothing definite is known about these poets or seers (*rishis*).

These epics are veritable encyclopaedias of ancient India. They contain most interesting and informative material on various aspects of social and cultural life, political organisation and philosophical systems of ancient Indians. These epics have been unrivalled in their popularity in India. But what is of significance is that in ancient time and in the middle ages these were well known even far beyond India's frontiers in Eastern and Southern Asia and in the Far and Middle East. Translations of the *Mahabharata* and the *Ramayana* into a number of European languages were widely acclaimed. Many outstanding figures in the history of Western and Oriental culture like Beethovan, Heine, Rodin, Gandhi, Tagore, and Nehru drew inspiration from them.

Even in the earlier periods, India maintained close links with both the neighbouring and the distant countries. These contacts were developed and consolidated over the centuries and Indian culture penetrated other ethnocultural zones and a process of mutual cultur enrichment ensued.

The earliest and deepest of these cultural ties were those linking India and Iran, which can be traced to as far back as the Neolithic times. The ancient Indians and the Iranians were closely related people, ethnically as well as linguistically. A period of particularly close Indo-Iranian ties began after the formation of the Achaemenic empire when certain areas of north-western India were integrated with that empire.

According to many scholars, the territory originally settled by the Indo-Europeans included certain parts of what was known till recently the Soviet Union. After the Aryan (Indo-Iranian) community took shape, Aryan tribes continued to inhabit these regions. Russian archaeologists have thrown new light connected with the migrations of peoples and in particular, the appearance of Indo-Aryans in the north-western part of Hindustan. Comparative linguistic studies of Vedic, Sanskrit and the languages of the Slav, the Baltic and the Iranian peoples have been very fruitful. The commonality of origin and a long period of cohibition by the Indo-Aryans and the remote ancestors of the Slavs explain the closeness of the Indian and Slav mythologies. A study of the culture of those peoples of the former USSR whose languages belong to the Iranian group, for example, the Ossetians, the descendants of the ancient Sarmatians, provides a wealth of comparative material.

In contemporary philological literature one may find arguments supporting the view that long ago there lived in the northern Black Sea area, not only Iranian-speaking tribes, but, in all probability, also tribes belonging to the Indo-Aryan group (the works of the Russian linguist Professor Oleg Trubachov provide an example). According to him, a whole series of names of the ancient Black Sea regions have a great deal in common, which can be explained by Indian onomastic data (for example, the locality near Khersones in the Crimea called 'Dandake', and the Indian 'Dandaka', the Scythian names Butonatos and Magadava, and the Indian Bhutanatha and Mahadeva, etc.) He even considers it possible to seek 'the beginnings of Hinduistic faiths' in the period when the 'Indo-Aryans inhabited the Black Sea regions', and speaks of the 'intensive cultural and ethnic ties' and 'bilateral communication' between the Black Sea regions and India in the distant past. In any case, the origin of the Indo-Aryans is bound up with the pre-history of what is now the European part of the former USSR and with that of some regions of Central Asia. Incidentally, the latter maintained relations with India as far back as the pre-Aryan Harappan period, of which the excavations in southern Turkemania, in particular, provide evidence.

Comparatively little is known of the relations between India and other countries in the remote past, but nevertheless, there can be no doubt about India's close links with the regions which now form part of the territory of the Central Asian Republics. Various trade routes were laid and states were formed which included both Indian and Central Asian regions. Most significant among them during earlier centuries was the Kushan state. Thus, in the time preceding the Muslim period, India exerted great influence on the material and spiritual culture of Central Asia.

Through the Graeco-Roman culture, a persistant image of India penetrated in to the literature of various countries—Armenia, Georgia, Russia, etc.—which is reflected in a large number of relics of the written and oral traditions of these people. Indian topics and traditions reached Eastern Europe via the literature of the Middle East, Byzantium and the Arab countries.

India-Central Asia Relationship

In the Middle Ages India maintained close trade, political and cultural relations with Central Asian regions, to some extent with Transcaucasia, and later with ancient Russia also, where several Indian colonies were established. Starting with the 11th century, a part of the territory of India and Central Asia was for some time incorporated in the same states, therefore, the cultures of these countries constantly exerted a strong mutual influence. Armenian merchants penetrated into India in the early days, playing an important role in the late Middle Ages not only in the country's economic life but at times in its political life as well. Beginning with the Middle Ages, many descriptions of India appeared in various languages of the peoples of Russia, including Russian. An image of India was gradually formed, and interest in the country began to grow.

Recent excavations made by Russian archaeologists in Central Asia show that there existed direct links between the southern parts of Central Asia and India in as early as the Harappan period and these became particularly deeper in the Kushana period. Central Asia's influence began to be felt in India as the Kushanas and the Shakas extended their sway, while Buddhism and other aspects of India's religion, culture and philosophy spread to Central Asia.

Judging by the inscriptions found in Central Asia, a large number of monasteries had been built during the Kushana and Gupta periods. The most striking demonstration of this is provided by the Buddhist monasteries at Kara-Tepeh (near Termez in the first century A.D.) and in Ajina-Tepeh (Southern Tajikistan, seventh century A.D.).

In the earlier centuries, trade links between India and China had grown apace, established by way of the Great Silk route and also by sea. Indian ambassadors and Buddhist missions were sent to China. In the third century A.D. Buddhist monasteries appeared in China and translations of Buddhist writings into Chinese had been undertaken.

Indian culture exercised a strong influence on literature, architecture and religion of a large number of countries. At an early stage, India had begun trading with many countries of South-East Asia, and later Indian settlements appeared in some of them. The settlers popularised the Sanskrit language in these regions and enriched the local culture, with the many achievements of Indian culture.

It would be relevant to stress that many crucial questions concerning the universe, man and nature were posed and solved through mutual exchange by Indian and the classical thinkers. This interplay points to the underlying pattern of cultural advance shaped by the processes of historical development in the ancient period. Therefore, when Jawaharlal Nehru said that Indo-Soviet relations were rooted in the history of the two countries he had these and other facts also in mind. It will not be, therefore, incorrect to say that cultural and economic relations between India and Russia, particularly with its Central Asian regions, can be traced thousands of years back. A large number of Buddhist architectural complexes, places of worship and monasteries dating back to the period ranging from the first century A.D. to the Islamic Middle Ages have been discovered in the Central Asian Republics of Uzbekistan, Tajikistan, Turkmenistan and Kyrgyzstan. This evidence also shows that the Kushan empire extended to the southern regions of what is now the Central Asia.

At the time of the famous Kushan King Kanishka and his successors, Buddhism spilled over from Hindustan to the north of Hindukush.

This would mean that as neighbours, people of India and Russia had been not only known to each other but had long been making cultural and economic exchanges. A thirteenth century book in Russian is aptly entitled *The Story of India, the Rich*. In the last quarter of the eighteenth century, Gerasim Stepanovich Lebedev, a Russian musician and dramatist, made his way to India. He not only learnt Sanskrit and Bengali but also wrote plays in Bengali.

The sweep of Changez Khan and the massive Arab invasions followed by Timur's conquests destroyed the Buddhist culture in these parts. Buddhist had also spread to some tribes residing in Siberia. They received it via Tibet, Ladakh and Mongolia, Ulan-Ude, the capital of Buriat, is a small 'autonomous region' situated on the bank of Baykal lake, on the border of Mongolia. Even today the people there are mostly Buddhists and have much in common with their coreligionists in the Ladakh area of India.

The whirlwind of Changez Khan swept through many a land. His thrust covered a vast area, including northern India which suffered calamities of plunder and loot along with the people of Central Asia. Timur made Samarkand his seat of power and was buried there after his death. His mausoleum is a beautiful piece of architecture and Humayun's tomb and Shahjahan's Taj Mahal were probably inspired by its design.

Historical Links between India-Russia

Though it is difficult to establish how knowledge about India reached Russia in this period of history. Indian scholars have not done enough work in this area. However, it appears that this happened both through published works and direct contacts. The Russian scholars hold that references to India are found in ancient Russian literature. In the early centuries, after conversion to Christianity, a stream of Greek and Bulgarian authors literally poured their books into Russia. It was due to translations of Christian literature that there appeared in Russian, Indian names, topics and motifs, as well as notions about India, which had taken shape several centuries earlier in Byzantium. Byzantium, in its turn, had adopted information about India from the writings of the 'Church Fathers', and the writers of the later Roman Empire in the 4th and 5th centuries, in which were interwoven fabulous legends from ancient Greek literature, and extracts from notes of the participants of Alexander the Great's campaigns. Christian writers of the yore were not only fascinated by the wonders of India and its religion but by the lives of the pious hermits and sages, the Brahmans and Shramanas, and the legends of conversion of Indians by St. Thomas. Information dating back to the period of active links between India and the Graeco-Roman world, to the time of Alexander's campaigns, the heyday of the Kushana empire and active sea trade via the Arabian and Red Seas, though distorted almost beyond recognition, reached Byzantium and later to Russia.

Original ancient Russian literature also developed, to a certain extent under the influence of Byzantium. One of its oldest works, *The Sermon on Law and Grace*, written in the first half of the 11th century by Ilarion, Metropolitan of Kievan Russia, 'a good and learned man much given to fasting' as he is described in the Chronicle, mentions of the baptism of Indians by St. Thomas. "The Deeds of Thomas", his building of a palace for the Indian ruler Gondophares and the latter's conversion to Christianity were well known in pre-Mongol Russia.

The author of the most ancient Russian chronicle *The Chronicle of Times Past* speaks about the distribution of nations over the earth, from Persian and "as far as India". Describing the manners and customs of the "Bactrians, otherwise called Rahmans or Islanders", the chronicle records that out of piety "they do not eat meat or drink wine, fornicate or do any evil". He contrasts the Indians who lack all these virtues with the 'Rahmans'. Both extracts are obviously borrowed from the Byzantine chronicle of George the Monk, which was translated in Russia in the middle of the 11th century. Information on

India and the Brahmans contained in it goes back to the period of late antiquity when the essay by Palladius, on the Races of India and the Brahmans, and its Latin translation by Ambrose, appeared. Similar information is contained in another work, well known in Russia the Chronographia of John Malalas.

A deep interest in nature, unusual animals, plants and stones was characteristic of Byzantine Christian literature. Wonders were explained as symbols assisting the interpretation of the holy books, the Old and the New Testament, while animal life served as a kind of 'symbolic mirror of man's spiritual world'. Stories by the authors of ancient times about the wonders of India, sometimes supplemented with legends from Arab literature became a most important source of the physiologus, well known in Europe in the Middle Ages. There were several variants of this ancient collection, among them being the Greek, the Syrian, the Coptic, the Ethiopian and the Armenian. A symbolic interpretation of the fantastic descriptions of the animals and birds of India is to be found in the works of Clement of Alexandria, 2nd-3rd centuries A.D. (the story of the Phoenix). In his works can also be found most valuable information on Buddhism in India and Bactria (including the territory of present-day Tajikistan). Reports on strange animals of India widely appear in Byzantine books, devoted to explanation of the Old Testament and a description of the universe according to Biblical cosmogony. The physiologus and similar works had an enormous influence on Russian ideas about India and other distant countries up to the 17th century. These ideas can be found not only in literature, but also in art and oral traditions.

Stories about the marvellous bird from India the Phoenix, which lived near the 'Sun-City' (Heliopilis), were particularly popular in Russia. The tales affirmed that the Phoenix lay without food on a tree, the cedar of Lebanon, for five hundred years, and then, induced by the priests of Heliopolis, set fire to itself. The physiologus contains many fabulous stories of the Indian 'ant-lion' (whose front half is that of a lion and rear that of an ant), of the kite which in India extracts the 'quick-birth' stone (easing childbirth), of the mythical bird Strafil (ostrich) and the curing stone with the help of which 'cunning doctors' removed the 'foul fluid'. India is frequently mentioned in the literature of the Middle Ages, although the information about it is often far from reality. Incidentally there are echoes of reliable information too about the strange animal world of India and about Indian medical knowledge.

The surprising animal world of India, abounding not only in real elephants and one-horned rhinoceroses but also in fantastic 'wild boar-elephants', 'ant-lions', 'nasihorns' and similar wonders, was mentioned in the *Christian Topography*, by Cosmas Indicopleustes (6th century), evidently translated in Russia during the Kievan period. This work, written in dispute with the Graeco-Roman theories of the Cosmas, contained an account of the Christian ideas of the Universe. In the descriptions of different countries, one can occasionally find reflections of accounts of travellers, in particular on India. A considerable number of the manuscripts of the *Christian Topography* have come down to use many of the illustrated.

The Romance of Barlaam and Joasaph enjoyed popularity in the 12th century Russia. It is well known that the Romance is transposition of the legendary biography of the Buddha, and the name Joasaph comes from the Indian word "Boddhisattva" (via the form Budashp). The legend of the Buddha was widespread in many regions of Central Asia in the first centuries A.D. It was popular among the Manichaeans in the middle of the first millennium. Mention of the Romance goes back to the 6th-7th centuries when it was recorded in Pehlevi at the command of the famous ruler of the Sassaind dynasty, Khusro Anushirvan (he displayed considerable interest in Indian culture and during his reign, according to legend, the fables of the *Panchatantra* were translated and the Indian chess (*shatranj*) appeared in Iran. The Pehlevi version of the Romance was subsequently lost, but an Arab translation, made in the 8th century, has survived. A Greek version appeared just a little later and has been ascribed to the famous Byzantine theologian of the 7th-8th centuries John of Damascus. The text of the Romance of Barlaam and Joasaph was later translated into Latin Ethiopian, Slavic and many West European languages. The Romance tells of the Indian prince's rejection of earthly blessings and temptations and his turning to a different, better world and retreat into the desert. The hermit Barlaam and the Indian prince Joasaph were canonised by both Western and Eastern Churches.

In Russia, subsequently, a religious poem was composed about Joasaph which became very popular. Some versions of this poem reproduce in detail the motif of the Romance, speaking of the meeting of the son of the Indian ruler Abner, with the 'blind leprous and toothless venerable old man'. The youth, hearing of the 'grief of the people, began to lament, and to talk of the unhappy life of the people' and then "himself put on monastic robes... and voluntarily became one of the destitutes". Other versions merely contain Joasaph's conversation with the hermit that is to say, his lamentation, prayer or praise for the hermit. To the question: "Yasakhvy, for whom are you abandoning your kingdom?", the prince replies: "The beautiful monter-hermitage, it is my temporary kingdom, but the Kingdom of Heaven is eternal".

Thus, one of the finest examples of Russian religious verse goes back to the Romance of Barlaam and Joasaph and is a reflection of the Indian legend of the Buddha. The 1681 edition of the Romance has engravings by the remarkable 17th century Russian artist Simon Ushakov. One of the earliest performances in the Russian court theatre at the beginning of the 18th century also reproduced the Romance. This motif, basically Indian in origin, inspired such well-known Russian poets of the 19th century as Vasily Zhukovsky and Apollon Maikov.

A definite Indian literary influence can also be felt in a number of other works of folk literature, in particular in the famous religious verse *Dove-Book* (Golubinaya Kniga), in which are posed, in the main, questions of a cosmogenic character: Where did the Earth appear from? How many parts went to create Adam; and so on? In the answers to these questions one can feel the influence of such works as the physiologus and The Story of the Indian Kingdom. The lines in some variants of this religious verse dealing with the origin of people are particularly interesting: "The rulers in our world came from the sacred head of Adam, the princely boyars from the sacred body of Adam, orthodox peasants from the sacred feet of Adam". These lines from the *Dove-Book* are reminiscent of lines from the *Purushasukta* the famous hymn of the *Rigveda* on the origins of the *varnas* (castes) which have frequently attracted the attention of researchers.

The famous Indian text on the origins of the castes most probably reached Russian folklore initially with the help of the Iranian Manichaeans and Christian heretics of the first centuries A.D. and then through Byzantine literature and Bulgarian Bogomils. Thus, Indian literary motifs and stories penetrated into Russia from two paths — from the West and through Iran. It would be no exaggeration to say that the ease with which 'Indian evidence' was accepted in Russia, is explained in no small degree by the ethnic, linguistic and cultural closeness and long-standing relations between the Slav-Russian population of Eastern Europe and the Aryan (Indian and Iranian) peoples.

India is mentioned in a number of ecclesiastical Slavonic texts too. A description of the life of the Brahmans or 'blessed' people was very popular in Byzantine and old Bulgarian literatures of the 10th-13th centuries. *The Narrative of Macarius of Rome*, for example, told of the journey of three youths to India to the country of the 'blessed', who live in a cave close to paradise itself, go about 'naked' and 'have white hair'. The description of the 'blessed' and the surrounding countries (on the side of them the canine-headed, and on the other the iron city beyond which lies paradise itself) is reminiscent of the description of the life of the Brahmans in late Graeco-Roman literature which served as a source for the Narrative.

One more work of a similar kind, well known in Russia, is the *Visit of Zosima* to the Rahmans. Knowledge of the naked wise men (Rahmans), taken from ancient Greek writer, is fantastically interwoven with reports about Biblical Rechabites. Much is made of the fact that the Rahmans inhabit the edge of the world, near the earthly paradise, and are therefore idealised. The influence of romances of Alexander the Great and stories about the 'blessed' Brahmans is also felt in the *Narrative of Methodius of Patara*. The location of the lands of the Brahmans is often quite fantastic at the edge of the world but Indian animals are to be found there too. Similar literature was also widespread in Western Europe.

The dissemination of essays on the life of the blessed Indian

Rahmans was connected with theological polemics and the struggle of ideas in medieval Russia. Proceeding from the tales about the Brahmans, the Archbishop of Novgorod, Vasily Kalika, in a letter to Bishop Fyodor set out to prove the existence of paradise on Earth. In the 15th century, the Russian writer, Yefrosin, composed on the basis of the Chronicles by George, the Monk, and other sources. *A Narrative of the Rahmans and their Amazing Life*. He emphasised the piety of the Rahmans, who knew no greed. This was an important problem for Russian social and political writers, as in Russia at the end of the 15th and the beginning of the 16th century, a sharp dispute had arisen over the question of monastic property and the greed of monks. Yefrosin writes of the Rahmans that they have "neither iron nor temples nor gold, nor wine, they eat no meat, have no ruler, no buying they live naked, eat a few vegetables, drink sweet water, ardently believe in God and pray continuously". A prominent 16th century ecclesiastical writer, Maxim the Greek, on the contrary, wrote about the 'false wisdom of the Rahmans'.

Under the influence of Christian writers, stories of the Brahmans or as they were called in ancient Russian works, Rahmans evidently received wide circulation. Tales of the Christians, the Rahmans who lived far beyond the seas even under the earth were long current in Southern Russia and the Ukraine. Judging by these tales, the Rahmans had no calendar, and celebrated Easter when the shells of Easter eggs cast into the water reached them. In Galicia there even appeared sayings like: "We fast like Rahmans", "On the Rahmans' great day" that is Easter Day. In the Ukrainian language the word 'Rahman' came to mean a righteous Christian and a pauper and in the Kaluga and Smolensk regions the adjective 'rahmany' is to be found, meaning 'meek, simple-hearted, strange'. According to some scholars, the Rahleiskoye kingdom of Saltan mentioned in Russian tales ('Of Bove the Prince', 'Of Yegory the Brave') originally read Rahmanskoya, i.e., the kingdom of the Rahmans.

There was no exact image of India in the Middle Ages, but on the basis of information gathered from Graeco-Roman literature, medieval authors created their own image of India, of a fabulous land inhabited by righteous people. It is interesting to note that in their description of India they also introduced the features found in reports of wonders and righteous people in other countries. All the knowledge they had of India they approximated to Old Testament traditions and gave them a Christian flavour. "Christianisation" of the image of India was quite widespread in the Middle Ages and had some influence on later literature too.

Russian legends while mentioning about 'fabulously rich country of India' made a special mention of certain other facts such as a bird with its nest on fifteen oak trees, wild elephants, unicorns, aurochs with golden horns camels and all kinds of ferocious elements. In some other legends, India was described as a country where people had six arms. This probably was an interpretation of iconography of Lord Shiva. Other legends mentioned that the rivers flowed in this country from paradise itself. Apart from mentioning pepper, India was described as a country which had 'everything in abundance', a country where there were neither thieves nor bandits nor envious persons. This was the image of India and its people in Russian legends.

Yet another story of Indian origin appeared in Russia in the 15th century *Stephanites and Ihnelates*, dating back to the *Panchatantra*. During the reign of the Sassanid king of Iran, Khusro Anushirvan, the *Panchatantra* was translated from Sanskrit into the Pehlevi language and later from Pehlevi into Arabic. It was titled *Kalilah wa Dimnah*. In the 11th century, on the orders of the Byzantine emperor Alexius I Commenus, it was translated into Greek by his court physician. Simeon Sythos (probably a Syrian by descent). The Greek version was the basis for the appearance, soon afterwards, of versions in Latin and a number of West European languages. Later, a South-Slav version, based on the Greek version, appeared in the 13th century and quickly reached Russia.

There are comparatively few sources of information on Russian-Indian relations in the 15th century, but one of these is very revealing. In his *Voyage Beyond Three Seas*, Afanasy Nikitin has given a graphic description of Indian life. His incisive mind could make out how Indian life had begun to change. He, for instance, has given details about their everyday rites—rules of taking food, caste prohibitions, the way personal names were given and the cult of cow and funeral rituals.

Though Russia had no official relations with India in the 16th century, individual Russian merchants did reach India. Indian merchants also went to Russia and there is evidence that at the close of the 16th century, the Russian ruler, Boris Godunov, gave them protection. A bronze vessel with an Indian inscription in the Gurmukhi script found in Orsk, southern Urals, possibly dates to the 16th century. It belonged to Bhola Singh, a Sikh engaged in trade in this area. Similarly, a Bengali merchant with a cargo of silk had also made an abortive attempt to reach Russia. It is, however, certain that in the 17th century trade relations between India and Russia started growing rapidly. Textiles, precious stones, incense and medicines from India were sent to Russia through Iran in large quantities. In this period, Iran itself was feeling the influence of Indian trading. There were colonies of Indian merchants, thousands strong, living in its large cities, such as Isfahan, Kandahar and Shiraz. A whole network of Indian colonies, interconnected by blood as well as business relations, encompassed territory from Transcaucasia and the Caspian Sea to northern India. Volume of trade was so considerable that in certain areas Indian trading 'centres' began to emerge.

Indo-Russian relations were raised to still higher level when a merchant from Astrakahn, Vaily Tushkanov, was sent to the Mughal Emperor Shahjahan, with the proposal that trading people should be allowed in the two sovereign states to carry on trade. Another significant development of this period was that Indian traders were permitted to perform their religious rites freely, and their traditional customs, such as the Panchayati system, were respected. Some Indians settled down in Russia and the whole group of Agrizhans are believed to be descendents of the mixed Indian-Tatar blood. Thus, towards, the end of the 17th century, Indo-Russian relations had reached a fairly developed stage. In 1675 a mission headed by Mohammed Yusup Kasimov was sent to the Mughal emperor, Aurangzeb. In addition to his other assignments, Kasimov was asked to bring to Russia vegetable seeds, small animals and birds and invite Indian experts on stone bridges and other such big undertakings.

Indian economy was fairly developed in the sixteenth and seventeenth centuries. Even in the smallest village rice, flour, butter, milk, beans and other vegetables, sugar and other sweets, dry and liquid were produced in abundance. Western historians have recognised the fact that before the British rule, India had achieved a fairly developed stage of industrial development relative to contemporary world standards. The Indian Industrial Commission of 1916-18 opened its report with the statement: "At a time when West Europe, the birth place of the modern industrial system, was inhabited by uncivilised tribes, India was famous for the wealth of her rulers and for the high artistic skill of her craftsmen. And even at a much later period, when merchant adventurers from the West made their appearance in India, the industrial development of this country was at any rate not inferior to that of the more advanced European nations".

Precisely in this period Indo-Russian trade started flourishing. The 1720s-1740s witnessed a sharp increase in Indo-Russian trade, and which was mainly carried on by Indians settled in Russia, either temporarily or permanently. The annual trade turnover of the Indians during this period sometimes exceeded 100 thousand roubles. Some of the Indian entrepreneurs possessed large fortunes. According to documents in the Russian archives, for example, when the Indian Sukhanand died in St. Petersburg, he left a fortune of 300,000 roubles.

Academic science developed in Russia in the 18th century. The St. Petersburg Academy of Sciences was founded in 1724. In the same year Daniil Messerschmidt got to know of an Indian merchant in Siberia and took lessons from him in Indian languages and scripts. This merchant had come from Delhi and was settled in Irkutsk. However, one of the first Russian scholars to work on Indian languages was Prof. Georg Jacob Kehr. He learnt the Devanagari alphabets and also knew Multani dialect, a dialect spoken even today in Pakistan. However, in the last two to three decades of the century, interest of Progressive Russian scholars and journalists in problems facing the Indian people increased, with the main focus on the exploitation of the people of this subcontinent by the British East India Company.

"Never had such a blessed people, which the Bengalis really are, been vanquished by another nation", and "this so rich and happy nation came so swiftly under its new ruler to decline and poverty that there is no example of this in history either", wrote Nikolai Novikov.

In 1788, a Russian translation of the *Bhagwadgita* appeared and with it began a new phase of keen interest by Russian scholars in Indian classics and literature.

The ties between India and Central Asia, the territories which constituted the Soviet Republics, before this integration of the USSR have existed since hoary antiquity. In fact, some historians contend that the Aryan tribes originally inhabited the region that comprises the present Tajik, Kyrgyz and Uzbek Republics. They gradually moved across to the present Iran, India and Europe. Alexander's route of conquests also lay across Uzbekistan. Later, the Kushans too came from the same region of Central Asia. Kanishka's empire covered a good part of north India today's Pakistan, Afghanistan and extended well into Tajikistan, Kyrgyzstan and Uzbekistan.

The sweep of Changez Khan and massive Arab invasions followed by Timur's conquests destroyed the Buddhist culture in these parts. Changez Khan's thrust covered a vast area including northern India which suffered calamities of plunder and loot along with the people of Central Asia. Timur's seat of power was Samarkand.

From the fifteenth century, European imperialism began spreading its tentacles in many directions. While India was subjugatec finally by the British, the Czar's empire extended to Turkmenistan From then on interrelation between India and Russia were excludec to a large degree by European politics. The mighty powers of Europe had their own wars and peace treaties in a series of changing fortunes By the middle of the 19th century, the British Empire had consolidated itself and incorporated Punjab, extending its rule right up t Khyber. This brought Russia and Britain face to face in open hostilit which continued till the World War I.

This notwithstanding, from the middle of the 18th century on ward, interest of Russian scholars in Indian literature in most of th languages, apart from Sanskrit kept on steadily increasing. As earl as in 1851, a Chair of Oriental Languages was created in Mosco University and in 1855 a Chair of Sanskrit was established

St. Petersburg. Progressive intellectuals and political leaders had watched with interest India's first war of independence in 1857. Significantly, the Russian scholar, Ivan Pavlovich Minaev, visited India a number of times.

But trade ties between India and Russia has a history far more ancient. In the Middle Ages, Indian pepper, ginger, products of sandalwood and handloom were well known to the Russians. For centuries, the overland trade among India, Central Asia, Russia and beyond was supposedly largely in Indian hands. In the capital of Azerbaijan, Baku, the great oil city on the Caspian sea a historical monument, a temple of fire worshippers, was established by Indian merchants. The earliest information about the Indian colony in Baku dates back to the 17th century. On the walls of this temple there are some 15 inscriptions in Devnagri and Gurmukhi scripts as also some phrases are in incorrect Sanskrit. An important factor is that most of the traders who were settled there or visited this place were Hindus and Sikhs. This is confirmed by the fact that in Baku at least two *sarais* (inns) built by Indian traders, still exist one of the *sarai* is still known as the 'Multani Sarai'. Fortunately, the original architecture and the interior decor of these inns have been maintained. One of them is now used as a tourist resort.

But all was not a one-way traffic. The Russian scholars have for instance, established that stable trading relations between India and Transcaucasia had existed in the 16th and 17th centuries. The Armenians were settled in almost all the major cities of India, e.g., Madras, Bombay, Calcutta, Delhi, Lucknow, Lahore, Dacca, etc. The chief judge in the reign of Akbar was an Armenian. One of Akbar's wife was also an Armenian.

From the middle of the 18th century, when the influence of the British East India Company had become firmly established in India, the British began to victimise Armenian merchants. During this period, Armenians living in India generally supported the freedom struggle against the British rulers. The military commander of the last Nawab of Bengal, Bihar and Orissa was Grigory Harutyunian, who fought against the British rule in the 1769s. He became one of the main heroes in the romance Chandrashekhar, created by classical

Bengali author Bankimchandra Chatterji.

All this show that in ancient Russia and image of India as a country of wisdom and wealth, had been formed, and over the centuries trade and cultural relations between Russia and India had developed and strengthened. Although till the 15th century, generally, it were the Indians who carried the torch of their cultural heritage to Russia, Russian travellers began to visit India after the 15th century and directly acquainted themselves with the natural environment, people, their way of life, languages, religion and above all, the rich heritage of the country. In certain areas, which constituted the USSR such as Central Asia and the Caucasus, interest in Indian cultural heritage, had been aroused very early in human history. But the 19th century witnessed a new urge among the Russian scholars to study ancient Indian civilisation, particularly the mutual influence of the Indian and Central Asian civilizations. It was on this edifice that cultural, economic and political relations between India and Russia has been shaping. Even after the disintegration of the Soviet Union, Indo-Russian relations have once again begun to grow, irrespective of the political dispensation in Moscow and New Delhi.

SECTION II

INDIA-CHINA:

Open Door Policy

9

India-China Relations: An Assessment

C.V. RANGANATHAN

As penetrating analysis has been made in the studies included in this volume on recent developments in India-China relations. I have attempted to provide a perspective from the point of view of a former diplomat who has had the privilege of serving in China in the sixties and late eighties and who dealt with China at the Ministry of External Affairs in the last three years of the decade of the seventies. One could highlight in brief, major events in China and in India during those years which influenced India-China relations as well as note briefly the changes in the international scene which had an impact on these relations.

From 1965-66, lasting almost a full decade, China went through the turmoil of the Great Proletarian Cultural Revolution, launched by Mao Zedong. Described as the lost decade for China, few foreigners can be as bitter about this strange period in contemporary Chinese history as the Chinese themselves. They have been open in acknowledging that this period coincided with the 30 per cent mistakes that Mao committed during his lifetime—a verdict passed by Chinese Communist Party in 1981. While internally the period was one of chaos and anarchy in China, externally China was seen as autarchic in its economic development, isolationist in its foreign policy and irresponsible in its behaviour towards foreign relations and foreigners in general with xenophobia and chauvinistic attitudes prevailing. Memories of the anarchy of the Cultural Revolution Years explain in large measure the warm welcome given to Deng Xiaoping—inspired reforms which were put in motion in 1978 as well as the acquiescence on the part of the majority of the Chinese population in the forcible measures used in 1989 to suppress demonstrators who gathered to protest at the Tien An Men Square. The Cultural Revolution only served to exacerbate poor India-China relations which witnessed armed conflicts in 1962 over the territorial question.

Indira Gandhi's Initiatives

In 1976, former Prime Minister Mrs. Indira Gandhi took the first step in signalling China that India sought a more normal pattern of relations with China when she took the decision to repost to China a full fledged Indian Ambassador, thus ending a hiatus of 15 years where diplomatic relations were downgraded to the levels of charge d'affaires from 1961.

In February 1979, the then Foreign Minister Atal Behari Vajpayee visited China at the invitation of the Chinese Foreign Minister Huang Hua. The significance of this visit was unfortunately lost on our political commentators and public opinion makers who were carried away by China's armed engagement with Vietnam which coincided with the tail-end of Mr. Vajpayee's visit when he was on a cultural tour after his official talks in Beijing concluded. Firstly the high-level exchange between the two countries was the first in more than eighteen years, the last such visit having taken place in 1960 when late Premier Zhou Enlai visited New Delhi. Secondly, the visit provided an opportunity to the Indian Foreign Minister to make a vigorous presentation of India's concerns vis-a-vis China. These included those elements of the relationship between China and Pakistan which harmed India's interests, China's moral and material support to a few disenchanted Nagas and Mizos who looked to China for assistance. China treating Sikkim as an entity separated from India etc. Thirdly, on the boundary question Vajpayee mentioned to Deng Xiaoping that since the status-quo on the boundary was disturbed significantly from the late fifties by Chinese movements, a conscious effort should be made to restore the status-quo of the period. On the positive side a request was made for the opening-up of Kailash and Mansarovar for pilgrims from India as a symbol of the improved relations between the two countries.

The above visit is recalled to show that there is a measure of domestic-political consensus in India cutting across political parties that in a world which is changing rapidly neither China nor India can profit from an attitude of hostility or detachment of the kind which characterised India-China relations for over two decades from the early sixties. At a time of possible political flux in India, this conclusion is important.

Rajiv's Visit: A Turning-point

It took another 9 years for an Indian Prime Minister to respond to the repeated invitations given by the Chinese to successively Morarji Desai, Mrs. Indira Gandhi and to Rajiv Gandhi, to visit China. The Rajiv Gandhi visit to China in December 1988 marked a turning-point in the normalisation of relations between the two countries. The domestic context in China was that from the early eighties China began to successfully implement the 'open door' policy for foreign investments in China initially in the Special Economic Zones abutting Hong Kong, Taiwan and Macau but later spreading to other areas as well. In agriculture and rural industry, the decommunication and de-Maoisation policies were yielding impressive results. In foreign affairs the major emphasis was on an 'omni-directional' policy which would ensure a peaceful and stable environment for China to pursue its liberalised economic policies at home.

Externally with the advent of Gorbachev on the Moscow scene, discernible changes in erstwhile Soviet policies towards the Western and Eastern countries were following with great rapidity. It was in this context that the late Indian Prime Minister Rajiv Gandhi, who was two generations removed from the trauma of the 1962, armed conflict with China, visited China in 1988. That visit followed by the visit to India in 1991 by Chinese Premier Li Peng, and by Mr. P.V.

Narasimha Rao to China in 1993 have brought in a large measure of political and military stability to a completely normalised pattern of India-China relationship. While the boundary question remains to be resolved to the satisfaction of both sides, working mechanisms have been put in place whereby civilian and military officials from both sides meet frequently to resolve the few discrepancies that exist over the actual lie on the ground of the LAC which separates the forces of both sides. On the positive side discussions relate to the implementation on the ground of confidence-building measures, improvements in communication facilities. Periodic meetings at authoritative levels of local force commanders of both sides take place.

The net effect is that ways and means are being pursued for each side to patrol and guard upto the limits of the LAC in a non-violent and non-provocative mode. If one recalls the events preceding the 1962 armed conflict, the military engagements post-1962 extending into the early seventies and the mini-tension of 1985-87 over pockets in the Eastern Sector, it is a noteworthy achievement that following the 1988 visit of Rajiv Gandhi to China, the atmosphere over the long India-China border is today neither relaxed nor out of newspaper headlines. In 1988 decisions were also taken to support border-trade between the Tibet Region of China and certain points in Himachal Pradesh and U.P. Although in the very nature of things it cannot be expected that volumes would be significant, the opening-up of border trade is symbolic of the intention to have peaceful commercial and cultural intercourse across areas which have witnessed armed conflicts.

Gorbachev's Proposal

It is not entirely fortuituous that India-China detente preceded the China-erstwhile Soviet Union detente. The political leadership in India were well informed about the implications of the several moves made by the former President of the Soviet Union Gorbachev towards China ever since he assumed office in 1985. The most significant signal he gave China of turning a new page in Chinese-Soviet relations came in a speech he gave in Vladivostok in the summer of 1986. Affirming the importance of the economic reforms in "Socialist

China", Gorbachev offered a break-through in the settlement of the long-vexed boundary dispute by offering the mid-channel principle on the large riverine border, clearly hinted at Soviet troop withdrawals from Afghanistan, undertook not to compromise China's position on nuclear arms-control in his conversations with the former US President Ronald Regan, offered better relations and communications with Japan and ASEAN countries (particularly over Vietnam's occupation of Kampuchea (now Cambodia) etc. Specifically during his visit to India in the winter of 1986, Gorbachev made it public in a Press Conference that India should settle boundary problems with China through negotiations and hinted that in the light of his new foreign policy, Soviet Union would extricate itself from entanglements in third country problems which affected Soviet national interests. Here again some sections of the then leadership in India and political commentators were unduly alarmistic. The realisation had not dawned in these circles that in a changed world ushered in by the several Gorbachev initiatives marking the beginning of the end of the cold war, the way was wide open for India to exercise flexibility in its foreign policy and to strengthen the independence of judgement and weight of India in international councils free from the hang-overs of the cold war period. It was in this context and perspective that the late Indian Prime Minister Rajiv Gandhi visited China in December 1988, a full six months before Gorbachev visited in May-June 1989. A bold initiative by any standards whose results are there for all to see.

Since the break-up of the Soviet Union, there has been vigorous continuity in the expansion of relations between China and Russia and between China and erstwhile countries of the Soviet Union, particularly between China and the Central Asian States atleast three of which border China's Xinjiang. The year 1966 saw many agreements between the two countries in the fields of sales of armed weapons, commercial and infrastructural areas. While each of these will have important political significance, perhaps the most important political agreement with security implications, is the one which Russia, China and the Central Asian States signed over borders, over maintenance of peace and tranquillity and for the intensification of overland trade and communication links.

This brings one to the question discussed in this book of possibilities of future cooperation among Russia, China and India on questions of global or regional importance. Here it would be sanguine if all thought of a formal grouping of the three is set aside. The national interests of all three would not necessarily be served by the sort of coordination of approaches to global or regional problems which would be perceived as confrontational or inimical to the interests of South-East Asian or East Asian countries or to Western Europe and USA. During the cold war years, the USA had placed itself closer to both Beijing and Moscow than either was to the other, thus giving it a better bargaining position vis-a-vis each. Developments in Russia-China relations since the end of the cold war signify the demise of that process. However, in terms of their fundamental interests, China and Russia cannot afford, inspite of domestic uncertainties in both countries, to distance themselves from the USA for all bilateral problems which each have with the USA. To a lesser extent the same logic applies to their relations with Western Europe, Japan, South-East Asia or East Asian countries. Under this broad premise there is, of course, ample room for closer dialogue on a whole range of economic, social, environmental and other issues which are peculiar to the three large societies of India, China and Russia, given their recent historical experiences and the implosions caused by their respective altered domestic economic policies. Cooperation which is issue-based could be strengthened across a wide range of issues which each of the three large societies face. To name just a few the struggle against terrorism and drugs, international trade and investment regimes, regional trade groupings, women's issues, environmental degradation and the intensification of bilateral or tripartite links in commerce, investments and communications, appropriate technologies to improve agriculture and horticulture yields, combating the onset of new diseases are some of the problems which could suggest themselves. The underlying philosophy which should inform dialogue and exchange of experience surrounding the areas suggested above, is that the globalisation and marketisation matrix cannot possibly find sustainable solutions to the new problems which arise in these areas.

10

India-China Relations: The Post Cold War Phase

SUJIT DUTTA

Since the December 1988 summit, India-China relations have entered a phase of confidence building and detente that today is at a fairly advanced stage. In spite of the unresolved problems that bedevil their relationship, this change in the bilateral dynamics is of great significance to the two countries as well as to the rest of Asia. India and China have increasingly begun to see each other and their relationship as crucial factors in their foreign relations. This in turn is also shaping the perception of other states towards the two states.

Stable relations between India and the People's Republic of China (PRC), are of considerable importance to the efforts to construct a peaceful post-cold war Asia. China and India are the largest Asian states, among the continent's most significant military powers, major economies and their largest emerging markets. Together India and China contain over a third of the world's population and, therefore, their future prosperity, security and progress can critically alter the fate of Asia and the world.

With cross border investments, trade and communications links spreading through the region and creating an increasingly intricate structure of interdependence in which India and China—along with the United States and Japan—are expected to play key roles, the future evolution of global capitalism would depend substantially on the stability and economic growth of the two countries. Consequently, both developing and developed states have significant interest in expanding friendly and cooperative ties with the two countries, as also in maintaining peace and cooperation between these two large Asian powers. As Asia struggles to cope with the effects of the sudden and dramatic end of the cold war, a prerequisite of security and stability in the new era would be the stability and prosperity of its largest economies—Japan, China, India, Indonesia—as well as peaceful, cooperative and stable ties among the major powers. Stable and expanding China-India relations are, therefore, important, both for the two billion people of the two countries and the rest of the region.

From India's perspective, constructing a successful China policy is among the most crucial diplomatic tasks. Only the policies towards the United States, the former Soviet Union (now Russia) and Pakistan have been more important in the past. This was largely because relations with China had gone into a freeze for over two decades following the 1959-62 phase of conflict. However, as the relations between the two countries entered a phase of detente, confidence building and widening cooperation in the post-Mao years, India's China policy has gathered greater weight. A series of confidence and security building measures, high level political and military exchanges, rising trade and investments, and cooperation in science and technology and in wider international issues have begun to lay the basis for a more stable and comprehensive relationship than in the past.

Border Problem with China

India has its longest land border with China. It, therefore, looms large on the security and geopolitical environment of India. China has disputed large segments of this border and continues to claim the whole of Arunachal Pradesh. It is yet to recognise Sikkim's accession to India on 26th April 1975 following the overthrow of the Chogyal by anti-monarchy and popular democratic forces. The PRC is the largest and the most important military and economic power in India's neighbourhood with extensive impact on both the subcontinental and the wider Asian strategic environment. Its ties, including those of military ones, with a large number of states around India—especially Pakistan and Myanmar—have significant implications for the Indian domestic, defence and foreign policies. China's tactical goals, strategic and growing force projection capability have a direct bearing on India's and the Asian security environment.

In turn, after Russia, India is China's second largest neighbour, the country with which it has the second longest border. From the Chinese standpoint, the nature of its relations with India has a direct bearing on the security of its troubled Tibetan autonomous region, on stability of its geopolitical environment, its ties with many of the states in the Southern Asia and with the non-Aligned countries. Beijing sees gains in increasing its interactions with India on global trade, environment, and human rights issues. It is also keen to expand trade, investments, technological, and military-to-military ties. Over the past decade of reforms on numerous micro and macro-economic issues and mechanisms of running a market and mixed economy, China has gained from India's advice and experience—as it has profitably from others. Since the end of the cold war and the post-Tien An Man Square difficulties in relations with the United States, China has stepped up its efforts to construct a friendly neighbourhood that serves as a security shield against big-power political interference and military pressure. Stable and non-antagonistic relations with India are, therefore, important.

Moreover, given the growing chorus of Chinese threats in sections of the Western and regional media, stable and peaceful ties with India are vital. India and Vietnam are the only two neighbouring states with which China has significant unresolved territorial problems, following the virtual settlement of the border problems with Russia in 1994. It has other unsettled border problems too—with Tajikistan over the Pamirs, Kazakhstan, Kyrgyzstan; Malaysia, Philippines, Brunei—over Spratlys; Indonesia—territorial waters; and Japan—Senkaku. But none of the disputes are as large and potent as those with India or Vietnam. If these two countries—with which China shares very long borders—feel confident about China's intentions and sincerity of its friendly pronouncements, the diplomatic pressures on China would reduce substantially and it would also influence the opinion of other states with which China has lesser problems.

The general direction of change in China's domestic and foreign policy strategy since the reforms began in the late 1970s, and especially since the end of the cold war, has been positive for peace and development in the region. This is valid despite China's war against Vietnam in 1979, its involvement in the Cambodian civil war and aid to the genocidal Khmer Rouge, its deep involvement in the Afghan war and the second cold war—all of which vitiated the regional security environment. However, the post-1978 modernisation and open door strategy by increasingly integrating the Chinese economy with the international system, and creating a complex network of interdependence with its neighbours has laid the basis for a potentially more peaceful China and a more secure regional order.

Thus, Beijing's policy of encouraging border trade in interior Asia has had a significant impact on improving both living standards in the peripheral provinces, stronger ties with neighbours, and an improvement in the regional security environment. The reform strategy has clearly given the PRC major stakes in the security, stability and prosperity of the rest of Asia and vice versa. And with the end of the cold war, the Cambodian and Afghan wars, the overall security environment has substantially improved.

A stable, peaceful, and externally responsible China is vital for Asian peace, security, and development. For the first time in a century China has secure and normal relations with all Asian states. If policies remain stable, the economies of the region—including that of China's—continue to grow, and a secure environment prevails, the whole continent will clearly gain in the coming decades. However, the PRC's great power ambitions, its ambitious military modernisation programme, its pattern of arms transfers in Asia, the way it is approaching or has approached its territorial and national unification goals, and the prospects of internal instability and power struggle — remain issues of great concern for the Asian security and to India. A substantial growth of China's power and influence is an inevitable consequence of its modernisation and unification. The world can live with it. The challenge to India and the rest of Asia is how that power would be used, how will China shape up, whether it will be responsive to the interests of others, and value the principles of common security, and the rule universally accepted norms and laws.

Uncertainty over China's future political and military direction, and concern about the effects on India of its nuclear build-up, its arms transfers, naval expansion, evolving regional military ties, and the unsettled territorial problem continue to hang over the relationship. What would be the effect of the growth of Chinese power and how would the post-Deng leadership use it, are crucial issues on which India's own strategy, the future of China-India relations, and the shape of regional politics and security would significantly depend.

This study argues that it is important for both India and China, as well as the rest of Asia, that the two countries continue to have stable and cooperative ties; that while their relationship has distinctly improved over the past six years, there are problems which must be addressed, and major challenges ahead could test it.

In order to construct a stable security order in Asia, balanced relations are essential among the most important powers in the region —the US, China, Russia, India, and Japan—in the coming years. It is urgent that India and China further involve themselves in the emerging regional economic structure of interdependence, abide by universally accepted legal structures and norms, forsake use and threat of use of force to settle external disputes, and constructively contribute to the making of a new cooperative system of post-cold war regional peace and security.

II

Confidence Building and Cooperation

India and China resumed their ambassadorial level ties in 1976 after a hiatus of 15 years. It came after a few months of the death of Premier Zhou Enlai, though some months before Chairman Mao Zedong passed away. K.R. Narayanan, a career diplomat then, had been sent to restore full-fledged ambassadorial ties as a result of discernible changes in the Chinese foreign policy. Since then the two countries have attempted to gradually construct a new relationship which is far more realistic, mature and without any romantic 'bhai-bhai' sentiments. The new approach is concretely concerned with building strong blocs that would withstand temporary shocks and pressures, enhance mutual understanding and cooperation, and be suitable for an immediate crisis management measure.

The resumption of political dialogue at the highest level has been among the most important factors bringing about this change in climate, and, of course, a principal confidence building measure. Late Rajiv Gandhi's visit to China in December 1988—the first ever visit at this level since Jawaharlal Nehru's visit in October 1954—was a landmark in itself. It led to the opening up of more frequent and closer political, economic, military, scientific and cultural exchanges, besides the setting up of the Joint Working Group to resolve disputes and expand cooperative ties. In December 1991, Chinese Premier Li Peng paid a return visit and in September 1993 former Prime Minister P.V. Narasimha Rao went to China to continue the interaction. From the Indian side, the important visits have included those undertaken by former President R. Venkataraman (1992), present Vice President K.R. Narayanan (1994), former Defence Minister Sharad Pawar (1992), former Deputy Prime Minister Devi Lal (1990), and former Commerce Minister Pranab Mukherjee.

Many a high level visits have been paid from the Chinese sides too. And the notable among the visitors, included Vice Premier Li Ruihuan (1993), Defence Minister Chi Haotian (1994), Minister of Trade Wu Yi, Vice Premier and Foreign Minister Qian Qichen (1990, 1994), and the recent visit of the Chinese President, Mr. Jiang Zemin (from 28th November to 30th November, 1996), who is also the General Secretary of the Communist Party of China and the Chairman of his country's Central Military Commission. He told the newspersons, "The Chinese and the Indian people joining hands will be a great force and an important guarantee for peace in Asia and the world at large."

Intensified political interactions, regular institutionalised negotiations on all issues of bilateral interest under the Joint Working Group framework begun in 1989, and the deepening of trade and other ties have laid the basis for a regime of confidence and security building between the two countries. A deciaration by the two countries that they would resolve their territorial differences peacefully through negotiations, would not take any measure to change the LAC, and maintain peace and tranquillity along it are some of vital measures that one can recall readily. The September 1993 agreement to Maintain Peace and Tranquillity along the LAC was a landmark development as it brought along political achievements of the entire phase of diplomatic negotiations that began in 1981, and paved the way for the political normalisation since 1988, and later led to discussions on confidence building measure in 1990s.

The direct contact between the defence establishments of the two states began in 1991 as a new phase of confidence building measure. This has involved exchange of visits by the Defence Ministers of the two countries, besides the Indian Army and Naval chiefs. It also brought the Chinese Vice Chief of Staff, a group of some 20 odd highest ranking generals of the People's Liberation Army to India.

These confidence and security building measures have laid the basis for greater stability and predictability, as far as the military situation along the frontiers of the two countries is concerned. They have also created a border security environment which is far more relaxed than it was in nearly four decades.

India-China Trade: Good Progress

Rising trade and investments have underpinned these changes in the political and military spheres. Indo-China trade has risen steadily since the signing of a Most Favoured Nation (MFN) agreement in 1984, but its real growth came about in the past three years. Trade touched 675.73 million dollar mark in 1993—a rise of 98 per cent over the previous year. Trade rose to 895 million dollars in 1994-95 and is expected to be around 1.2 to 1.3 billion dollars in 1995-96, which will be the highest ever. The Indian exports to China increased from 180.99 million dollars in 1992 to 416.57 million dollars in 1993 —a rise of 169.9 per cent. Trade balance did favour China in 1994-95, and is likely to remain so in 1995-96 too. Mineral products and iron and steel were the two largest items of export to China. Other Indian exports include chemicals, jewellery and semi-precious stones, raw hides and skins, and possibly rice too in near future. The bulk of Chinese exports was taken by raw silk for the booming Indian textile industry. The level of investments is not large, but is definitely growing. An Indian drugs and pharmaceuticals firm, Ranbaxy, is opening up a venture in Beijing, and China is investing in a medium steel plant in Orissa.

The two sides have also set up a joint committee for cooperation in science and technology. Significant exchanges of visits have taken place at the highest level in the past few years, especially in the areas of space, aerospace, nuclear power, agricultural science, milk and dairy development and others. The Indian purchase of low enriched uranium from China for the Tarapur Atomic Power Station earlier in 1995, following the refusal of the United States and France to continue with the supplies, was the outcome of the changed perceptions of the two big sized neighbours.

Politically, Chinese position on several regional issues and on Kashmir, have been more positive in the post-Tian An Man Square, post-cold war phase than earlier. There has also been a discernible unwillingness in Beijing to foment India's differences with its neighbours, or take partisan positions, despite the fact that the reportage of the official media remains heavily biased against India in its subcontinental reportage. On Kashmir, China since 1990 has accepted the Indian position that the issue should be peacefully and bilaterally settled between India and Pakistan as called for by the 1972 Simla Agreement. In January 1994, for instance, China clarified that it was against an independent Kashmir, and by mid-year it had refused to support a Pakistani attempt—which had to be given up though—to move a resolution at the Human Rights Commission in Geneva over the alleged human rights violations in Kashmir. All this came in stark contrast to China's pro-Pakistan postures and its calls for Kashmir's self-determination in the Maoist phase, and the deliberately hazy articulations of the 1980s in which it sought to please both Pakistan and India by mentioning both, a bilateral settlement and the UN resolutions, in the same breath.

The end of the cold war, the normalisation of China-Russia relations, the end of the Afghan and Cambodian conflicts, India's growing ties with the United States, the ASEAN states, Europe and Japan, and the economic reforms and liberalisation initiated by the Narasimha Rao government—have all had their impact on creating a new environment, facilitating an upturn in the India-China ties.

There are, however, several issues that need to be addressed if India-China relations are to move forward from the confidence building measures stage to a more interdependent stage.

III

While significant movement in improving the overall climate of negotiations has been achieved, the two countries have yet to reach the stage of resolving the key differences and disputes—principally concerning the border and territorial issues. These pending problems would have to be positively and meaningfully tackled in the coming years if bilateral relations are to move forward from confidence building to a meaningful detente and a framework of stable security.

KEY ISSUES INVOLVED

(a) Stability in Ties and Policies

For building stable and cooperative ties between India and China, long-term continuity in cooperative policies is essential since the Chinese foreign and defence policies have been prone to radical swings in the past owing to internal instability and power shifts within the Communist Party of China's leadership. Mao himself was instrumental in initiating extreme swings in policies with grave impact on China's internal situation and external relations. The extreme left-wing and ultra-nationalist policies that were launched by Mao after 1957 significantly contributed to the deterioration in relations with India, which resulted in the break-down of diplomacy, and the resultant conflict. The post-Mao reform years have witnessed a far greater stability in policies than ever before, though they have not been free from pressures and pulls, and instability. As Deng Xiaoping and the older generation pass away, it is of crucial importance to India and others that China stays on a stable, peaceful and reformist course. That, of course, cannot be said for certain now.

(b) Growth of Military Power

Although the post-Mao leadership presented its reform and liberalisation strategy as the "four modernisations", it has principally been concerned with the twin-modernisations—of the economy and the military. The modernisation of agriculture, industry and science and technology—the first three of the so-called 'four modernisations' —was, in fact, a disaggregated way of presenting what essentially amounts to economic modernisation—possibly done to secure the support of the peasantry, the industrial working class and party-managerial cadres, responsible for industry both at the enterprise and the ministerial levels, and the intellectuals.

The modernisation of armed forces has, thus, been among the major goals for the Chinese reforms led by Deng Xiaoping. While economic reforms have certainly been the key Dengist goal, in large areas China's economic and military reforms in fact merge. Politically, the reformers never lost sight of the importance of China's military power in providing it a strategic and diplomatic leverage that could be used to advance its twin modernisations plans. Military power was also essential both for maintaining internal stability through the difficult transition period of a command to a market economy, which at the best, revealed the bloody role the People's Liberation Army in suppressing the nation-wide urban upheaval in April-June 1989, and in maintaining the so-called nationalism and national prestige as internal ideological factors that legitimise the continued rule of the Communist Party of China. And finally, with the vast segments of the economy run by the military, economic reform was also in a way a reform and modernisation process of China's sprawling military-industrial complex. The leadership believes that military power and the Communist Party's control of it are essential if the Party has to survive the difficult post-Deng transition period.

Since 1989 China's official defence expenditure has grown dramatically—ranging from 12 to 25 per cent per annum, which is among the steepest in the continent. But even this does not give the complete picture of its actual military growth as large segments of the total military allocations are not covered by the Central budget.

There is little transparency in overall defence allocations, and most international estimates place actual expenditure at three to five times higher over the official defence expenditure estimates. Thus, while the 1991 Chinese official defence expenditure stood at 33.03 billion yuan or a little over 6 billion dollars, the US Arms Control and Disarmament Agency placed it at 51.04 billion dollars, or eight times higher than what was officially given out. By 1994, the official defence expenditure had gone up dramatically to 54.35 billion yuan, which at current exchange levels was shown at 6 billion plus dollars. It presents thus a huge grey area in understanding the reality. This lack of transparency is clearly not conducive to regional peace.

(c) Transfer of Arms

Arms' transfers present yet another dimension of the rise of China's military profile in the region. Weapons' exports are increasingly an important source of revenue for People's Liberation Army, while as the defence linkages prove valuable in expanding China's external influence. China is not a globally dominant exporter of weapons, as the US, Russia, and Europe are far ahead of it. Nor is its military technology the most sophisticated or lethal one. But Beijing has not hesitated from exporting lethal weapons, such as missiles, if it has brought economic or military gains.

From India's perspective, Beijing's arms transfers in the region are not always a peaceful, commercial exercise, but they have significant politico-military impact on its security environment.

The bulk of China's arms exports are to a group of countries around India. These countries are: Pakistan, Iran, Myanmar, Bangladesh and Thailand. With all these countries China has strong defence ties, besides the naval cooperation. It has also sold naval vessels to Sri Lanka. Its first sale of weapons to Nepal in the late 1980s had caused a serious breach in Indo-Nepal relations. The Chinese sale of M-11 missiles to Pakistan and the Intermediate Range Ballistic Missiles to Saudi Arabia, and its involvement in Islamabad's missile and nuclear programmes are serious issues for regional stability, and also compromises the global efforts at non-proliferation of weapons of mass destruction.

The recent China-Myanmar military cooperation has not only

strengthened the Myanmar's military regime, but has raised fears in India of growing naval cooperation between them as it poses a fundamental change in the strategic environment, as it happened way back in 1960s when it helped Pakistan in a similar fashion. Myanmar's neutral and non-aligned status is important for India's security in the east and in the Bay of Bengal, and, in fact, in the Indian Ocean region. Any Chinese attempt to forge a strong strategic relationship with Myanmar thereby alters the latter's non-aligned status and thus would clearly have an adverse reaction in India. It is not in the interest of China-India cooperative ties.

(d) The Nuclear Factor

China has often brought to bear the weight of its position in the first tier of the global security system to enhance its political, military, and economic interests, as well as in its dealings with the major power players such as the United States. The US offer—made by Defence Secretary William Perry during his visit to Beijing in December 1994—of simulation technology for testing nuclear weapons, should China agree to sign the CTBT is the latest example of the distance the major powers are willing to maintain the two-tier security structure. It also depicts their balatant disregard for the security of the non-nuclear weapon states.

India's position on the Non-Proliferation Treaty (NPT) is not centred around China—as, for example, Pakistan's is vis-a-vis India—and is based upon political, security and disarmament logic. It is deeply troubled by the production of weapons of mass destruction per se; as it is by their possession by the handful of powerful states, as well as the Pakistan's clandestine nuclear-weapon programme. But it cannot be denied that the Chinese weapons are of particular concern to India, notwithstanding the fact that the country has lived with such a reality ever since 1964. India has lived with the reality of Chinese weapons uneasily being ever wary of its negative military-security, political and diplomatic implications for the country. The increasing evidence of deep and ongoing collaboration between China and Pakistan in the area of nuclear technology and equipment, which have both civilian and military uses, and in Pakistan's missile programme, have made a mockery of China's adherence to the Nuclear Non-Proliferation Treaty (NPT) and the Missile Technology Control Regime (MTCR). Such a reality cannot be wished away as it certainly has the most direct implications for India's nuclear and missile policy.

(e) APEC and Asian Multilateralism

Active involvement of India and China in both bilateral or multilateral security related and strategic dialogues are necessary if Asia is to remain stable and peaceful. The process has already begun. The India-China Joint Working Group, the ASEAN-China dialogue in 1996, China's involvement in the ASEAN Regional Forum, the US-China security dialogue, the Russia-China confidence building measures, and the current negotiations on China's entry to the World Trade Organisation (WTO) are all important.

The two countries along with the other regional powers would simultaneously have to stress the observance of law and international norms, and oppose states that violate them. Adoption of an Asian convention on non-use of force or making such threats to settle disputes, including disputes over sovereign rights, would facilitate this process. Establishment of a regional security forum, such as a Conference on Security and Cooperation in Asia (CSCA), agreement on a set of norms for conduct of cooperative and peaceful external relations in the Pacific Asian-Indian Ocean region, and concerted and time-bound efforts at universal nuclear disarmament and so on are other steps that would enhance post-cold war Asian security. China has joined both the Asia Pacific Economic Cooperation (APEC) and the ASEAN Regional Forum (ARF). With India poised to join both these organisations in the coming years, multilateralism will get a major boost in the region and elsewhere.

There are strong reasons why China should continue to seek peace and cooperation with the outside world. Its modernisation, economic well-being, and national security depends on a peaceful foreign policy. Statements by most of its leaders do express China's interest in deepening long-term peace and security in the region.

President, Jiang Zemin, who is also the general secretary of the

Communist Party of China at a meeting with the president of the Japanese newspaper, *Asahi Shimbun*, in August 1993, put forward China's position on establishing a security framework for the Asia-Pacific region and his support for conducting "multiform, multi-layer, and multichannel security dialogues" so as to increase understanding and trust. President Zemin also maintained that China believed that "countries in the Asia-Pacific region should treat each other as equals and get on well with each other on the basis of Five Principles of Peaceful Coexistence; should not seek hegemony or sphere of influence; should not establish and participate in any military bloc directed at other countries; all countries should enhance mutually beneficial cooperation, expand bilateral, subregional and regional cooperation, achieve common prosperity and development, enforce disarmament and arms control in accordance with the principles of fairness and reasonableness, oppose arms race and border disputes; and other controversial issues between Asian countries should be settled peacefully through negotiation in accordance with the relevant international conventions and oppose resorting to arms or the threat of arms".

Much of this is in tune with India's goals. Yet there has often been a problem between China's international principles and practise. China's active push to cross-border trade and investments, its promotion of confidence and security building measures with India and Russia, reopening of dialogue with Vietnam, its formal joining of the ARF and the APEC, and its participation in bilateral and multilateral security dialogues are in keeping with the Deng's statement that 'peace and development' are interdependent and the major trend of the times. However, Beijing's first preference remains bilateral measures, but, if and when they fail, unilateral actions are there to attain its goals. Multilateralism is a new process concept for China and it would take time before it finally digs in.

World View

Current Chinese international and strategic thinking raise a series of issues that need attention. These are:

• Most Chinese analysts see the emergence of a five power

multipolar world following the collapse of the bipolar power world. However, they do not critically examine what are the implications of such a five power multipolar world order. Is it a system based on balance of power or a five power hegemonic concert, with spheres of influence? one wonders.

• China's current military strategy for local and border wars do have a direct bearing on the security of its neighbours. Would it not promote military build up and fears in the region? Is it in tune with its professed need for peace to promote development and cooperative ties with neighbours?

• Does Chinese irredentism—seemingly aimed against its neighbours, most of whom are developing countries—match with its principles of friendship and solidarity with the Third World, or with its attempt to have a friendly, secure and stable neighbourhood?

• Does its policy of support for a non-discriminatory global order and nuclear disarmament square with its current role within the NPT system, or the continuous modernisation of its nuclear forces, or even with its silence on concrete alternative to mechanisms for bringing about a global non-proliferation?

• Can domestic issues be totally segregated from external relations as China wants, as it espouses for the inviolability of sovereignty? The absence of rule of law in China, for example, directly affects its external business ties and also the investment environment. Foreign states, which have trade and investment ties with China, should surely have the right to insist on the maintenance of contractual obligations in letter and spirit.

• What kind of message does it want to send to the rest of Asia by its display of military power on the Taiwan issue?

Prospects

Over the past few years it has become increasingly clear that both India and China have enormous interest in the development of their burgeoning relationship. The rest of Asia, and the world at large, too have strong interests in the growth, prosperity and peaceful policies of the two major Asian powers.

Most predictions about the shape of the next century place Asia at the centre of global growth, trade and development. The World Bank's forecast is that by 2020 China, the United States, Japan, India, and Indonesia will be the largest economies. According to these forecasts, six of the world's biggest economies will emerge from Asia. The reality could be far more complex and the hierarchical order quite different. Yet the historical trend holds that there would be a major reassertion by the Asian power and civilisations, and it cannot be denied. Such an outcome would not only restore what was the long pattern of historical evolution till it got distorted by the Western capitalism and colonialism, but would be in keeping with the size, resources, and civilisational strengths of the Asian people.

However, such a future cannot materialise if the antagonism and conflict or fears and suspicions among the Asian powers persist. Theories of hegemonic stability and the continued use of force by the big powers, including China, to achieve their national goals are not conducive to a long term peace in the region. An Asian century can emerge in true sense only if strong cooperative bridges are constructed across the continent, and with the outside world. That would entail peaceful defence and foreign policies, a synergising of strengths, and the adoption of a philosophy of common security and prosperity. An asymmetry of wealth and power within societies and between states is a sure cause for continuing internal and external conflicts in Asia. India and China—the two largest states in the continent and the world—have a special role to play in constructing an alternative, but more peaceful and prosperous, future. But the uncertainties that continue to cloud the region's future can be removed only through joint efforts of all the states, major and small, of the vast continent.

11

India-China Relations: Past to Present

SHRI PRAKASH

Any analysis of India's relations with the People's Republic of China today must at the outset state the major differences in the global situation, domestic policies and perceived national security interests which set the 1950s and the 1990s apart, especially with reference to Asia. The world is no longer embroiled in a bitter cold war between the two superpowers, competing with each other for superiority in military power, strategic reach and political influence. The political disintegration of the former Soviet Union has major implications especially for the geopolitical map and the geostrategic situation of Asia. To begin with in terms of size, China and India are now more comparable to Russia and are considerably larger than any of the other numerous nation-states of the CIS. In terms of contiguity with India's borders in the North remain the same, China's western frontiers now run alongside those of three new states, Kazakhstan, Kyrgyzstan and Tajikistan. The overall political environment in the countries surrounding China has undergone a dramatic and decisive transformation with the exception of Myanmar and Vietnam. All the other States like, Mongolia, Russia, the three CIS states, mentioned above, and India, as well as Pakistan, have multiparty Parliamentary democracies. While all these countries are friendly with China, excluding Myanmar and Vietnam, these states have undergone a change from a one party ruling states to multi party political systems. It means that interaction among these countries and mutual communication within them and with China are inevitably bound to influence the Chinese people in the long run, thus enhancing the chances of a sort of political liberalization taking place in China too. Further it may usher in a socialist democracy there, but through peaceful means. It must be emphasized that there are significant sections, within the Communist Party of China as well as outside it, who are for a further political liberalization on the lines of the economic reforms. A senior Chinese academician Xing Bensi recently observed: "Reforms of the political and the economic structures must be interdependent and mutually complementary. Without political reforms, economic reforms will not get anywhere. In recent years, we have searched for ways and means to perfect democracy and the legal system, while carrying out economic reforms. Besides we have abolished defacto life tenure of the cadres, reformed the leading structures and Government. All these are reforms in the political field. Only a higher development of socialist democracy can enable socialism to both take over (absorb) productive forces created by capitalism and serve the interests of the whole society and all the people, and not that of just a minority".[1]

China's New Policies

The present phase of economic liberalization in China shows that its efforts are to base itself on future national development on the strategy of promoting a socialist market economy. China's new foreign policy of seeking peace in the world as a whole instead of promoting people's war or militant peasant movements and other forms of class struggle as in the past is accompanied by its simultaneous efforts to improve trade, investment and other forms of economic as well as cultural interaction with neighbouring and distant industrialized as well as Third World economies with its dominant agrarian and mining labour intensive sectors. This striking change in the Chinese policies has made it much more appreciative of India's national development efforts through a mixed economy. China's new policies also create an objective basis for a greater exchange of experience with India in the formulation and implementation of national development and management strategies. This process is slowly progressing in such economic and scientific areas where either India or China lag behind. Such a bilateral political environment and relationship stands in sharp contrast to the 1950's when, despite the euphoria of the post decolonization phase and the much touted *Hindi-Chini Bhai Bhai* (Indians and Chinese are brothers) slogan, and the doctrine of *Panchsheel* (peaceful coexistence). China viewed India's security interests and political ambitions as being too close to the Western powers and later on to the Soviet Union, with which it subsequently developed a highly antagonistic relationship and took sharp turn for a strategic and trade relations with USA, Canada and the EEC countries. Hence, today China no longer holds India's foreign policy, designed to serve its own national interests in a multipolar world, against itself as she herself is following a similar foreign policy. Such a situation again enhances the possibility for a potential China-India cooperative relations in many myriad spheres

India-China Relations in the Pre-1947 Phase

Not much can perhaps be written about China-India relations in a period when both were not independent sovereign nations. There is enough evidence in the statements of leaders of the National Liberation Movements of both countries that they deeply sympathized with their respective popular struggles to put an end to colonialism. An indication of the mutual regard they held for each other is unfolded in a letter Mao Dezong wrote to Jawaharlal Nehru in July 1940, when the two countries were in the midst of their national struggles to throw away the foreign and the feudal yokes. "The emancipation of the Indian people and the Chinese will be the signal of the emancipation of all the downtrodden and oppressed",[2] wrote the Mao. Messages expressing similar sentiments were exchanged by many notable Indian and Chinese personalities, like Kang Youwei, Liang Qichao, Rabindranath Tagore, Gandhiji and Dr. Dwarkanath Kotnis

How did the British-Indian colonial government view its rel

tions with China? British India's concern with China was peripheral and mainly a product of its strategic concerns about the possible danger of Russian expansionism southwards, beyond Mongolia and into Tibet, as well as delineating, even though roughly, the Northern and North-Eastern borders of British India from the Chinese influence. By 1850, and subsequently after overcoming the 1857 Indian revolt, the British Empire in India had achieved sufficient stability for its rule and its functionaries to explore the North-Western, Northern and North-Eastern frontiers of the subcontinent which formed the natural boundary. The British efforts to know both the natural boundaries and the recognized and acceptable historical frontiers materialised in the form of mapping of the routes and rivers as well as watersheds and mountain passes and towns in the first instance. Strachey in 1851, Walker in 1854, Johnson in 1865 and Ardagh in 1897 gathered information which later became the basis for various settlements among the British-Indian Government, Tibet and the Chinese Manchu Government.[4] On the basis of these route surveys and expeditions, like the young husband expedition to Lhasa in the 1890s, several agreements were concluded. The Anglo-Tibetan convention of 1904, the Anglo-Chinese convention of 1906 and finally the Anglo-Russian convention of 1907 expressively recognized China's suzeranity over Tibet while giving the British Raj facilities for trading marts".[5]

In 1910, covert activities of the British forced the Chinese to move forces into Lhasa, which resulted in the first flight of Dalai Lama to India and the outbreak of the revolution in China that finally led to the fall of the Manchu dynasty. The British Raj then concluded a Simla Agreement with China and Tibet in 1913, conceding Chinese Suzeranity over Tibet, though demanded autonomy for it. This convention was never ratified by China as it continued to claim complete suzeranity over Tibet on the basis that it was a part of the Manchu Empire during the 13th century A.D. Interestingly, there is no disagreement between the People's Republic of China and the Republic of Taiwan on this issue. Both assert categorically that Tibet is a part of China since the 13th century. Indeed, on the question of where did the historical border run between India and Tibet, there was no difference between the position taken by the People's Republic of

China and the one outlined by the pre-1949 government of Tibet. Professor Noor Husain points out that after the transfer of power in India in August 1947. "The Tibetan Government sent a message to the Indian Government, demanding the return of extensive territories spreading from Assam to Ladakh, including Darjeeling and Sikkim. A similar demand was made by Peking, (Beijing) in later years".[6]

It only means that the Chinese government only agreed with the pre-1949 position of the Tibetan Government on the issue of boundaries between India and Tibet. A fair settlement would have to be worked out through negotiations in order to resolve the border dispute even if India were hypothetically dealing with a free Tibet. The Dalai Lama's case for the Tibetan self-determination does not rely on the actual treaties signed by the British India government with the then Chinese government in the presence, and with the concurrence of, the local Tibetan administration. Recently, the Dalai Lama published a paper on "Tibet's case for self-determination"[7], in which he asserted that "Tibet was an independent country before its occupation by China. It had its own government, now in exile, its own judicial and administrative systems; its small army, postal system, currency and taxation. Tibet maintained independent relations with other countries, especially those in the region, by whom it was recognized. There is no justification for claiming that Tibet was a 'part of China' as Beijing claims today". The Dalai Lama's version, however, does not refute or explain how did the British India government sign several agreements with the Tibetan and the Chinese governments, recognizing China's suzeranity over Tibet. In fact, at present China, instead of regarding the Dalai Lama as a religious leader, calls him a political exile, who wants to break up China.

Second Phase of India-China Relations: 1949-62

Once both the countries, India and China, become independent they did not begin to see themselves in a fresh light with hope only but as nations with their own ambitions, which did not always harmonize with each other. To begin with, China thought that compared to its own, India's independence from the foreign yoke was not all that decisive, since it continued to be a member of the Commonwealth and accepted aid from the Western countries. The Communist Party of China also expected the Communist Movement in India to make a rapid progress, and so much so that it wrongly took the Telengana peasants' movement of 1948 in Andhra Pradesh and the Tebhaga peasant movement in West Bengal of 1949 as the harbinger of the Communist march to power in India. In his reply to a message of greetings to the Indian Communist Party in October, Mao Dezong hoped that "India would certainly not remain long under the yoke of imperialism and its collaborators". He went on to say that like free China, free India would one day march into the socialist and people's democratic family. "That day could be the end of the imperialist reactionary era in the history of mankind", he had remarked. However, this cannot be taken as the only dimension of the China-India relationship. The second element of this relationship still rested upon Chou en Lai's deft handling of Third World diplomacy. The enunciation of the Panchsheel Declaration at the Bandung Conference in 1954—signed both by India and China—set out in clear terms principles of the post-colonial global order with which both agreed and wanted to be accepted by the ex-imperial powers. These principles were: Mutual respect for each other's territorial integrity and sovereignty; mutual non-aggression, mutual non-interference in each other's internal affairs; equality and mutual benefit and peaceful coexistence. The Panchsheel Declaration clearly signified that there could be an appropriate policy framework for peaceful relations between India and China, as it took into account the legitimate national, economic as well as security interests of both the countries.

India's view of China was to a great extent shaped by Nehru's ability to pursuade the pro-West Indian elites to try and take an objective view of both the positive and negative aspects of Chinese nationalism. It is quite wrong to suggest that because of his overt commitment to socialism Nehru had a biased view of China. While Nehru undoubtedly was sympathetic to the mass content of the Chinese experiment at social modernization with the promise to remove mass poverty, illiteracy, control unchecked population increase, build the infrastructure to promote the growth of modern industry and agriculture, he was also aware of the fact that nationalistic ambitions of these two big states could lead to rivalry. His advocacy that both had to have a conscious policy of accommodating each other's interests in such a way as to coexist peacefully, was fine tuned to this aspect which, however, received a jolt with China's unprovoked attack on India in 1962.

There is ample evidence to show that Nehru was aware of the potential conflict situations which could bedevil the efforts at building constructive China-India relations. In his book, *The Guilty Men of 1962*, Dr. Mankekar states that at the time of his visit to Peking in 1954 during his discussions, Nehru had said "that some day or the other these two Asian giants, were bound to tread on each others' corns and come into conflict and that would be a calamity for Asia. That was an eventuality which we should all strive hard to avert".[8]

More recently, Frank Moraes in his book, *Witness to an Era*, wrote that in 1952, when he went as a member of a cultural delegation to China, Nehru in his briefing had said "never forget that the basic challenge in South-East Asia is between India and China. That challenge runs along the spine of Asia".[9] In one of his speeches in Parliament, Nehru in December 9, 1959 referred to the Border Committee, which was appointed in 1951, and said that since 1950 the picture of the two powerful states coming face to face with each other on a tremendous border had been before the government. They might have "differed as to the timings in our minds as to when that would happen; whether in five years, ten years, fifteen years or thirty years."[10]

Nehru and other Indian leaders had to shape a policy towards China. From 1947 to 1949 Nehru was preoccupied with military action in Kashmir and Ladakh. China was proclaimed in October 1949 and was duly recognized by India. India's strengthening of its border defences in Ladakh in 1948 and in Sikkim in 1949 was perceived by China as a threat to Tibet and its vulnerable Western link to Chinese Sinkiang. China's reaction was thus sharp and sudden. Chou En-Lai reiterated his government's determination to "liberate the People of Tibet and stand on guard at the Chinese frontiers".[11] In spite of diplomatic pressure from India, China moved into Tibet in late 1950s. Apparently, China was also apprehensive of the

Indian activities in Nepal, Bhutan, and the North-East Frontier Agency (NEFA).

Moving cautiously, Nehru consolidated India's relations with Nepal, Sikkim and Bhutan. Finally in 1954, he signed an agreement with China that recognized the Tibet Region of China, removed Indian military personnel from Gyantse and Tatung. And against compensation, gave up rest houses and communication facilities and conceded the China's right to have trade agencies in Calcutta, Kalimpong and New Delhi on a reciprocal basis. Despite these positive developments and a conciliatory agreement, events occurred which led to a deterioration in China-India relations. In 1956, a revolt broke out in Lhasa. Chou En Lai accused Nehru of trying to reap the benefits of British imperialism by inciting a revolt in Tibet through the Khampa tribes and infiltrating guerrillas with Western help from the Kalimpong base in India. In 1959, the Dalai Lama fled from Lhasa and was granted political asylum in India. The result was the end of the promising China-India friendship. Some 50,000 square miles of territory became openly disputed along the 3000 kilometre frontier stretching from Aksai Chin across Uttar Pradesh, Himachal Pradesh, Punjab and NEFA and also along China's boundary with Nepal, Sikkim and Bhutan, which China regarded as outside the Indian sphere of security interests.

The boundary dispute between India and China has for a long been the single biggest issue in their relations. In order to understand the China-India border dispute and its various ramifications, it has first to be realised that there is a marked difference in the terrain on the Indian and the Tibetan sides of the border. The Indian side gets fairly heavy rainfall and the mountains are covered with dense forests. There is thick snow in the winter. The Tibetan side is bare and cold, with light snowfall. It has an easy access and construction of arterial roads with link roads to the border had been taken in hand since 1951 and had been well established on the Chinese side by 1960. India set up the Border Road Development Board only in 1960 and it takes time to construct roads in the prevailing terrain conditions. Only a start had been made in the prevailing terrain conditions by 1962.

Although in the eastern sector, after the cessation of hostilities, the Chinese withdrew behind 'the McMohan Line', though the Chinese formally do not accept the McMohan Line as the indicator of the border between India and China. They contend that China was not signatory to the Simla convention of 1913-14, which mapped out the McMohan Line. Further, there is dispute over the alignment of the McMohan Line. In the Thagla Ridge-Khenzemane area, China holds that the line runs through the Drokung Samba bridge. There are differences also in the alignment of the border in the Western (Ladakh) Sector and the Central (Himachal Pradesh and Uttar Pradesh) Sector. There was protracted and exhaustive correspondence between Jawaharlal Nehru and Chou En Lai between December 1958 and December 1959. The two leaders met in April 1960. Subsequently, three rounds of discussions were held among the officials of India and China by November 1960, but no progress had been made and the matter was left unresolved.

Basically, China maintained that the China-India boundary is not formally delineated and some differences exist between the boundary lines drawn on the maps of the two countries which require survey and mutual consultation. India contended that in three different sections—Ladakh, Sikkim and NEFA, covering much the larger part of the border—the boundary as shown on its maps was supported by geography, and in some cases by tradition and treaties, like the 1842 treaty between Kashmir and the Emperor of China, and the Lama Guru of Lhasa in respect of the Ladakh Sector; the Anglo-Chinese Convention of 1890 in respect of Sikkim and the McMohan Line in case of NEFA. The remaining portion from the tri junction of Nepal to Ladakh is also traditional and follows well-defined geographical features. The meeting of the two Prime Ministers in April 1960 could not devise a way out and the official talks failed. It is believed tha China indicated that it would accept the McMohan Line in the eastern sector if India would accept the LAC in Ladakh.

Many other divisive issues complicated China's relations with India during the 1950's and early 1960's. One issue was China' 'special relations' with Pakistan as also the large scale supply o Chinese military hardware to Pakistan. Another issue which was no so well known to Nehru was the growing China-Soviet dispute which definitely accelerated the progress of Indo-Soviet relations. If this had been known to Nehru he could have solicited greater support from the Soviet Union in seeking to restrain China. It was only in September 12, 1959 that Nehru referred in Parliament to the Soviet neutrality in the case of the China-India dispute. In his speech Nehru said that "the issue of a statement (the Tass statement of September 9) itself shows that the Soviet government is taking a calm and more or less objective or dispassionate view of the situation considering everything. We welcome that".[12]

Subsequently, the border dispute between India and China became a matter of heated discussion between Khrushchev and Chinese delegate Peng Chen at the Bucharest meeting of June 22, 1960.

Khrushchev visited India in February, 1960. It is extremely unlikely that he and Nehru did not exchange views on relations of their countries with China. Subsequently, in April-May, 1962 there were a number of border incidents on the China-Soviet border in Sinkiang. According to the Chinese, several tens of thousands of citizens of Ili region were enticed into the Soviet Union. The Soviets charged the Chinese with more than 5000 violations of the Soviet frontiers in 1962. By this time the Soviets had already repudiated the treaty they had concluded with China on the development of nuclear weapons in July, 1959. One can see the correlation in time between the Soviet repudiation of this treaty and their neutrality over the China-India border question.

'Forward Policy'

There has been considerable discussion in and outside of India about the wisdom of the so-called 'forward policy'. It is important to remember that the term was first used by Neville Maxwell, a Western critic, who has argued in his book, *India's China War*, that this was a provocative act on India's part which invited Chinese retaliation leading to the short lived border war of 1962. What is meant by the term "forward policy"? During the years 1959-61 the Chinese were constantly trying to move forward up to their 'claim line'. At that stage they put forward two 'claim lines', the second one claiming more areas than the first. In addition, they brazenly claimed that they were in occupation of areas which indeed were known to be in the control of the Indian security forces. The so-called 'forward policy' was nothing more than increased patrolling and surveillance of regions in the river-valleys of the Indus basin and the trans-Karakorum area at quite some distance from Aksai Chin and the Chinese roads to Sinking. This patrolling and surveillance was done by setting up an additional line of checkposts on the territory under Indian control, but claimed by the Chinese. The 'forward policy' can at best be described by quoting from the decision recorded in the Prime Minister's directive of November 2, 1960. "So far as Ladakh is concerned, we are to patrol as far forward as possible from our present positions towards the international border. This will be done with a view to establishing our posts which should prevent the Chinese from advancing any further and also dominating from any posts which they may have already established in our territory. This must be done without getting involved in a clash with the Chinese, unless this becomes necessary in self-defence". A similar policy was later adopted in Arunachal Pradesh.[13]

The fact that India's so-called 'forward policy' in Ladakh and later in NEFA was not intended to be a purcussor to hostilities of any kind could be seen from other macro indicators. The Chinese Communists were adept at the use of the army since they had come to power through armed struggle and believed in Mao's dictum that "political power flows from the barrel of a gun". They had openly declared their intentions of recovering territories they had to give up because of the 'Unequal Treaties'. India on the contrary had primarily believed in using non-violent methods for winning its success during its national liberation struggle. It wanted a peaceful settlement of disputes with its neighbours. In any case India faced a major military threat from Pakistan and was hardly likely to start hostilities on two broad fronts especially at a time when it was poorly equipped to fight a high altitude mountain war. Although a committee headed by General Himmat Singh was constituted in 1952 to study the military threat to our northern borders, its recommendations, even in regard to creating the communications infrastructure, were pursued with no urgency. The Border Road Development Board was set up only in 1960. No thought was given to raise, train and acclimatise forces for operational tasks in high altitude areas. The Indian Army, which was over two million strong during the Second World War, had been drastically run down after the war. In the 1950's an army of 300,000 was being talked about. Because of India's adverse relations with Pakistan, the actual strength in the period 1960-62 was about 500,000. It was only after the 1962 hostilities with China that mountain divisions, organised to operate on India's northern border, were raised and the strength of the Army, according to the Military Balance of London, went up to 900,000 in 1970. Far from preparing for any war, with China, India had spurned all offers from the West to join Military Pacts like SEATO or CENTO and was actively developing its policy of building up the Non-Aligned Movement by spreading its philosophy of Non-Alignment among Third World countries. Indeed, just before the outbreak of hostilities in October 1962, both India's Prime Minister as well as India's Defence Minister V.K. Krishna Menon were touring abroad in September 1962. The Chief of the General Staff, Lt. Gen. Kaul was on leave. The Director of Military Operations was sent for a cruise abroad the Air Craft Carrier, *Vikrant.* All evidence points to the high probability that the Chinese action was the result of a deliberate decision taken in Beijing, well in advance to humble India. The Chinese forces could not have been assembled in such great strength to carry out the operations just within a few days. Some American scholars, notably Harold Hinton, have also hinted at a time correlation between the Chinese attack on India and the confrontation between the Soviet Union and the United States over Cuba. China took advantage of this fact which accounted for the Soviet neutrality rather than intervention in the China-India dispute.

The Chinese attacked in two waves in NEFA and Ladakh beginning from October 20, 1962. After several dourly fought battles they succeeded in occupying about 5000 sq. miles of the Indian territory. Due to tremendous international pressure and for fear of advancing deeper into better populated Indian territory, which would have been much more difficult to hold, China declared an unilateral ceasefire in

November 10, 1962 and withdrew behind the McMohan Line in the NEFA sector.

As a result of the 1962 War China gained about 3000 sq. kms. of the Indian territory. However, according to Chinese version, it does not occupy even now a single inch of the Indian territory. In May 8, 1986, the official Chinese News Agency, Xinhua, published a pamphlet called "introduction to the Sino-Indian Border Issue". In it outlined the Chinese view point about the history of the border dispute, asserting that more than 90,000 square kms. of the Chinese territory was still under the Indian occupation.[14] Still India agreed to an unilateral ceasefire because it wantcd a peaceful and negotiated solution to the border problem. If India had wanted to continue the war it could have got the support of both the Soviet Union and the USA. At that time China was having poor relations with the Socialist Bloc, led by the Soviet Union, and the West, led by the US. Hence, China was extremely isolated and not in a position to fight a long drawn out frontier war with India.

Period between 1962 and 1981

The China-India relations, soured by an emotion charged border dispute, embittered by a war and accelerated by conflicting political perspectives and foreign policy perceptions, remained in a deep freeze all through 1962-68. Because of India's close relations with the Soviet Union and her leadership of the Non-Aligned Movement, China saw India as a political rival in the Third World and constantly tried to denigrate her in Afro-Asian Forums. At that time Beijing was engaged in a vituperative campaign against India. The Chinese media attacked practically all aspects of the Indian policies and developments. India's economic policies, political developments within the country, political and economic relations with South and South-East Asia, incidents with regard to Tibet and Taiwan and of course ties with the two big powers, the USA and the USSR, the US and the Soviet economic assistance to India was criticised. "The Indian reactionaries had sold out their national interest for aid from the 'U.S. Imperialists and revisionists' and were living entirely by begging and borrowing from them. When an unofficial delegation came from

Taiwan to take part in some private celebration programme on Mahatma Gandhi's birthday, not only did the Chinese Charge d'Affaires lodged a strong protest with New Delhi, as Beijing regarded it as a grave crime by the "Indian reactionaries" and charged India with efforts to create two Chinas "under the instigation of the US imperialism". When Soviet Premier Alexai Kosygin came to represent the Soviet Union at the funeral of President Dr. Zakir Husain, it was termed by China as "a plot to step up military cooperation with the reactionary Indian Government and to hatch a fresh anti-China plot". Similarly, Mrs. Indira Gandhi's visit to Indonesia was sharply criticised. Beijing denounced both ASEAN and the proposal for creation of a Ministerial Council of ECAFE, supported by both India and Indonesia. The proposal was described by China as a prelude to the establishment of an anti-China military alliance manipulated by the US Imperialism and the Soviet revisionism.[15]

Even more serious from India's point of view was the assistance extended to insurgency in India—whether they were hostile elements like the Naga rebels or Marxist-Leninist groups trying a Maoist type of revolution in India. The rebel Nagas were given training in arms and provided with weapons and funds to carry on armed rebellion in India. Beijing also, in its propaganda, would have the world believe that India was going through an acute revolutionary phase and extended vociferous support to the Naxalite movement which was waging a so-called armed revolution on the pattern of the Chinese revolution, acknowledging Mao as their leader.

However, gradually another undercurrent seem to emerge in China's policy. Whereas line I was based on the assumption that India and China were political rivals in the Third World, line II seemed to open up possibilities of cooperation. After the complete isolationism of the Cultural Revolution Days, China was making a turn towards befriending old enemies like the USA or neutralizing others like India as a strategy for promoting peace that would permit more concentration on economic development and also as a counter strategy to the alleged Soviet strategy of encircling China. Apart from its newly acquired friendship with Western countries, China also needed to play a larger role in the Third World and conflict with

India did not particularly help. The Indian opposition to military alliances and unwillingness to support proposals for collective security arrangements in Asia, that could be construed as anti-China, made some impression on the Chinese. In addition, on certain issues Mrs. Gandhi had not changed India's stand. On Taiwan and Tibet and on the representation of the People's Republic of China in the United Nations, India maintained her traditional standpoint, supportive of China. In one of the most important indications of the new thinking and in what was undoubtedly meant as a message to the Chinese, Mrs. Gandhi had said in January 1, 1969 that India's problems with China would not be solved by taking a rigid position.

The Chinese response came at the annual Parade at the Tinanmen Square in Beijing in May 1, 1970. The Indian Charge d'Affaires was ushered in the presence of Chairman Mao Zedong who chatted with him for a while, talked about the traditional friendship between India and China and hoped for the revival of friendly relations.[16] This was followed by the Indian Government's decision to raise the level of representation to ambassadorial level and Mr. K.R. Narayanan, now Vice President, was sent as ambassador to China after a gap of almost two decades in April, 1976. Soon after Beijing announced its decision to appoint an ambassador in New Delhi. The process for mending relations had thus begun.

A further step in improving China-India relations was taken during the tenure of the Janata Government. Its Foreign Minister Atal Behari Vajpayee, guided by then Foreign Secretary Jagat Mehta, visited China. But the visit had to be cut short because of the outbreak of hostilities between China and Vietnam.

Mrs. Gandhi returned to power in January 1980. In the emerging situation, the Chinese were ready to welcome talks with her and no longer exhibited the old animosity against her. The thaw was helped by a meeting between Mrs. Gandhi and then Chinese Premier Hua Guafeng in Belgrade where both had gone for the funeral of Marshal Tito. The meeting was followed by a visit to India by then Chinese Foreign Minister Huang Hua in June, 1981.

The importance of Huang Hua's visit lay not only in that it set a procedure for the beginning of a dialogue between the two countries, but also because, from India's point of view, China recognized the importance of resolving the boundary question between the two countries. Huang Hua himself set down three principles in search for a reasonable settlement. These, according to him, were "historical background, existing realities and rational sentiments" of the people.[17] The basis of the Chinese position on the border issue had earlier been spelt out by Deng Xiao Ping to an Indian journalist in June 1980.

"So long as both sides are sincere", Deng had said, "respect the present state of the border, and be tolerant towards each other, the Sino-Indian boundary question can be solved through peaceful negotiations". As a matter of fact, ever since negotiations on the boundary question began, China has never asked for the return of all the territory that it had maintained had illegally been incorporated into India by the old colonialists. Instead, China suggested that both countries should make concessions—China in the eastern sector and India in the western sector, on the basis of the actually controlled border line so as to solve the boundary question in a package plan, thus fully demonstrating the spirit of mutual understanding and concessions. India has, however, not accepted this position. In July 1980, then Foreign Minister P. V. Narasimha Rao had told Parliament that India had never accepted the premise of linking "concessions" of territory by the Chinese in the eastern sector — a territory in their occupation in exchange for the Indian territory in the western sector.

Gradually the Chinese and the Indian side came around to the position that while they should continue with talks and negotiations about the border dispute, this process should not be allowed to prevent the expansion of the relations on issues of economic cooperation, trade, cultural exchanges and political cooperation on issues of global concern to Third World countries in general. This is what Deng Xiao Ping had told a delegation of the Indian Council of Social Science Research led by late G. Parthasarthi, who was the Chairman of Policy Planning in the External Affairs Ministry. This is the process that has gradually been developing through official talks and exchanges during the 1980's and 1990's. The five-day official talks in 1983 January 23 to February 1, yielded progress on expanding economic, trade, scientific and cultural exchanges. For the first time in two decades, a six member official delegation went to Beijing in June 1984 for exploratory talks about cooperation in the tea sector and to see whether they could coordinate their moves for an international tea agreement and for a common marketing strategy. The two countries also reached an agreement on bilateral cooperation in the field of standardization. The Indian Standards Institution and the China Association for Standardization proposed exchange of national standards as well as information and teaching material concerning standardization.[18]

Congenial Atmosphere

The fifth round of boundary talks were held between September 17 and 22, 1984 in Beijing. These talks yielded the general understanding that pending a final settlement of the two countries would maintain tranquillity on the border and neither would take any action that could disturb the peace. In October 31, 1984, Mrs. Gandhi was assassinated. China sent weighty politbureau member and Vice Premier Yao Yilin as special envoy of the Government to New Delhi for the cremation ceremony. It might be recalled that it was Yao Yilin who had negotiated the first break-through in China-Soviet relations when he had signed a major trade agreement in Moscow. Yao had a talk with late Rajiv Gandhi, who had been sworn as new Prime Minister and invited him to visit China. Rajiv Gandhi had told the Chinese leader that India wanted to have good relations with China.

While the overall environment was becoming more hopeful and helpful, quite against the run of the events, the Sumdorong Chu border incident took place in the Kameng division of Arunachal Pradesh in July 15, 1986, just on the eve of the seventh round of talks scheduled in Beijing for July 19. However, both sides played down the incident and insisted that it was accidental rather than international. India, at the same time, conferred full statehood on Arunachal Pradesh in December 8 and 9, 1986 with the Lok Sabha and the Rajya Sabha adopting a legislation to upgrade the Union Territory into a full-fledged State. China claims this area as its own on the assumption that it had been conquered and ruled by Tibet in the past.

Despite these developments, the process of peaceful negotiations was not halted. The then new Foreign Minister N. D. Tiwari visited Beijing in June, 1987. In their joint statement both he and the Chinese Vice-Foreign Minister Liu Shuqing emphasized that peace and friendship were far more important than any differences.[19]

Tiwari's visit was followed by the important visit of the then Prime Minister Rajiv Gandhi to China between December 19-23, 1988. This led to the setting up of the Joint Working Group (JWG) on the border issue, headed by the respective foreign secretaries. It was later raised to the level of Ministers of State for External Affairs. One of the new tasks assigned to the JWG was to undertake a fresh survey of the border to see how to arrive at a consensus about its demarcation and to think of military confidence building measures that would reduce tension and preserve the peace on border of the both countries. Since 1988 the JWG has had four meetings and undertook many a confidence building measures, including that of joint meetings of the Chinese and Indian military personnel on a regular basis and reduction of troop levels. The next meeting of the JWG was held in June 1993. Further confidence building measures have been agreed upon for the readjustment of checkposts.[19] These measures include prior notification of military exercises, prevention of air intrusions and redeployment of forces along the LAC. Furthermore, there was an agreement to open another trade point at Shipkila Pass in Himachal Pradesh in addition to the one at Lipulekh in the middle sector of the boundary.[20]

Another permanent committee created during Rajiv Gandhi's visit was the Joint Commission on Science, Technology and Trade. The meetings of this Commission, and the signing of several agreements between the two governments, have led to exchange of expertise relating to space technology, dairy industry and agriculture. Similarly, a protocol for educational exchanges too was initialled at the highest levels. A delegation of Chinese Vice-Chancellors has visited India. The Indian Defence Minister has visited Beijing. Former Indian President R. Venkataraman visited China. So did former Prime Minister P.V. Narasimha Rao. Numerous exchange of visits of senior Parliamentarians and political leaders on both sides have taken place. A festival of China was organised in India during December 1992. In November 28, 1996 the Chinese President Mr. Jiang Zemin came to India with high-level delegation led by the Chinese Vice Premier and Foreign Minister, Minister for Foreign Trade and Economic Cooperation, Minister for Civil Affairs and the Chairman of the Tibet Autonomous Region's Government. Jiang focused on common interests.

Trade with China has increased though it remains a small share of the total value of the external trades of India and China.

Recent value of trade between India and China

(in Rupees Million)

Year	*Export to China*	*Import from China*	*Balance of Trade*	*Total Trade*
1989-90	391	658	–267	1049
1990-91	327	556	–229	883
1991-92	1162	526	+636	1688
April-August 1992	472	249	+223	721
1993-94	380	240		

Source: Directorate General of Commercial Information and Statistics DGCIS, Govt. of India, New Delhi.

During the three years of 1981-83, the average per year value of China-India trade was 29 million US dollars. During the next three years of 1984-86, this annual trade average was 22.6 million US dollars. In the three years between mid-1989 to mid-1992 the annual average value was 42 million US dollars or about 35% more than the average for the early 1980s. However, compared to the overall trade value of the two countries, this constituted a very small share. Between September 1989 and September 1990, the value of China's foreign trade was 91,200 million US dollars.[21] In that year the value of trade between India-China was 33.8 million US dollars or just 0.038% of the value of China's foreign trade. In 1991-92 it was only 0.07% of the value of India's foreign trade.[22]

The Indian imports from China at this time mainly consisted of silk, silkyarn, pulses, petroleum and petro chemical products, resin, dyestuffs, tyres and tubes and a number of engineering products. China mainly buys from India iron ore, chrome ore, tea, coffee and urea. The Annual Trade Protocols lists the possibility of exporting hydrogenerating and thermal power equipment and transport equipment like trucks and railway equipment. There is potential for increasing trade between India and China. A delegation of the Federation of Indian Chambers of Commerce and Trade has identified a list of 50 items for export to and import from China. Several points on the China-India border have been reopened to promote border trade with Tibet.

In the future India can hope to compete for a further share of China's imports of wheat, sugar, coffee, tobacco, cotton, electrical and non-electrical machinery and transport equipment. It can hope to import petroleum products, rolled steel, manufactures of metals, oil seeds and nuts to produce edible oils, aluminium and aluminium alloys.[23] There is scope for investments in each other's economies, and putting up joint ventures in SAARC countries as has been witnessed with the setting up of a joint Indo-China factory in China to produce washing machines there.[24] Another joint venture has been finalized between the Indian Essar Corporation and the Chinese Metallurgical Import and Export Corporation to set up a medium scale steel plant of one million tonne capacity in Orissa.[25] After the implementation of South Asian Preferential Trade Agreement (SAPTA) by the SAARC countries, the ground has been prepared not only for negotiating South Asian Free Trade Area (SAFTA), but giving a thought to the creation of another North Asian Free Trade Area (NAFTA), including Central Asia, South Asia and China. Apart from initiating trade and investment liberalization measures, China and India can cooperate in supporting each other's case for entry into WTO and APEC respectively. They can try to propose joint or multilateral strategies for relief from and reduction of Third World debts. A prospective agenda for trying to evolve a common perspective and position as well as a timetable for action on some vital issues of global concern could be considered on the following lines:

(a) Reforms of the UN: Expansion of the number of permanent members in the Security Council; Implementation of the

UN's socio-economic goals.

(b) China's admission to the WTO; India's admission to APEC: A common future programme for promoting a New International Economic Order.

(c) Fight against international terrorism and drug trafficking.

(d) Formation of a North Asian Free Trade Area, comprising China, Central Asian States and the South Asian Countries.

(e) A functional view of environmental conservation and regeneration in the specific context of the Third World countries.

(f) Population control measures.

(g) Women's issues and implementation of rights of children.

(h) Continuance of negotiations for the settlement of the border dispute between India and China and implementation of new strategic confidence building measures to avoid conflicts in future.

(i) Containment of military expenditure through maintenance of strategic parity and ensuring mutual and equal security without getting involved in an arms race.

(j) Promotion of confidence building measures, transparency and cooperative security in Asia.

(k) Promotion of nuclear weapons non-proliferation and a programme for the global elimination of nuclear weapons.

References

1. Xing Bensi, "Certain Theoretical Issues Concerning Social Transformation in Contemporary China", in Prof. Manoranjan Mohanty *Chinese Revolution: Comparative Perspective on Transformation of Non-Western Societies*, Ajanta Books, Delhi.
2. K. Subramanyam, Nehru and the India-China Conflict of 1962 in *Indian Foreign Policy, the Nehru Years*, ed. B.R. Nanda, p. 110, New Delhi, 1992.
3. Prof. Wang Hongwei, *The Relationship between China and India Facing the 21st century*, The Institute of the Asia Pacific Studies, p. 1, Beijing, November 1992.
4. K.K. Mojumdar on *Sino-Indian Relations: Images and Reality*, Deptt. of Chinese and Japanese Studies, University of Delhi, March 22-24, 1993.

5. Noor A. Husain, India's Regional Policy: Strategic and Security Dimensions, in *The Security of South Asia: American and Asian Perspectives*, p. 37, ed. by Stephen Philip Cohen, 1987, University of Illionis Press.
6. Ibid., p. 38.
7. The Dalai-Lama "Tibet's case for self-determination", *The Asian Wall Street Journal*, April 2, 1991.
8. Dr. Manekar, *The Guilty Men of 1962*, p. 110, Bombay, 1968.
9. Frank Moraes, *Witness to an Era*, pp. 220-21, London, 1973.
10. Prime Minister on Sino-Indian Relations, *Lok Sabha Debates*, vol. XXXV, pp. 2186-2214, 1959.
11. Bhabani Sen Gupta, *The Fulcrum of Asia*, p. 104, New York, Pegusus, 1970.
12. Minister of Indo-China Relations, *Lok Sabha Debates*, p. 8125, vol. XXIV, 1959.
13. K. Subramanyam, Nehru and the India-China Conflict of 1962, in B.R. Nanda, ed. *Indian Foreign Policy, the Nehru Years*, p. 125, Radiant Publishers, reprint, New Delhi, 1990.
14. *Xinhua* (English), 8 May, 1986.
15. Gargi Dutt, India-China Relations, in A.K. Damodaran and V.S. Bajpai, ed. *Indian Foreign Policy, the Indira Gandhi Years*, pp. 97-98, Radiant Publishers, reprint, New Delhi, 1990.
16. *The Statesman*, New Delhi, June 8, 1970.
17. Ibid., Feb. 17, 1982.
18. V.P. Dutt, *China after Mao*, pp. 366-67, Vikas Publishing House, New Delhi, 1991.
19. *Patriot*, June 16, 1987, New Delhi.
20. *The Hindustan Times*, June 12, 1993, New Delhi.
21. Report on "India-China take Major Peace Steps on LAC", *The Times of India*, pp. 1 and 9, June 29, 1993, New Delhi.
22. Statistics from the State Statistical Bureau, *China's Foreign Trade*, Beijing, Jan. 1991.
23. Statistics, *Economic and Political Weekly*, Bombay, p. 2276, vol. XXVII, no. 42, October 17, 1992.
24. Shri Prakash, Economic Dimensions of Sino-Indian Relations, *China Report*, pp. 230-31, SAGE, vol. 30, no. 2, 1994.
25. *The Economic Times*, July 19, 1989, New Delhi.
26. *Indian Economic Diary*, 26 March-1 April, 1992.

12

Evolution of Russia-China Relations

V.D. Chopra

The friendship between the Russian and Chinese peoples dates back to the 17th century, when relations between the two countries were first established. These relations were always marked by warm feeling and interest in each other's life and culture and struggle for liberation. The greatest Russians including Pushkin, Belinsky, Chernyshevsky, Tolstoy and Gorky repeatedly voiced the feelings of warm sympathy for the Chinese people.

Dmitri Mendeleyev, a great Russian scientists who was an ardent champion of close relations between the Russian and Chinese peoples, once wrote: "Alliance between Russia and China appears to me to be if not the best, then *the surest and simplest guarantee of the peaceful progress of not only these two countries but of the whole world*". (emphasis added) This perhaps is relevant today.

Lenin: A Charismatic Figure

Lenin made tremendous theoretical contribution to the Chinese revolution. His teaching on the national-colonial revolution, his theoretical and practical advice to the participants in democratic youth movements in the oppressed countries of the East, the Chinese Communists included, was of great importance to the revolutionary movement in the East as a whole and to China in particular.

In his article "Inflammable Material in World Politics" (1908), Lenin made a brilliant prediction of the development of the Chinese revolution. He wrote: "In China, too, the revolutionary movement against the medieval order has made itself felt with particular force in recent months. True, nothing definite can yet be said about the present movement because there is such scanty information about it. But there can be no doubt about the vigorous growth of the 'new spirit' and the 'European currents' that are stirring in China, especially since the Russian-Japanese war; and consequently, the old-style Chinese revolts will inevitably develop into a conscious democratic movement."

Three years later, in October 1911, a revolution broke out in China toppling the Manchu Ching dynasty.

Russia: Inspired the Chinese

In olden times the development of friendship between the peoples of Russia and China was obstructed by the reactionary policies of the feudal governments, of Tsarist Russia and Ching China which fomented national strife between the two peoples, suppressing their longing for closer relations and mutual support in revolutionary struggle.

The October Revolution in Russia swept away all the obstacles placed by the Tsarist regime. The Soviet state immediately announced the principles upon which it would base its relations with the oppressed peoplcs of the East. These principles equality and friendship of all peoples were new to history. The Soviet Union became an ally of the Chinese people in their struggle against the imperialists colonial brigandage. It repealed the unequal treaties Tsarist Russia had concluded with China and declared its desire to establish friendly relations.

In July 25, 1919, the Soviet government issued an address to the Chinese people and to the government of South and North China reiterating the principles of its policy in relation to China and expressing the Soviet people's friendship towards the Chinese people.

The revolutionizing influence of the October 1917 Revolution in Russia and the growth of friendly feelings for Soviet Russia among the Chinese people alarmed the ruling circles of the imperialist powers and China's reactionary government in Beijing, which set out to erect a barrier between the two countries.

The first years following the victory of the October Revolution (the period from 1917 to 1924) witnessed the struggle of the Soviet and Chinese peoples and of China's progressive organizations, above all the Communist Party, for the establishment of normal relations between the two states and for wider contacts between the two peoples.

An important contribution to the dissemination of information about the Soviet Union among the Chinese people in the 1920s was made by those who pioneered this work Professor Li Ta-Chao, one of the founders of the Communist Party of China (CPC); Chu Chiu-po a CPC leader and a prominent publicist; the writer Lu Hsin, and other progressives, who were the first in China to write truthfully about the October Revolution, about Lenin and the situation in the USSR, and to fight the falsehoods that were being circulated.

In the early twenties there appeared in China the first public organization aiming to promote contact with and extend knowledge about Soviet Russia. In July 1920 a Society for Marxist Studies was founded in the town of Changsha, Hunan Province. A Society for Russian Studies was also set up, its character declaring that: "The principle objective of the Society is to study all ideological currents existing in Russia. The tasks of the society included: (1) publication of books about Russia based on reliable material; (2) organization of fact-finding trips to Russia; (3) adoption of measures to have students sent to Russia for purposes of study".

In 1921 the Society sent a group of young people to study in Soviet Russia. Subsequently some of these formed part of the leading core of the CPC.

The progressive Chinese press being in need of truthful information about Soviet Russia in 1921 a Chinese-Russian Agency was instituted in Shanghai to translate relevant materials from foreign periodicals. The same year, also in Shanghai, Russian language courses were opened for students of Marxist literature. Liu Shao-Chi was among those who attended the courses.

An earnest attempt to spread knowledge of Soviet Russia was begun in the early 1920s by Hsin Chingnien, Meichou Pinglun and a number of other progressive periodicals.

In 1922 members of the Chinese parliament organised a Society for the Promotion of Chinese-Soviet Relations. In addition, seventeen public organisations sponsored a Chinese-Russian Association which advocated the establishment of relations and rapprochement with Soviet Russia. In 1923 a Union for Chinese-Soviet Diplomatic Relations and a People's Diplomacy Society were set up.

In the period of its cooperation with the Communist Party, the Kuominatang, under the impact of the revolutionary events of 1924-26, took some steps towards closer relations with the Soviet Union. Sun Yat-Sen who was a convinced champion of friendship between China and the USSR called for alliance with Soviet Russia. Addressing the members of the USSR Central Executive Committee in March 11, 1925, shortly before his death, he wrote: "Parting with you, dear comrades, I wish to express the hope that the day will soon come when the USSR will greet a friend and ally in a mighty free China, and that in the great struggle for the liberation of the oppressed peoples of the world, the two allies will advance hand in hand towards victory".

By 1924 the struggle of the democratic movement in which the young Communist Party had gradually begun, from 1921 onwards, to play an active part, compelled the Beijing government to establish normal diplomatic relations with the USSR.

In May 31, 1924, the Agreement on General Principles for the Settlement of issues was signed between the USSR and the Chinese Republic. Thus, China's first-ever treaty (based on equality); dealt a serious blow to the imperialist powers system of unequal treaties. Two factors created conditions favourable for the development of friendship between the peoples of these two countries and for the spread of knowledge about the Soviet Union in China.

The first was the establishment of diplomatic relations between the two countries in keeping with the May 31 agreement and the second was the important successes achieved by the revolutionary armies of the South during the famous Northern Expedition of 1924-

26 in which Soviet military advisers invited by Sun Yat-Sen, who then headed China's revolutionary government in Canton, took part. However, Chiang Kai-shek's reactionary coup in 1927 heralded a rein of reaction and terror. Anti-Sovietism was rampant, the mere mention of the Soviet Union could bring on ruthless reprisals. This campaign became vicious after the Kuomintang had broken off diplomatic relations with the USSR.

In the 1930s, faced with Japanese aggression, the Kuomintang leaders toned down their anti-Soviet campaign some what, since they needed Soviet support for the war against the invaders.

Set up in 1935, with branches in Nanking, Shanghai, Beijing, Tientsin, Changsha, Kunming, Lanchow, Kweilin and other major cities, the Chinese-Soviet Cultural Society on the whole united those who in the face of the Kuomintang reactionaries advocated friendship and cultural cooperation with the USSR.

A treaty concluded in August 22, 1937 stabilized political relations between China and the Soviet Union. During the war against the Japanese aggressor the Society intensified its work considerably.

In 1941-45, during the Great Patriotic War against Nazi Germany, the Soviet Union's prestige in China rose particularly high, and so did the interest of broad sections of the Chinese population in the life of the Soviet people.

The Communist Party of China took considerable effort to foster friendship with the Soviet Union. The first societies for friendship with the USSR were organized in 1924-26 under its guidance.

From 1927 until liberation there existed in China along with the 'White regions', large democratically-governed territories controlled by the CPC and the Chinese Red Army. In 1927-37 these regions were called Revolutionary Strong-holds. Beginning with the anti-Japanese war and the third civil revolutionary war, these Liberated Regions, as they had come to be called, were being extended.

Societies of friends with the USSR were established by Communists-internationalists in the democratic regions. Translations of Soviet publications appeared in large editions. Much was done to promote Chinese-Soviet friendship in the Liberated Regions of the North-East (Manchuria). During that period Soviet troops were stationed there (1945-46) Chinese-Soviet friendship societies emerged in a number of cities such as Dalny, Port Arthur, Changchub, Harbin, Tsitsihar, Mutankiang, Kiamusze and Fushun.

In 1924-27 large-scale activity developed in China which internal reaction and foreign imperialism strove to contain in every way. The trade unions in the USSR responded by organizing a mass 'Hands off China' movement.

Following Japan's predatory invasion of Manchuria in 1931 the movement of solidarity with China spread throughout the Soviet Union. Thousands of North-Eastern Volunteer Army troops and civilians found hospitable refuge in the Soviet Union.

Important Chapter of Friendship

During the anti-Japanese war of 1937-45 the Soviet Union, in keeping with its policy of solidarity with peoples fighting against imperialist oppression, rendered substantial military, material and other assistance to China. In 1938 it granted her two credit loans, of 50 million US dollars each and in 1939 another credit of 150 million dollars.

The Soviet Union's entry into the war against Japan in 1945 and the liberation of Manchuria by the Soviet Army added one more glorious page to the history of Soviet-Chinese friendship. Mao Zedong, said in his speech at the 7th Congress of the CPC: "The Soviet Union was the first country to renounce unequal treaties and sign new, equal treaties with China. During the period of the Kuomintang's First National Congress called by Sun Yat-Sen in 1924 and the subsequent Northern Expedition, the Soviet Union was the only country that gave aid to China's war of liberation.

In the rout of the Japanese armed forces in Manchuria, the decisive contribution made by the Soviet Army acting in close cooperation with the Mongolian People's Liberation Army of China, and Korean guerrillas, need to be recapitulated.

It should be stressed that with the collapse of the Kwantung Army, that bulwark of Japanese militarism, the centre of the Chinese revolution, both in economic and military-strategic terms shifted to Manchuria. It is region had been preserved and safeguarded as a revolutionary base against US-Chinang Kai-shek aggression by the people's liberation forces of China. The presence of Soviet troops in Manchuria (1945-46) and the naval base of Port Arthur (1945-55) was a valuable support for the revolutionary forces of China and played an important part in strengthening the people's democratic system in the liberated North-East.

The active preparation of the People's Revolutionary Army, of cadres and of communication routes was begun between 1945 and 1949 in Manchuria.

In that period the revolutionary troops in Manchuria were equipped with ammunitions captured from the Kwantung Army. General Wedemeyer, the US President's special envoy who inspected the situation in China in July-September 1945 regretfully reported that the Soviet Union's actions in Manchuria had strengthened the position of the Communist Party of China and that this had an extremely adverse effect on the activity of the Kuomintang government on the political, military and economic fields.

The Chinese revolutionary forces entered the civil war unleashed by the Kuomintang in 1946 properly organized armed and trained.

The Soviet Union's political and diplomatic activity in the international arena prevented US from directly interfering in the internal affairs of China and thwarted its attempts to arrest the development of the Chinese revolution. The firm stand which the USSR took on the Chinese question was repeatedly reaffirmed in the UNO at meetings of the foreign ministers in Moscow in 1945-47.

The Soviet assistance in the restoration and improvement of military and economic communications was an important contribution to the strengthening of the revolutionary base in Manchuria; it greatly facilitated the general offensive of the People's Army against Chiang Kai-shek's troops. Various forms of Soviet military, political and economic assistance enabled the Chinese revolutionaries to strengthen their forces and consolidate their authority throughout the country and made possible the decisive assault which led to quick victory.

An analysis of the facts and events of 1945-49 shows, that the North-East was the base of China's liberation, that the northern regions (above all Manchuria with her industrial potential and considerable working class concentration) directly adjoining the Soviet Union became the strategic jumping-off ground from which regular units of the People's Liberation Army of China launched an irresistible southward offensive and dealt a mortal blow to the decaying Kuomintang regime, thus frustrating the plans of its imperialist patrons.

It was in Manchuria that the United Democrating Army (UDA) the revolution's principal shock force was created. It was formed in favourable social conditions on the basis of alliance of the industrial working class and the toiling peasantry.

The combination of these various positive factors: the military-industrial potential of the Manchurian revolutionary base, the workers' and peasants' armed force, the active assistance and support of the world socialist movement and above all of the Soviet Union, and the large-scale activity of the people all over the country helped the CPC to carry the struggle to a victorious end.

It can be said it conclusion that the military-revolutionary base in Manchuria built up by the Chinese Communists and its army was vastly instrumental in bringing about the victory of the Chinese. With this base, and led by the Communist Party, the reorganized, re-equipped and well-trained People's Liberation Army crushed the reactionary Kuomintang regime and drove the American imperialists out of China.

With the victory of the Chinese revolution and the establishment of the People's Republic of China a new stage in Chinese-Soviet friendly relations began.

In October 2, 1949, the day after the proclamation of the People's Republic of China, the Soviet government established diplomatic relations with the new state, initiating international recognition of the Chinese people's democratic state.

In February 14, 1950, a Treaty of Friendship, Alliance and Mutual Assistance between the USSR and the PRC was signed. An agreement granting long-term Soviet Credit to China was another important factor for the development of Chinese-Soviet relations. Mao Zedong declared at a sitting of the Central People's Government in April 11, 1950: "The new Chinese-Soviet treaty and agreements have put a juridical seal on the friendship between the two great states China and the Soviet Union and have given us a reliable ally. They have facilitated our work of internal construction and joint opposition, in the name of preserving world peace, to possible aggression on the part of the imperialist powers".

Assistance in Various Fields

Within three years, with active Soviet assistance China had completed the rehabilitation of her national economy, thus defeated the blockade imposed by the imperialist powers. Soviet-Chinese economic cooperation took most diverse forms; mutually advantageous trade, technical assistance, credits, exchange of production experience, scientific and technical cooperation, etc. Trade was growing from year to year. Soviet assistance in the construction of industrial and other projects was the most important form of this cooperation.

By 1960 the USSR had given the PRC technical assistance in the construction and modernization of 291 large industrial enterprises.

In the first decade of its liberation about 11,000 Soviet specialists were sent to China, at the Chinese government's request, to give help in building in organizing new types of production, promoting science and culture and training personnel. In addition more than 7,000 Chinese engineers and skilled worker received further theoretical and practical training in the Soviet Union.

Scientific and technical cooperation between the two countries developed on an ever increasing scale. This included exchange of experience, technical documentation and information on research work, and exchange visits by scientists to enable them to acquaint themselves with the scientific and technical achievements and the latest work of the other country. Between 1954 and 1958 the Soviet Union made the PRC a gift on more than 7,500 technical documents.

With the help of Soviet blueprints more than 400 large enterprises in the metallurgical, engineering oil and coal industries, and communication projects were designed in China. The USSR kept China informed of the latest findings and achievements in science and technology, with Soviet assistance China organized research in nuclear physics and work on the peaceful application of atomic energy.

In January 18, 1958, the governments of the two countries concluded an agreement on joint research in vital branches of science and technology. The agreement envisaged joint work on more than 120 major scientific and technical problem over the period 1958-62.

II

In the late fifties and early sixties the relations between the Soviet Union and China began to reflect tensions. Subsequent developments confirm the conclusion that these conflict had not only political but also ideological basis. They can be traced to subjectivism.

In fact it appears that the leadership of the communist movement in both the countries had a different perspective of building socialism. In both the countries estimate about concrete realities began to clash and personality cult compounded the situation.

Political pluralism, tolerating different views within the communist and socialist movements, different countries have to evolve different paths of socio-economic development, all these questions receded into the background. Rigid dogmas and theories were evolved and that too at a time when expectations from the communists and aspirations of the people were rising.

It was in this background that in the autumn of 1957, Mao Zedong demanded in the central committee of the CPC that Soviet experience of socialist construction should be abandoned. He called for an end to the 'superstitious' attitude to Soviet experience. This ideological offensive was launched under the banner of 'struggle against blind faith in established technical rules and standards, in foreign experience', 'struggle against conservatism', etc. In this essay one cannot go into the merits of this criticism. But it also cannot be denied that there was an objective basis for this criticism. However, as its attack on the Soviet model increased, narrow nationalist passions among Chinese people began to be fanned.

It was in this context that Chinese leaders promised to build a communist society in three years. The Soviet leaders did not agree with this assessment. However, the Soviet leaders themselves suffered from this deviation. Nevertheless, the cleavage between the Soviet and Chinese leaders began to widen.

It became clear in early 1960s that the leaders of the CPC had failed in their attempts to eliminate the country's economic backwardness within the shortest possible period by voluntaristic methods, including the 'big leap' and 'people's communes'. The prospect for turning China into a powerful military nation was becoming even dimmer.

Though in this period Soviet-Chinese relations began to deteriorate both the countries had common perception on certain international problems. For example, in April 13, 1958, the Chinese government declared that it fully supported the Soviet government's decision of March 31, 1958, to be the first to discontinue the testing of all types of atomic and hydrogen weapons, and the Soviet government's proposal to this effect made to the governments of the United States of America, Great Britain and other nations. All said and done, the triangle of relations among Soviet Union, USA and China began to change in late fifties. However, in the early 1960s sharp differences surfaced between China and Soviet Union on various international issues such as peaceful coexistence between capitalism and socialism. This led to division in the international communist movement. It was in this period that the theory of 'inevitability of world war' was put forward by the Chinese leaders.

In November 1960 a Meeting of Representatives of Communist and Workers' Parties took place in Moscow, marking an important stage in the struggle of the world communist movement for unity and cohesion.

The differences between the Soviet Union and China on international situation became sharp during the Caribbean crisis in the autumn of 1962 when Cuba was faced with the threat of American intervention. It was in this period that an armed conflict between India and China took place. The Soviet Union on this conflict took the stand that it could not align either with a 'friend or a brother'. However, there was something more to this formulation of 'friend and brother' as has now become clear. The stand taken by the Soviet

Union behind the scene led to termination of this conflict.

This shows that in the early 60s, Soviet-China relations began to deteriorate rapidly. This had its own impact on the economic relations between the two countries. The share of the socialist countries in China's foreign trade dropped to 25 per cent in 1966, as against 68 per cent in 1959. At the same time, the share of capitalist and developing countries in China's foreign trade rose to 75 per cent. It is noteworthy that China's trade with the Federal Republic of Germany in 1965 exceeded that with the German Democratic Republic more than three times. This shows that Chinese leaders began to follow a pragmatic policy in economic relations with other countries as early as in the mid-sixties. This had its own impact on the attitude of the Western and American experts towards China.

Another fact which should be mentioned here is that in the first ten years of the existence the PRC, the Soviet-Chinese border was one of the friendship and good neighbourliness. The population of the border areas in both the countries maintained extensive contacts, trade and cultural exchange. This process was reversed in the 60s. The situation on the borders deteriorated and border skirmishes between the two countries began to take place. In 1961-62, several thousand border incidents were reported. In 1963 over 4,000 border incidents took place.

In the mid-sixties, economic relations between the Soviet Union and China further worsened. China decided to discontinue all work on projects set down in agreements signed by the USSR and China, while its turn over was reduced to under 300 million roubles a year. This shows that China began to look at economic relations with the Soviet Union in terms of its own national interests.

Chinese leaders began to look at international developments from a fresh angle. In August 1963, the Soviet Union signed an agreement with the United States and Britain. The Treaty Banning Nuclear Weapon Tests in the Atmosphere, in Outer Space and Under Water was one of the important agreements. This step of the Soviet Union evoked a sharp response from China. China accused the Soviet Union of conduction a policy of 'alliance with the forces of war to fight peace', of 'alliance with imperialism to fight socialism', of 'alliance with the United States to fight China', etc.

Again in practical terms, the policies of the Soviet Union and China on American aggression on Vietnam did not coincide. The United States back in October 1964, directed its aggression against the Democratic Republic of Vietnam by launching systematic bombing raids on its cities and villages. The Soviet Union not only took a firm stand on this development but gave all possible military help to the fighting forces of Vietnam. This stood as a complete contrast to the practical policy of China.

Though in this essay, any evaluation of the Chinese 'Cultural Revolution' will be irrelevant, it had a clear anti-Soviet bias.

In the late sixties, Soviet-China relations touched their lowest ebb. In 1967 for instance, for the first time in the history of Soviet-Chinese relations, no plans were made for cultural and scientific exchange or for cooperation between friendship and tourist organisations. Beginning with 1968, no more protocols on trade between the two countries were signed. But there is something more to it.

In this period border conflicts between the two countries took a serious turn. In February 1967, China's Foreign Minister Chen Yi commented on prospects of Chinese-Soviet relations: "It is possible that the relations will be broken off, *it is possible there will be a war*". (emphasis added) In March 26, 1967, in a speech before representatives of democratic parties, Chou En-lai held that 'besides big wars, there are also border wars', and that 'a border war between China and the USSR will start earlier than a war with the United States.' This confirms the conclusion that within one decade, from late fifties to late sixties, Chinese-Soviet relations had taken a turn in which the possibility of an armed conflcit could not be ruled out. In March 2, 1969, shortly before the opening of the 9th CPC Congress, an armed conflcit between the two countries took place on the Island of Damansky. Another major border incident involving arms took place near Zhalanashkol, a settlement in the Semipalatinsk region in August 13, 1969.

By mid-seventies, Chinese-Soviet relations took a dangerous turn. At its first session in 1975, the National People's Congress adopted a new PRC Constitution, which included the provision that the country must set its sight on confrontation with the USSR over a 'long historical period'. Article 15 of the first section of the Constitution said that the armed forces of China must fight against 'social imperialism'. Its implication is too obvious.

After Mao Zedong's death, the Soviet press stopped (between September 1976 and May 1977) to publish articles criticising the Beijing leaders' foreign policy in order to create better atmosphere for improving relations between the two countries. This did not evoke an immediate positive response from the leadership of China. In fact there was no change in the perception of leaders of China about the policies of the Soviet Union and the hostility between the two countries continued to grow. A close study of the policy declaration of Chinese leaders leads one to the conclusion that it is in this period that China's relations with the United States began to take a concrete shape, which in turn created serious misgivings in Moscow about China's role in the international affairs. In a speech to graduates from the Chinese diplomatic academy, Geng Biao, vice-premier of the State Council, said: "Today, let the United States protect us from the influence of Soviet revisionism... But when we find that the time is ripe, we shall tell Uncle Sam: "Be so kind and pack up." This shows that in the assessment of the Chinese leaders at that time China and America had some commonality of interests. Notwithstanding the fact that dialogue between the two countries continued in this period to resolve their differences, particularly hotting up of the situation on Soviet-China border, no improvement in the relations between the two countries took place.

China's armed conflict with Vietnam in February 17, 1979, signified a qualitative change in Soviet-China relations. The Soviet Union came out in support of Vietnam.

This was followed by non-renewal of the Agreement of Friendship, Alliance and Mutual Assistance between the Soviet-China signed in 1960. The non-renewal of the Agreement of 1950 was perhaps the most important development, which highlighted how the relations between the two countries had almost reached a dead end.

The Western countries, the United States in particular did not conceal their satisfaction over this conflict between China and the Soviet Union. On the contrary, China's relations with the United States began to register an upward trend. Thus for nearly one decade, the relations between China and the Soviet Union continued to deteriorate. Nevertheless, the history of Soviet-Chinese relations shows that there are no objective reasons for alienation, much less for confrontation, between the two countries. On the contrary as the recent development have shown, there are all the necessary conditions for restoring good neighbourly relations and cooperation between the two countries, conditions which stem from the vital long term interests of the Russian and Chinese people from their need to regenerate their economies for the welfare of their people.

III

Before we examine the present phase of Russia-China relations, it is relevant to mention that the third period in the post-war history of the communist movement, according to Chinese researchers, began in the mid-1970s and lasted till the late 1980s. During this period, communist parties began to seek their own path of development, making use of the experience and lessons, they had learnt from the past. They sought to uphold their independence 'against the diktat of the leading centre and the leading party', and applied the fundamental tenets of the Marxist teaching with an eye to the specific situation in their respective countries. These parties were seeking to build a new type of relations between the communist parties, building these relations on the basis of independence and equality.

On the other hand, the Soviet scholars began to advocate that their party and leadership should discard a lot of long-established stereotypes and ideological dogmas. What sort of reforms should be introduced in the Soviet Union and China? "When we started renovating society, we began to cross the river, groping for stones on its bottom. Each nation should carefully study its neighbours' experience, both positive and negative, not to repeat their mistakes and to make use of the best practical achievement", a Soviet scholar underlined.

This fresh approach between the Chinese and the Soviet scholars paved the way for steady improvement of the relations between the two countries.

The evolution of Russian-China relations can be subdivided into several basic stages; close relations, amounting to an alliance in the 1950s. These relations were based on a common ideology and socio-economic system and the overall strategic objective of opposing imperialism. The next phase began with the ideological and political controversy of the mid-1960s. This turned into global strategic confrontation of the late 1960s and 1970s. The new phase is marked by a gradual improvement of relations.

Lack of understanding and controversies in the 1960s and 1970s stemmed largely from the fact that the USSR and PRC were at different stages of socio-economic development. For this reason they had totally different views of the ways and means of building socialism. Each one of the two countries believed that their path of building socialism was correct not only for their country but also for all other countries. Therefore, the leadership of the two countries came to believe that they had the "monopoly of truth and wisdom". This understanding led to sharp ideological differences. This conflict extended to other spheres, including in state to state relations. But more important than this approach was that in practice, the leadership of the two countries came to believe that their interest were totally incompatible. For a long time the USSR and the PRC each believed that their relations could improve only when the other side radically changed its domestic policy and ideology in conformity with the 'only correct' formulae.

Balance and stability, therefore, could only be achieved if the Russia and China delinked their bilateral relations from the ideological bias and built them on a correlation of interests. The past has shown that lecturing one another or claiming to be more socialist than the other leads to an impasse and hampers solution of problems. This in turn builds up tension.

In the 1950s the USSR and the PRC recognised it as their common strategic interest to resist pressure from US imperialism; in the 1960s the Soviet policy for improving relations with the United States was regarded by China as a policy of 'collusion' infringing upon Chinese interests. But in the 1970s China sought to set up a 'broad united front', the US included to contain 'Soviet expansionism'.

In the late 1970s the situation changed radically; China was recognised by the vast majority of states, it came to have its own nuclear weapons and occupied a legitimate seat in the UN Security Council. As a result the Chinese leadership became more confident of its strength. It became less apprehensive of the prospect of some country or other threatening China's security interests through political manoeuvring. Chinese foreign policy was built on the rational calculation based on economic feasibility. It, therefore, decided to concentrate on economic growth. This created a stable and peaceful atmosphere for economic reforms inside the country and ensured external security at minimal economic costs. This was the basis of China's independent foreign policy and its resolute line towards non-participation in military-political blocs. This policy even today holds good.

That being the situation in the late 80s, normalisation of their relations with the USSR did not upset the world balance of forces. On the contrary, both the countries sought to improve their strategic positions within the obtaining pattern of alignment of world forces.

The Current Phase

Another distinctive feature of the new-type of Russian-Chinese relations in the current phase is the assumption that the Russia's cooperation with its friends and allies will not be employed to 'contain' China, while China will not use its relations or ties with other countries to 'restrain' Russia. Thus a new basis and new parameters have been created in building Russian-Chinese relations. After the disintegration of the Soviet Union this basis has been further consolidated. This implies that the model of Russian-Chinese relations has its owned specific features, which are different from all the previous periods of the relations between the two countries.

The new model of Russian-Chinese relations has led to a gradual lowering of the level of military presents along the Russian-Chinese border. This has both regional and global significance. This may help to bring down the level of military confrontation elsewhere in Asia

It also shows the way towards mutual advantageous agreements on conventional arms reductions. The current level of these two countries relations provides each side with certain advantages, enabling them to conduct a more flexible and manoeuvrable policy, while dealing with other partners, the Western world included. Both countries have made remarkable headway in their bilateral relations in the spring of 1996. Such a 'dash' or 'spur' did not come like a bolt out of the blue. It took the two countries almost a decade to prepare for this noteworthy achievement.

Russia and China have moved to establish the required international-legal base of bilateral relations, which encompasses a wide range of problems of interest to both sides, from the border-line settlement and border-line military confidence-building measures to common environmental protection and nature-conservation measures. The number of bilateral treaties and agreements now stands at more than 200. And intensive work is currently proceeding apace to fill such documents with practical content.

Throughout 1996 Russian-Chinese interaction was supplemented by a number of new spheres, e.g. peaceful use of nuclear energy, creating the appropriate power-industry infrastructure, intellectual-property protection, space exploration, anti-monopoly policies, etc. Both countries seem to believe that their armies border-control forces and law-enforcement agencies would continue to strengthen friendly and practical contacts.

The two nations are likely to carry on bilateral military-technical cooperation, within the framework of their own international commitments. The recent agreement on strengthening border-line military confidence-building.

SECTION III

INDIA-RUSSIA-CHINA:
Economic Relations

13

Indo-Soviet Economic Relations: A Critical Estimate

ARVIND VYAS

From the Soviet side, foreign trade was based on the so-called 'nul saldo' principle implying that as output levels expand in a centrally planned economy (CPE) the volume of imports would decline. The argument does not hold where the CPE simply does not produce certain commodities like jute, black pepper, cashewnuts, tea (of the Indian type). More formally, the above argument can be expressed in terms of the system of material balances, taking into account foreign trade, i.e. gross output + imports = intermediate use + final demand + exports.

On the Indian side, foreign trade planning was highly asymmetric—almost 90 per cent of exports were from the private sector, which was guided by prices and profitabilities, while the bulk of imports from the USSR were to the public sector.

Old Edifice of Economic Cooperation

While today, it has become fashionable to discredit the public sector in India, it is pertinent to draw the readers attention to a Tata Consultancy Services report which mentions that in the past several years, fruitful cooperation developed between the two countries in a large number of areas including steel, coal, oil, power, non-ferrous metallurgy, machine-building, communications, irrigation, and science and technology. Some of these public sector projects, set up with the Soviet assistance, were also the first of their kind in India. Projects built with the Soviet collaboration in India, accounted for as much as 40 per cent of India's steel output, 32 per cent of aluminium production, roughly 80 per cent of metallurgical equipment, 40 per cent of mining equipment, 55 per cent of heavy power equipment, 35 per cent of crude oil production, 40 per cent of oil processing, and 10 per cent of power generation. The commoditywise composition of the Indian exports and imports were broadly as follows: On the side of exports, there were basically three categories of goods: primary goods, e.g. tea, coffee, pepper, spices; secondary manufactured consumer goods: textiles, garments, shoe uppers, etc.; and finally, other manufacturers' articles which had been the fastest growing items since the 80s. However, its share in the total Soviet imports of machinery and equipment was not significant—the main suppliers being the then Germany—formerly German Democratic Republic (GDR), Federal Republic of Germany (FRG), Finland and former Czechoslovakia.

In short, till the early 80s, the Indo-Soviet relations functioned in a healthy trading climate. India emerged as the leading trading partner of the USSR overtaking the USA, the UK, Japan, etc., as far as exports were concerned. However, by the mid-80s, the economic relations ran into heavy weather, mainly because of oil prices which started declining from 1982 and remained depressed till 1987, resulting in a significant reduction in the generation of rupee resources for the USSR. It imparted a rude shock to the Indian exporters. If we also take into account the fact that during the same period the bulk of the Indian exports from the USSR (almost 85%) consisted of the so-called 'hard goods'—oil, fertilizer, newsprint, coal, steel scrap, chemical products, etc., it would not be an exaggeration to say that the Soviet aid, trade and loans made an invaluable contribution to the development of India's infrastructure.

What was, therefore, the nature of interaction between a CPE and mixed developing economy of the Indian type? Initially, it led to an astronomical increase of trade turnover from 1970 till the early 80s. The trade turnover increased from 364.9 billion roubles in 1970, to 1,739.8 billion roubles in 1980 to 3,072.2 billion roubles in 1985! The corresponding figures in the Indian currency are: Rs. 316 crore in 1970-71 and Rs. 3,784 crore in 1985-86.

Indo-Soviet Relations between 1985-90

During this phase, the Indo-Soviet relations proceeded from stagnation to a state of virtual collapse. The following figures elaborately depicts the decline.

Table 1
Decline in Indo-Soviet trade

(billion roubles)

Year	*X*	*M*	*X + M*	*X – M*
1985	1,572.6	1,499.6	3,072.2	+ 73
1986	957.6	1,233.6	2,191.2	–276
1987	1,105.4	1,073.1	2,178.5	+ 32.3
1988	1,128.7	1,123.3	2,252.0	+ 5.4
1989	1,147.2	1,770.6	2,917.8	–623.4
1990 (Jan.-March)	NA	NA	NA	
1991	230.8	385.1		–154.3

Where,

X = Exports from USSR
M = Imports from USSR
X + M = Trade turnover
X – M = Trade balance
NA = Not Available

Source: Annual issues of the USSR Foreign Trade.

Figures from the Indian sources point out even a more depressing picture. Exports to the rupee payment area—mainly the former USSR and later on the Russian Federation—declined between December 1991 and April-May 1992 by more than 50 per cent. It came down from Rs. 7,800 crore to Rs. 3,600 crore during this period.

Developments from 1992-96

The following are the newly emerging pattern of trade and economic relations:

(i) Trade and economic relations would be conducted on the principle of economic accountability. This is an inevitable consequence of the Russian Federation shifting from a command—administrative economy to a market economy. This obviously has implications for widening income distribution, regional disparities—in short, marketization, globalization and privatization, considered as a package of measures. The shift in trade to hard currency was inevitable to that extent. In addition the Indian side was and is interested in massive borrowing from International Monetary Fund, World Bank and also direct foreign investments from Germany, the USA, Japan, the South Korea—from the advanced capitalist countries in short. It portrays a short-sighted policy on both sides to my mind.

(ii) Trade and economic relations would be conducted mainly through private companies, joint stock and organization companies, as also there would be joint ventures.

(iii) The following are the main trends: Exports from India (a more detailed commodity composition of exports and imports is given in the statistical appendices).

Table 2A

	Main commodities for Export to Russia	*Company dealing with the Russian Federation*
1.	Paper, cardboard and pulp	International Consortium—Mekor, Bombay.
2.	Automobiles, garments, chemicals, engineering and financial services	DCM (overseas) Ltd., Moscow
3.	Ashraj exports coffee	Coffee, Asraj Exports, Bombay, India and Coffee Board of India
4.	Engineering thermoplastics	Joint Venture of Greaves Ltd., Bombay
5.	Wide range (10) of construction activities for details see Appendices	Larsen and Toubro Ltd. Construction Group
6.	Chemimpex	Chemimpex India Pvt. Ltd.

Table 2B
Imports from the Russian Federation

(i) Output of Ferrous Metallurgy (10 units)	Tyazhprom Export (Foreign Economic Association (Moscow))
(ii) Non-ferrous metallurgy (95 units)	
(iii) Pumps, equipment and machine tools	Gidromash, Moscow offer from CIS routed through
(iv) Wide range of machine tools (11)	Dalal Machine Tools Agency Pvt. Ltd., Bombay
(v) All other imports from Russia	Elixir Corporation, Moscow
(vi) Compressors, spare parts, Marine and ship-building equipment, spare parts, pulp, plywood and cardboard	Harley International, Moscow
(vii) Insurance Company	*INGOSSTRAKH*, Moscow
(viii) Services, anciliaring of Indian rupees through *Vneshcombank* manufacture of readymade garments for reexport to USA/Europe, Customs clearing and warehousing facilities.	Bentimi AO, Moscow
(ix) Cholrpyriphos	AIMCO Pesticides Ltd., Bombay
Accumulator batteries	*SOVELECTRO* FT Joint Stock Company Moscow.

(iv) Defence deals: This will take the following forms:

(a) upgrading of 600 MiG 21s and four squadrons of MiG-23 aircraft.

(b) Purchase of a small number of MiG-25 as an interceptor aircraft.

(c) purchases of MiG-27 and MiG-29.

(d) MI-25 and MI-35 attack helicopters, and light-combat aircraft.

Finally, the Indian Navy is interested in long range reconnaissance aircraft.

Problem Areas in Trade and Economic Relations

A brief examination of some of the main problem areas in Indo-USSR/CIS trade and economic relation. For the reasons of brevity, one shall only list them as follows:

(a) The question of the rupee-rouble exchange rate.

(b) The reluctance on the part of the Russian Federation and the now so-called independent states to supply hard currency items to India.

(c) Supply disruption in CIS, owing to a highly unstable political climate. (Refer to tables on GDP growth and inflation in Russia and CIS)

(d) The problem of defence equipment and spares and repayments—the latter problem has apparently been sorted out, after January 1993.

(e) The Government of India's ban on the supply of high and medium technology items—where the import content exceeds 30 per cent—to the CIS.

(f) Slow use of intergovernmental credits on the part of India, owing to a shortage of rupee funds in India.

(g) A manifestly awkward situation, where India on the one hand, extends technical credit to Russia so that the volume of trade does not decline, while on the other hand, India has a massive accumulated foreign trade debt of the former USSR, on account of repayment of mainly military credits. The repayments of this credit is to continue till 2030. The debt is of the order of Rs. 38,000 crore. The Reserve Bank of India had earlier stated that no more technical credit would be extended to Russia. However, the trade protocol between India and Russia for 1992 allowed a technical credit of only Rs. 850 crore. The question of the rupee-rouble rate enters the picture here, and we need to turn our attention to it.

(h) On the whole, the so-called golden days of Indo-Soviet trade are over. There would hence forth be basically two criteria for trade and economic relations. These are: prices of exports to and imports from the Russian Federation should be internationally competitive. It should be so in terms of quality too. It had made the picture more complex.

(i) The Rupee-Rouble Exchange Rate: At the outset, it is important to note that in a bilateral trading system—even under Rupee trade — there are multiple rates of exchange. It is because each of which has a different function to perform. In addition, the following points are worth mentioning. (i) As far as 'hard goods'—oil, newsprint, fertilizer, steel scrap, etc.,—are concerned, the prices are quoted in terms of a basket of 16 Western currencies. However, earlier, it was done in the US dollar terms, which were later converted into non-convertible rupees so that the rouble did not enter the picture. (ii) The above arrangement does not apply to the repayment of military and civilian credits, where it dominates the rouble. Incidentally repayments are made at the commercial rate of exchange, currently Rs. 32 for one rouble. (till January 1993 it was Rs. 20 for a rouble). It is in accordance with the devaluation of the rupee and the November 1978 protocol. (iii) Finally, it was a deferred payment rate of exchange, and another for tourists and embassies.

Who is to blame for this? It is because both sides are enamoured of Western Europe, the USA, Japan, South Korea, Taiwan, Singapore, etc. Elsewhere I have argued that export-led growth for India is probably the road to economic disaster, whereas for Russia it is less so. However, Russia lacks political stability conducive to market reforms, though its infrastructure is far more developed than India's. It also has a much better raw material base.

(j) India made a fatal mistake in the 80's by heavily relying on imports of 'hard' currency items — oil, fertilizer, newsprint, steel scrap, chemicals etc. and not on machinery and equipment, from the former Soviet Union during the period of rupee trade. One cannot forget the former Soviet Union's warning not only to India but also its Communist bloc partners like Cuba and Vietnam, way back in 1985-87 that it could no longer supply hard currency items nor build major investment projects on concessional terms. India, trying to be too 'clever' by relying on the then Soviet Union mainly for its exports. For imports and loans it sought IMF, World Bank, non-Resident Indian and direct foreign investments. At the moment there are not more than 8 to 10 commodities which have a market at international prices in Russia or CIS. These items are: tea, coffee, spices, jute, leather goods, garments, textiles, shoe uppers, and some engineering goods. Even in the case of tea and coffee India has lost out to Sri Lanka. Earlier we used to supply 65 per cent of tea output to Russia. The figure has now fallen to barely 10 per cent! Regarding food and beverages, the picture is bleak.

(k) The exposure to high quality Western goods has made the Russians to look at the Indian commodities with suspicion —this applies, particularly to garments and coffee, where Indian prices are exhorbitant and poor in quality.

Most of the Indian companies prefer to deal with Russia through Singapore or the Gulf countries in the interest of quality. Hence all figures relating to the Indian exports to Russia have to be taken with a pinch of salt.

In this connection it may be useful to quote a so-called 'success' story — a Singapore Corporation worth 500 million US dollars engages in the following export and import activities: Food processing and packaging, pharmaceuticals and some manufacturers, are its exports. It imports fertilizers, metal, chemicals, hides and skins, crude oil and oil products.

(l) The role of the Indian companies and Joint Ventures in Russia is also not impressive—especially in 46 regions of Russia. The main problem seems to be the effective management of foreign investments. Besides, India simply does not have the technical know-how to modernize Russian industry save a very few branches.

(m) Last but not the least, we have the ticklish question of the

> repayment of military credits. The Russian side would like to auction part approximately Rs. 3,000 crore per year of its accumulated rupee stocks. The Indian side is unhappy about this, to put it mildly. It feels that the Russian side (private companies and financial institutions might resort to unscrupulous trade practices by converting rupees into the US dollars as the rupee has become convertible for trading purposes. One such auction took place some time ago, and the rate was Rs. 14 for rouble. Results of more recent auctions are awaited.

The collapse of rupee trade was an inevitable consequence of the transition from a command administrative economy to a 'market economy' in Russia. A shift away from the public sector to liberalization, privatization, globalization, export-led growth in the case of India. The costs of the transition process are and would be painful. It has led to unemployment, hyperinflation, besides the emergence of the social maladies like mafia in Russia and hawala deals in India. Widening or flight of capital abroad and income differentials. It is said that all commodities are available in Moscow but only for 15 to 30 per cent of the population. In India 40 per cent or more of the population lives in the conditions of abject poverty.

A pragmatic approach towards the Indo-Russian trade and economic policies, coupled with 'sensible' internal economic reforms, India and Russia could become prosperous states. But one must caution that the road to prosperity is always very difficult, though not impossible?

Statistical Appendices

As far as possible the author had tried to obtain data from both Indian and Soviet/CIS sources. The differences are due to the classification, and also because trade data in the former USSR were in f.o.b., whereas the Indian data are in CIF. This, however, does not affect the overall conclusion of the study.

Appendix A1

India's trade turnovers with the USSR till 1992

Table of Actual and Estimated Trade Values (Turnover)

(Billion roubles)

Year	*Actual Y*	*Exponential trend*	*% error*	*Linear trend*	*% error*	*Quadratic trend*	*% error*
1970	364.9	323.52	11.31	-90.30	124.7	386.75	-6.0
1971	372.1	377.39	-1.4	99.35	73.3	285.59	-3.6
1972	451	440.23	2.4	289.01	35.9	411.68	8.7
1973	588.8	513.54	12.8	478.67	18.7	465.04	21.0
1974	615.5	599.05	2.7	668.32	-8.6	545.65	11.3
1975	685.6	698.79	-1.9	857.98	-25.1	653.53	4.7
1976	647.5	815.15	-25.9	1,047.63	-61.8	788.66	-21.8
1977	926	950.88	-2.7	1,237.29	-33.6	951.06	-2.7
1978	771.4	1,109.21	-43.8	1,426.95	-85.0	1,140.71	-47.9
1979	1,035.1	1,293.91	-25.0	1,616.60	-56.2	1,357.63	-31.2
1980	1,739.8	1,509.36	13.2	1,806.26	-3.8	1,601.81	7.9
1981	2,397.9	1,760.69	26.6	1,995.91	16.8	1,873.24	21.9
1982	2,514	2,053.86	18.3	2,185.57	13.1	2,171.94	13.6
1983	2,322.6	2,395.86	-3.2	3,275.23	-2.3	2,497.90	-7.5
1984	2,809.5	2,794.79	0.5	2,564.88	8.7	2,851.12	-1.5
1985	3,072.2	3,260.15	-6.1	2,754.54	10.3	3,231.59	-5.2
1986	—	3,803.00	—	2,944.20	—	3,639.33	
1987	—	4,436.24	—	3,133.85	—	4,074.33	
1988	—	5,174.92	—	3,323.51	—	4,536.59	
1989	—	6,036.61	—	3,513.16	—	5,026.11	
1990	—	7,041.76	—	3,702.82	—	5,542.89	
1991	—	8,214.29	—	3,892.48	—	6,086.93	
1992	—	9,582.07	—	4,082.13	—	6,658.23	

Notes:
1. All data have been compiled from annual issues of *Vneshnaya Torgovlya*.
2. We have taken a geometric mean of the exponential and quadratic trends.
3. Estimates for 1992 are inaccurate, as a result of the formation of CIS. Actual Y stands for the total trade turnover (X+M).
4. A detailed breakdown between exports and imports is available in Sen and Vyas (1989) *op. cit.* in the statistical appendices.

Table

India's exports, imports and trade turnover with USSR/CIS (1970-71 to 1990-91)

(Rs. crore)

Year	*X*	*M*	*X + M*
1970-71	210	106	316
1980-81	1,226	1,014	2,240
1985-86	2,006	1,678	3,684
1986-87	1,867	1,006	2,873
1987-88	1,963	1,608	3,571
1988-89	2,609	1,258	3,876
1989-90	4,463	2,038	6,501
1990-91	5,255	2,548	7,803

Notes: X : stands for exports to USSR/CIS.
M : stands for imports from the USSR/CIS.
X + M : total trade turnover.

Appendix A2

Share of India's Exports in USSR's Trade (Selected Years in %)

1970-71	*1980-81*	*1985-86*	*1986-87*	*1988-89*	*1989-90*	*1990-91*
13.7	19.2	18.4	14.9	12.8	16	16

Note: Thus in the mid-80s, India was USSR's largest trading partner ir terms of exports, which to an extent puts paid to the hypothesis in th(introduction to the study.

Source: *Ibid., loc cit.*

Appendix A3

Share of India's imports in USSR's trade (Selected Years in %)

1980-81	*1985-86*	*1986-87*	*1987-88*	*1988-89*	*1989-90*	*1990-91*
15.7	8	5	7.2	4.4	5.7	5.8

Source: Government of India, Ministry of Finance, *Economic Survey o India* 1991-92, pp. S-87-88.

Appendix A4

Percentage Utilization of Soviet Loans to India

Year	*Percentage*	*Year*	*Percentage*
1980-81	6.7	1987-88	7.8
1983-84	52	1988-89	2.8
1985-86	9.5	1989-90	10

The very low percentage of utilization reflects the shortage of fund re sources in India to carry out the necessary infrastructural investments.

Source: *Ibid., loc cit.*

Table
Direction of India's Trade with Selected East Asian Countries

(percent shares)

Country	Exports 1991-92	Exports 1992-93 (April-March)	Exports 1993-94	Exports 1993-94 (April-Sept.)	Exports 1994-95	Imports 1991-92	Imports 1992-93 (April-March)	Imports 1993-94	Imports 1993-94 (April-Sept.)	Imports 1994-95
1	2	3	4	5	6	7	8	9	10	11
Indonesia	0.8	0.7	1.0	1.0	0.9	0.3	0.3	0.5	0.4	—
Malaysia	1.1	1.0	1.1	1.3	1.0	2.0	1.9	1.1	1.0	2.2
Hong Kong	3.4	4.1	5.6	5.8	5.4	0.6	0.8	0.8	0.8	0.8
South Korea	1.4	0.9	0.9	0.9	1.1	1.7	1.6	2.4	1.6	2.0
Singapore	2.2	3.2	3.4	3.4	2.9	3.6	2.9	2.7	2.5	2.8
Thailand	1.1	1.4	1.6	1.4	1.5	0.3	0.3	0.2	0.3	0.8
Chinese Taipe	1.0	1.0	1.2	1.4	1.1	1.5	1.0	0.7	0.8	0.9
Total	11.1	12.3	14.8	15.2	14.1	9.9	8.7	8.4	7.4	10.7

Source: Compiled from DGCI &S, Calcutta.

Table
Direction of India's Trade with Russia

(percent shares)

Country	Exports				Imports			
	1992-93	*1993-94 (April-March)*	*1993-94*	*1994-95 (April-Sept.)*	*1992-93*	*1993-94 (April-March)*	*1993-94*	*1994-95 (April-Sept.)*
1	*2*	*3*	*4*	*5*	*6*	*7*	*8*	*9*
UK	6.5	6.2	6.3	6.5	6.5	6.6	7.0	5.6
Germany	7.7	6.9	6.9	6.6	7.6	7.7	7.3	7.3
Other EC Countries	14.1	12.9	12.2	12.9	16.1	15.7	17.6	11.0
USA	19.0	18.0	18.5	19.8	9.8	11.7	10.5	9.9
Japan	7.7	7.8	7.7	7.7	6.5	6.6	5.9	7.3
Russia	3.3	2.9	2.4	3.0	1.2	1.1	0.9	1.3
East Europe	1.1	0.9	1.0	0.6	1.4	0.6	0.6	0.6
OPEC	9.6	10.7	10.4	9.5	21.6	22.4	24.8	21.5
LDCs	20.8	24.1	24.5	23.2	15.2	15.3	13.7	21.5
Others	10.1	9.7	10.2	10.1	14.2	12.4	11.7	14.6
Total	100.0	100.0	100.0	100.0	100.0	100.0	100.0	100.0

Sources: DGCI&S, Calcutta
The Economic Survey of India, GOI, Annuai issues of 1994-95 and 1995-96.

NOTES

1. This study is based on my following works: (a) - cf(C), (f)h, (2), (k), pp. 372-83, *Pioneer*, 16 September 1994. 'Has India's trade with FSU/CIS peaked?'
2. See (k), pp. 373-74.
3. *Khozraschet*—Russian team-wrongly translated as *uchyet* (economic accounting). The text translation is more accurate.
4. See sections 1-4, (a) to (1).
5. By 'sensible economic reforms' we mean the development of a strong infrastructure, higher literacy rate in India and stabilization of inflation and modernization of industry and the service sector the Russian Federation. The key to the above problems lies in the growth of GDP (picking up albeit very slowly in 1995-96) and the elimination of widespread shortages which adversely affects growth and income distribution.

REFERENCES

1. Granovski, A.E., *Indo-Soviet Relations in the Period of Transition*, 1991, mimeo.
2. For a more detailed analysis, see Pronab Sen and Vyas, Indo-CMEA Economic Relations (Phase II), ch.1, part of a report submitted to the Ministry of Commerce, August 1989; also by the same authors, "Indo-Soviet Economic Relations" in V. D. Chopra (ed.) et al, *Socio-Economic Reforms in the USSR*, Patriot Publishers, New Delhi, 1990, and finally Bibek Debroy and Varshney, *Indo-Soviet Economic Relations in the Next Decade*, Idem.
3. Import Possibilities from the USSR, Tata Consultancy Services Report, p. 20, vol. 1, Bombay, 1988.
4. For further details, see Sen and Vyas (1989) op. cit., statistical appendices, also Suresh Kumar (ed.) Indo-CEMA Economic Relations, Ashish, New Delhi, 1987.
5. Ibid.
6. However, if we take into account countertrade, private trade, etc., the fall apparently between December 1991 and April-May 1992 was only 30 per cent. I am grateful to Dr. Granovski for drawing my attention to this phenomenon.
7. There is a vast and confused literature on the problem which I tried to clarify in *The Times of India* and 10 February, 13 March and 7 May 1992, see also Pronab Sen EPW: Rupee-Rouble Exchange Rate, 24 March 1990.
8. a.f. Granovski (1991), *op. cit.*

9. The Rupee-Rouble rate was changed in January 1992 when the market rate of exchange came into operation. Currently the market rate is fluctuating between 390 roubles = 1 US dollar, 417 roubles = 1 US dollar. Under these assumptions, India can buy a MiG-29 or T-72 tank for only US $ 3,000 — obviously a proposition which will be unacceptable to the Russian side. Negotiations were renewed in June 1992 which apparently broke down. Currently the rate 55,000 = 1 US $. The problem was resolved during Yeltsin's visit to India in January 1993 as mentioned in the text, see section 14, and elsewhere.
10. For sources regarding this problem have relied heavily on press clippings for the relevant periods.
11. The architects of these policies are two eminent economists: Dr. Manmohan Singh, the former Union Finance Minister, and Dr. M.S. Ahluwalia. Their basic argument is that the countries of South-East Asia have made spectacular progress whereas India has been lagging behind (incidentally GDP fell between 1991-92, *The Times of India*, 16, January 1993). The advocates of the South Korea as an ideal 'model'.

14

India-Russia Trade: New Opportunities in Joint Ventures

R.L. VARSHNEY

The former USSR was an important trade partner of India. Both were able to develop a unique phenomenon by developing the rupee trade. It kept the dollar and other hard currencies out of all transactions between them. This was basically a barter system which worked quite effectively. As a result trade between the two increased from Rs. 1.3 crore in 1956 to Rs. 900 crore in 1990. India's exports increased from Rs. 1,700 crore in 1982 to Rs. 5,400 crore in 1991 and its imports increased from Rs. 1,150 crore to Rs. 4,330 crore over the 10 years period. The USSR accounted at times, for about 15 per cent of India's exports.

The trade designed in the Indian rupees benefited both the countries immensely. India, like the Soviet Union, derived greater advantage as its need to source imports without spending foreign exchange was perhaps even more than that of the USSR. India obtained substantial quantities of crude oil and kerosene and defence equipment and spares from the erstwhile Soviet Union.

India's exports consisted of processed food, spices, jute, and coir goods, hosiery, leather goods, paints, chemicals and cosmetics, tea, coffee, pepper, tobacco, drugs and pharmaceuticals, detergents and toilet material. In many of these products, India's dependence on the Soviet Union was substantial. What is more, there was a high degree of instability in the Soviet demand. However, the Indo-Soviet trade led to diversification of India's export markets and better terms of trade.

Disintegration of Soviet Union

The disintegration of the Soviet Union led to a disruption for many Indian business sectors. Though some steps have been taken to repair the damage, the Indo-Soviet trade is bound to undergo a dramatic change.

A five year trade agreement was signed by former Commerce Minister P. Chidambaram, now the Finance Minister, and Russian Secretary of State E. Burbulis in May 1992. It is historic inasmuch as it marked the end of Rupee Trade era from January 1993, and ushered in a new phase of convertible currency trade between the two countries. It was also decided to set up an Inter-Governmental Commission for cooperation in trade, economy as well as science and technology. India also extended Rs. 2.5 billion credit line for the purpose of exporting tea, coffee and tobacco to Russia.

In January 1993, the then Indian Prime Minister P.V. Narasimha Rao, and the Russian President Boris Yeltsin, signed an agreement that the Indian debt to Russia would be repaid through export of the Indian goods and services to Russia. The Indian debt had been evaluated at Rs. 31,377 crore. Out of this, Rs. 19,044 crore is to be repaid in over 12 years. It carries an average rate of interest of 2.4 per cent. The remaining Rs. 11,734 crore is to be repaid at nil rate of interest over 45 years beginning April 1993. Each year India is to credit Rs. 3,000 crore to the 'special account' of Russian Bank of Foreign Economic Affairs.

In addition, the Government of India has taken some other steps to promote trade with Russia. Countertrade has been permitted for all items that do not figure in the Exim Policy negative list. The Government of India has also decided to withdraw the stipulation of 233 per cent value addition on all exports to Russia that was imposed in November 1990. The Reserve Bank of India allowed exporters to Russia a period of one year to realise proceeds on consignments. The exporters will have to apply to the Reserve Bank of India for this facility and it would be allowed provided the proceeds are realised in free convertible currencies. Moreover, this facility would be available only to the exporters who have a satisfactory track record. The following table provides data about India's trade with Russia.

India's Trade with Russia

Year	*India's exports*	*Percentage share of India's total exports*	*India's imports*	*Percentage share of India's total imports*
1992-93	1,759	3.3	737	1.2
1993-94	2,037	2.9	807	1.1
1994-95	2,541	3.1	1,572	1.8

The table shows that significance of Russia in India's foreign trade has declined precipitately. But now it has more or less stabilised in exports at three per cent and the share is increasing in imports.

There are good prospects for increasing Indo-Russian trade because of the following:

(1) The State Bank of India and the MMTC have decided to jointly set up a Bank in Moscow to overcome the procedural hassles being faced by the Indian and Russian businessmen. The Canara Bank will also have a presence in Moscow.

(2) Russia has eased currency transfer rules. Permission would be no longer needed to pay hard currency for imports with a delivery period of more than six months.

(3) Russia has received a loan of 10 billion dollar from the International Monetary Fund. The Indian goods are a long accepted factor in the Russian market and if trading conditions are made easy and mutually satisfactory, they will have good prospects in Russia. Among the new products which can be introduced in the Russian market are pharmaceutical goods. The Indian Ayurvedic medicines too hold good prospects in the Russian market.

Among the imports, there are good chances of importing many minerals from Russia. Russia is endowed with vast resources of metals like nickle, zinc and scrap in addition to rough diamonds. All these products could be imported at a lower price than from other sources.

In addition, India has ample opportunities to collaborate in many joint ventures in Russia. The areas include petrochemicals. The Russians have invited the Indian expertise in telecommunications and development of port facilities in the Black Sea region. Departmental stores, fast food chains and hotel industry offer investment possibilities in Russia. The Indian joint ventures in Russia can also help us in penetrating the European Community market.

Many Indian firms are already going to Russia in a big way. Lakme has several distribution outlets there. Hindustan Lever and Ganpati Exports have increased their exports substantially. The Alpha Groups, Procter and Gamble and BPL are a few of the firms that are bidding for a tie up with the Russian trade organisations to set up manufacturing units.[1]

Problems and Suggestions

The most important problem faced in Russia is that most of the Russians are broke. The Indian exporters find that the demand for their goods gets restricted for lack of purchasing power of the Russians and the scarcity of hard currency in Russia. Again, the Russian market is now open and the trading is in free currency. It means the Indian exporters will have to compete with other suppliers to Russia, specially from South Korea and China. The Indian exporters will have to improve the quality of their products also to generate demand there.

Another problem faced by the Indian exporters is the increasing mafia gangs there. Their presence is felt right from the point of entry (ports) to the point of trade. Groups of mafias have taken the control of the financial institutions in Russia as well. If 'speedy money' (bribes) is not paid, the entire consignments get stuck enroute to the trading points for months.

The Russian consumer market is among the largest in the world. There is a similarity in the Indian and the Russian markets. The emphasis is on basic needs instead of the glamour and sophisticated packaging. The Indian exporters should never compromise on promised quality, for they face stiff competition there. Prices have to be competitive enough as the Russians are hard bargainers. There is a long and hard struggle to negotiate a contract. The Russians have an excellent market intelligence network. They enjoy bargaining and so this aspect has to be borne in mind for the price fixation mechanism. However, due to overall shortages in Russia, this factor may not be that important for the present. But it can be ignored only at the cost of exporters in the long run. There should also be a concerted attempt to build up brand images for the Indian goods. A friendly ambience towards India can be exploited for the Indian exports but without relaxing on quality.

The PHD Chamber of Commerce and Industry has cited non-availability of warehouses in Russia as a factor which hampers India from taking advantage of the fast emerging opportunities for consumer products. The Chamber has suggested that warehousing should be declared as an export activity. Loans may be made available for the creation of warehousing facilities on terms and conditions of export credit. This will enable exporters to provide off-the-shelf delivery.

It must, however, be admitted that despite all efforts, the value and volume of the Indo-Russian trade may not reach the pre-1990 levels.

Reference

1. *The Economic Times*, January 12, 1995, p. 9.

15

India-China Trade: Beginning of A New Chapter

R.L. VARSHNEY

Sweeping reforms introduced in China in 1978-79, included, among others, relaxation of planning controls, increased reliance on market forces in setting price mechanism and output, decentralization of decision-making, encouragement to the private sector and the opening up of the economy to private foreign investors. Since the economic reforms and opening up, China's economy has developed very quickly. The average annual growth rate of GDP up to 1990 was about 8.9 per cent, which rose to 13.6 per cent, 13.4 per cent and 11.8 per cent respectively in 1992, 1993 and 1994.

Mutual Trading Relationship

The policy changes had its effect on China's foreign trade. Exports went up to 150 billion dollars in 1995 and imports went up to 132 billion dollars, leading to a trade surplus of about 17 billion dollars. However, export growth is likely to slip in 1996 because government cut export tax rebates twice in 1995. On the other hand, imports are likely to jump up by 25 per cent in 1996 as a result of tariff cuts on 4,000 products. The trade surplus is likely to dwindle to around 6 billion dollars.

Active steps have been taken by both the Indian and the Chinese governments to encourage mutual trading relationship. They have been signing annual trade protocols. The 1994-95 protocol identified the items of import by the respective countries, though it was stated that the trade exchanges would not remain confined to these items alone. However, no value or quantity was fixed for the items to be imported or exported by the two countries.

The table below gives an indication of India's trade with China.

India's Trade with China

(Rs. crores)

Year	*Exports*	*Percentage to total Exports*	*Imports*	*Percentage to total Imports*
1990-91	33	0.1	64	0.1
1991-92	119	0.3	51	0.1
1992-93	409	0.8	374	0.6
1993-94	875	1.3	947	1.3
1994-95	800	1.0	2,368	2.7

The above table shows that there has been a rapid rise in bilateral trade between the two countries. What is more significant is that China's share both in India's exports and imports is more than India's share in world imports and exports. India has now become China's largest trading partner in South Asia.

The major products India export to China are: Iron ore, other ores and minerals, marine products, primary and semi-finished iron and steel, iron and steel bars and rods and pharmaceutical products. Other items listed for import by China are tobacco, tea, coffee, cotton, rice, spices, bulk drugs, agro-chemicals, power generation and signalling equipments and spare parts for railway rolling stock, oil field equipment, electronic components and computer software, telecommunication equipment, open cast coal mining equipment, commercial vehicles, two-wheelers, auto components and other engineering products.

The major products of the Indian import from China are: Bulk drugs and chemicals, raw silk, coal coke and briquettes, medicinal and pharmaceutical products, textile yarn, fabrics and fabric articles, pulses, machinery other than electrical, inorganic chemicals, pulp and waste paper and pearls, precious and semi-precious stones. Other items listed for import are spices, resin, light industrial products, petroleum products, tyres and tubes, fresh water cultivated pearls, power station equipment, oil drilling equipment, long wall mining equipment, trolley buses, pharmaceutical products and newsprint.

Another significant development has been the setting up of the first China-India joint venture in India by Mideast Steel Company in Orissa in 1995. This steel plant, established with the help of Chinese technology, would have one million tonnes steel production capacity. Four more medium-sized steel plants, being set up in India with Chinese technology, are at various stages of implementation.

Prospects of Increasing Bilateral Trade

China has in recent years witnessed an increase in its GDP. It has naturally led to an increase in per capita incomes. This will obviously give rise to the demand for consumer goods. Even otherwise China, because of its high population, provides a large market for consumer goods. The planned reduction in tariffs will also lead to a surge in Chinese imports.

The US-based Centre for the Global Trade Development, in a report, pointed out that "India and China had a bilateral trade potential of many billions of dollars and this potential has remained untapped because companies and enterprises in the two countries had traditionally ignored each other's markets".[1] The report had also predicted that the Chinese and the Indian entrepreneurs would form a large number of joint ventures and exchange technologies to boost trade. In fact, under the trade protocol with China, signed in January 1993, India and China agreed on the need to identify specific technologies for transfer between the two countries as well as jointly to third countries. The two sides agreed to further strengthen their bilateral trade relations through joint market surveys, identification of goods and commodities which could help to increase the trade volumes, to undertake trade promotion measures such as organising of exhibitions and trade fairs in each other's country, the exchange of trade delegations and the establishment of representative offices in both the countries. They also agreed to undertake consultancy services.

A good potential exists for joint ventures between the two countries in machinery and construction, engineering consultancy, power generation equipment, railways, iron and steel processing and computer software.

Suggestions

1. Countertrade and buy-back arrangements: China is actively encouraging countertrade its Ministry of Foreign Economic Relations and Trade has set up its own countertrade division. It is interested in joint ventures and buy-back arrangements. India should explore the possibilities of importing goods from China under countertrade arrangements either for her own use or for sale in third countries.

2. Arrangement should be made for opening more points for border trade in addition to Pithoragarh centre in U.P. The Chinese authorities have also pleaded for a more favourable treatment for border trade.

If concerted efforts are made, increase in trade volumes can be generated for the mutual benefit of the two countries.

Reference

1. *The Hindu*, June 16, 1994, p. 1.

16

Economic Development in China: Some Lessons for India

Guljit K. Arora

China and India are the most ancient and sophisticated Asian civilisations of the world today. For thousands of years they had comprehensive economic systems, government set up and administrative patterns.[1] They not only made a number of technological inventions but also played a predominant role in international trade.[2] Though they witnessed frequent wars, famines, destructions, inept kingdoms, and corrupt bureaucracies, they were not underdeveloped in the modern sense, of the word.

Identical Problems

It is also generally agreed that both China and India had more or less the same per capita income, life expectancy, poverty, mortality rates and industrial development in the 1940s.[3] Both these countries had a slow growth of population and income, and poor capital and industrial base. China and India were not only at a similar stage of development in the early 1950s but also adopted somewhat similar development strategies.[4] Both the countries articulated a development strategy that had in early years a considerable Soviet influence.[5] In addition to instituting the Soviet style of inward oriented governmental planning, both the countries pursued self-reliance, import substitution and industrialization by relying on strong controls on investment through investment licensing, and foreign trade through import quotas.

Though China and India, had similar problems and adopted a common development strategy (at least to start with), both have had altogether different historical roots and socio-economic-politico characteristics. China, a state of a amazing continuity, began its existence on the banks of the Yellow river around 221 BC whereas India got unified initially in the third century BC under the Mauryan Empire, though it remained under the domination of different foreign rulers—Aryans, Mughals and Europeans.[6] Since 1949, China had a communist dictatorship and a command economy whereas India had representative democracy with market oriented mixed economy since 1947. China had to be nearly entirely rebuilt in 1949 because the Chinese people had a long history of foreign interferences, civil wars, warloads and devastating famines unlike India where partition pains were really serious but not greatly prolonged.

After the Communist regime had been established in 1949, China experienced acute ideological pressures during the Great Leap Forward (1958-60) and the country was pushed to the verge of collapse and suffered a worst famine, leading to the death of 20-30 million people.[7] During the period of Cultural Revolution (1966-71), China suffered further from anarchy and its education system deteriorated. The dramatic events of Tien An Man Square further jeopardised the well-being of the nation.

India, on the contrary, had shown a relative stability though it also had to pass through very tough and difficult times. Events like the excesses of emergency resulted; and peoples' rise against the government which led to its defeat in the poll battle, assassination of Prime Minister and a former Premier followed by the communal riots, and political instability thereafter, the reservation imbroglio and widespread demonstrations and immolation attempts all over the country by the students and so on were really painful. It is also important to note that India also exhibits a vast degree of diversity with respect to languages, religions, castes, political entities and ethnicity. In China, for instance, Hans are a majority community, whereas national minorities consisting of nearly 56 ethnic groups—Tibetan, Kazaks, Mongols, Muslims to name a few—account for only 6 per cent of the total population and generally live in marginal and sparsely populated regions.[8] In contrast, India has more than 2000 ethnic groups, castes, tribals and the minorities constitute more than one-fifth of its total population.[9]

By now these two heavyweight Asian countries have gathered four and a half decades of growth and development experience and have a number of achievements to their credit. It would, therefore, be interesting and useful to make a comparative study, particularly of the human resources, in the socio-economic development and bring out the role of different forces to explain this interlinkage.

The Growth and Structure of National Income

Though the thinking on how development should be defined has undergone a sea change during the past forty years, still per capita income continues to be one of the most important and acceptable quantitative measure of growth and development. Development measured through the growth of the per capita income though cannot be considered as an adequate index of national welfare of a country, still the analysis of national income, its growth and sectoral composition along with the occupational structure can capture some of the basic characteristics of the development process of a country.

While both China and India are categorised as low-income economies in World Development Report, China is ahead of India both in terms of per capita income level and its growth. China's average annual growth rate of per capita GNP was 8.2 per cent as against 3.(per cent for India during 1980-93. These rates were exactly half in both the countries during the period between 1965-80 (Table 1).

China has not only shown a sustained rise in national output, bu also a high rate of structural transformation of its economy. Thougl agriculture is a critical sector in both the countries, both have shifte(away from agriculture. The share of agriculture in GDP in Chin: registered a decline of 79 per cent during 1970-93 whereas th(corresponding figure for India was just 45 per cent for the sam(

period. At present, the share of agriculture and industry in China is 19.5 per cent and 48 per cent respectively, whereas the percentages are 31 and 27 for India. China's sectoral distribution of income at present shows that the share of industry is followed by services and agriculture respectively. India, on the other hand, does not show the same pattern. The share of agriculture continues to be high and is higher as compared to industry's share. In fact, the share of services sector (which historically should rise once the share of industry has increased) is found larger than that of the agriculture as well as industry.

It is important to point out that in China the fall in the share of agriculture sector to GDP by 15 percentage points over the period of 23 years was matched increasingly by the share of industry (10 percentage points). In the case of India, on the other hand, the decline of 14 percentage points was taken over largely by the service sector (8 percentage points) and the industry (5 percentage points).

It is distressing to note that industrial sector in India instead of absorbing the labour force released by agriculture laid off its own share by one percentage point. As a result, the share of labour force in the service sector increased to 27 per cent in India during 1970-92. The excessive growth of service sector in comparison with industrial sector in India may generate either inflationary tendencies or encourage high imports with an adverse effect on the balance of trade.[10] This may even dampen the saving propensity since saving propensity falls as the share of the services goes up in GDP.[11]

The 'leading role' played by the industrial sector, particularly the non-state township and village industries, in transforming the Chinese economy is well known. One finds that a considerable percentage of labour force freed by the agriculture sector found occupation in the industry—a pattern of development predicted by Colin Clark.[12] In addition, the solid agriculture foundation created through well-implemented land reforms, comprehensive agricultural infrastructure built up by the communes and particularly employing the labour force in irrigation works, helped China in building up its impressive grain production sector and the redistribution of income. The rural industries consisting of enterprises run by local governments, firms, hotels and shops that are cooperatives and private establishments also played a very crucial role in checking the rural to urban migration. The strict controls on migration had a great impact. The process of rural transformation into urban and semi-urban areas was also greatly influenced by the participatory decentralisation. The decentralised rural development, i.e., local development by local enterprise and local effort, decentralisation of productive activities and the egalitarian social structure (recently changing) brought through asset and land redistribution, public distribution and consumption and welfare guarantees achieved through equitable distribution of public services and depressing the relative prices of basic food necessities all played a key role in China's economic transformation.[13] This really did not happen in India.

Role of Human Resources in Development

Development is expected to put the human beings at the centre of all concerns, be it economic growth, trade employment, political freedom or cultural values. This is because human beings are both the means as well as the end. How human resources are being managed in the process of economic development or what role have they been given can to a large extent indicate the pace or the character of economic development.

In the present context, human resource development both in China and India is adjudged with respect to the following three related and interdependent aspects. (Table 2)

Demographic Profile

Since population and its related characteristics can prove both stimuli and an obstacle to economic growth and development, the management of population and its growth assumes a very important role. The experience of China in controlling population is noteworthy and can offer much in designing the population policy. The annual rate of population growth is much lower in China (1.4 per cent) compared to India (2 per cent). It should be pointed out that though the birth and the death rates have declined in China and India, the birth rate as compared to the death rate is higher and any further decline in death rate would only add to the population problems of these countries. However, the problem is likely to be far more serious in the case of India as death-rate-birth-rate difference is higher.

The most important factors for the slow population growth in China appear to be the following:

(a) *Family planning education to women*: By extending education to women, China could increase the marriageable age of women and convince them to adopt methods to avoid early child birth. For instance, the percentage of married women of child bearing age using contraception is as high as 83 as compared to 43 in India. The use of contraceptive is probably the highest in China.

(b) *Health and nutrition standards*: By improving the health and nutrition levels of the people, particularly of women, China could increase the female life expectancy. It is much higher in China (71 years) as compared to India's (61 years). China could also reduce the maternal mortality rate tremendously by investing in the health of the people and improving their living standards. Consumption of daily per capita calorie is 14 per cent higher in China than in India. Also the proportion of household food consumption is in China is 17 per cent than in India. This indicates the importance of integrating the production and distribution of food.

(c) The implementation of family planning programmes, particularly in the rural areas, have reduced the infant mortality rates tremendously in China (30) in contrast to India (80). In China, 94 per cent of the child births are attended by trained health personnel as compared to India's 33 per cent. Thus, schemes such as rural cooperative health insurance, barefoot doctors, non-pecuniary incentives, mass motivation under collective organisations and community participation in preventive health programmes and the political commitment under the Communist leadership help to extend health services to rural areas along with reduction in the degree of human deprivation. The better health facilities and education have freed the women from prolonged period of child bearing.

(d) *Role of education*: Education is the principal institutional mechanism for developing human skills and knowledge. It improves people's ability to innovate, acquire and use information, as it deepens their understanding of themselves as consumers, producers, and citizens besides strengthening their ability to meet their wants and those of their families.

The education statistics show China ahead of India in general literacy level, though the all level enrolment (first, second and third level) are the same in both the countries. China, no doubt had to face several ups and downs in devising a system of education, but the most important aspect of China's education policy is female education, indicating that China had gone a long way in fulfilling its constitutional commitment. Female illiteracy in China is 38 per cent as compared to 66 per cent in India. The same story emerges in the case of female education enrolment both at primary and secondary school level. Better educated women benefit the society not only by improving the health and life expectancy of children and reducing the family size. It also helps in removing gender bias. Participation in the economic activities of the society is other vital aspect in this direction.

(e) *Labour supply and sectoral distribution*: Human resources development benefits the labour supply as it brings a change in the population size and its age structure. It is important to note that the availability of labour force is one thing and its absorption into useful activities is another. The unabsorbed labour force and its growth has got economic, social and political dimensions. Feeding the unemployed labour force not only exhausts the economic resources, it deprives the society of the material output it would have otherwise created. In addition, a continued unemployment problem; when once becomes chronic, can even pose a serious political problem. This explains the need for adopting the development model which can create job opportunities sufficient to employ both the existing as well as the future labour force. By raising the general employment opportunities, the labour productivity and wages, it leads to development which can reduce poverty and inequalities between men and women, ethnic groups and even the geographic regions.

In the context of China and India, three points are worth noting (Table 2) :

(a) Labour force in China constitute about 60 per cent whereas it is just 38 per cent in India. This suggests not only a relatively higher dependency burden in India but also the differences in the growth pattern of population and the interplay of social, economic and institutional forces influencing the fertility rates. One can also not underplay the role of government in mobilisation of people, particularly during the initial years. By doing so China could give employment to its entire workforce particularly at the time when the population was growing at a relatively higher pace. As a result, it could raise the average productivity of the entire labour force by fully realising the potential of its human force. This did not happen in India at all though such an attempt was made in the late 1960s and early 1970s.

(b) The female share in labour force and its participation rate are very high in China as compared to India. Females constitute about 45 per cent of the labour force whereas this share is just 24.5 per cent in India. Similarly, percentage of participation of female labour force is 80 per cent for China and 31 per cent for India. The differences are equally glaring in the case of employment. At present, in China the female share of labour force in employment is 43 per cent as against 25 per cent in India. It is a matter of great concern that female share of labour force in employment in India has come down from 30 per cent in 1970. China, on the other hand, shows a marginal increase. The differences between China and India are more glaring in the matter of female labour force participation raaei ntris 80 per cent for China and 31 per cent for India. Thus, it is clear that education of women along with better health facilities and family planning motivation emancipated the Chinese women to increase their share in labour force.

(c) China showed a distinct change in its sectoral distribution of labour force. Labour force employed in industry increased from 8 per cent in 1965 to 14 per cent in 1992. India, on the other hand, experienced a marginal decline in its labour force employed in industries—from 12 to 11 per cent. Though both China and India registered a decline in the share of labour force dependent on agriculture, China could absorb 75 per cent of the agriculture released labour force into industry, whereas India could not do that at all. The agriculture released labour force in India has gone to the non-agriculture-non-industrial sector i.e., service sector. This is a phenomenon which is generally found in industrial countries.

Synopsis

The statistical record of economic development measured through the growth and structure of national income both in China and India show that China in general has done much better than India. In the comparative perspective, some of the primary considerations on which China appears to have heavily relied during the course of development are worth noting for India to draw some lessons from.

First, high rate of structural transformation was obtained by shifting a considerable proportion of labour force from agriculture to industry by improving the agricultural productivity and building up rural industrial base through town and village industries and through high capital formation rates and infrastructural development. In this transformation, human capital development played a key role. It not only checked the population pressure on agriculture by reducing the population growth rate but also made available better quality labour force, particularly the women, to take up the work of mechanised agriculture, industrial development both in rural and urban areas and modernisation.

Secondly, higher rate of human capital development was achieved through providing education, including to the women, which helped improving the quality of labour force and promoting socio-political integration and modernisation; creating better health facilities, popularising the family planning programmes which in the long run helped in reducing the dependency ratio and mobilising people into useful and productive activities, particularly in building the agricultural infrastructure.

Thirdly, the interlinkages of the different socio-economic variables further show that the process of economic growth and development in China probably was not divorced from the social and political attributes and other non-economic factors. In post 1949 era, a majority of poor and non-elite groups, consisting of special interest groups, not only enjoyed political influence but also dominated the decision-making in many key areas. This paved the way for an institutional structure of cooperatives and communes with little disruption of the economy in rural areas. This in turn mobilized labour and resources which helped in transforming the countryside and creating a remarkable economic base for its national superstructure. India no doubt is better recognized as far as its political, legal and judicial institutions and their democratic strength are concerned, but India has always been slow in adapting to changes unlike China which has been quick in learning from its past mistakes and adopting changes required to meet the future needs. There is no doubt that the democratic institutions—the press, the opposition parties—provide checks and balances by compelling the government in power to modify the ongoing plans to formulate new people-oriented policies and take preventive measures whenever required, but the role played by disciplined leadership possessing an ideology capable of mobilizing people, workers, peasants and intellectuals in the nation's restructuring and economic modernisation cannot be ignored.

Table 1

Per Capita Income and Growth in China and India

National income and structural change	*China*	*India*
Income (1993), GNP per capita, dollars	490	300
Income growth (1980-93) avg annual % of GNP per capita	8.2	3.0
Income growth (1965-80) avg annual % of GNP per capita	4.1	1.5
Agricultural growth rate (1980-93), avg annual %	5.3	3.0
Agricultural growth rate (1970-80), avg annual %	2.6	1.8
Industrial growth rate (1980-93), avg annual %	11.5	6.2
Industrial growth rate (1970-80), avg annual %	8.9	4.5
Services growth rate (1980-93), avg annual %	11.1	6.4
Services growth rate (1970-80), avg annual %	5.3	4.6
Share of agriculture in GDP, % (1993)	19	31
Share of agriculture in GDP, % (1970)	34	45
Share of industry in GDP, % (1993)	48	27
Share of industry in GDP, % (1970)	38	22
Share of services in GDP, % (1993)	33	41
Share of services in GDP, % (1970)	28	33

Source: World Development Report 1995 and World Human Development Report 1995.

Table 2

Economic Progress in China and India

Human Resource Development Indicators	*China*	*India*
Demographic Profile		
Population (mid 1993), millions	1178.4	898.2
Pop. growth (1980-93), average annual % growth	1.4	2.0
Crude birth rate per 1000 pop. (1993)	19	29
Crude death rate per 1000 pop. (1993)	8	10
Births (%) to women aged under 20	4	11
Married woman of child bearing age using contraception	83	43
Infant mort rate (1993) per 1000 live birth	30	80
Life expectancy at birth years (1993)	69	61
Female life expectancy at birth years (1993)	71	61
Births attended by trained health personnel, % (1983-93)	94	33
Education		
Adult literacy % (1992)	79.3	49.9
Female literacy % (1992)	62	34
Enrolment ratio for all levels, %, age 6-23 years (1992)	55	55
Female enrolment ratio for all levels, %, age 6-23 years (1992)	52	46
Total primary edu. enrolment % (1992)	121	102
Female primary edu. enrolment % (1992)	116	90
Labour supply		
Labour force growth rate (1980-93), avg. annual, %	2.0	1.9
Female labour force share in total labour force, % (1994)	43	24
Female share of labour force in employment % (1993)	43	25
Male labour force participation rate % (1995)	96	90
Female labour force participation rate % (1995)	80	31

REFERENCES

1. Etienne, Gilbert et al (1992): *Asian Crucible*, Sage Publications, New Delhi.
2. For instance, cotton textiles, silk, iron and steel were invented both in China and India; zero in India and; gunpowder, printing press, the compass etc. in China.
3. Etienne, Gilbert et al (1992), *op. cit.*
4. Bhalla, A.S. (1992): *Uneven Development in the Third World — A Study of China and India*, Macmillan, London.
5. Kumar, D., quoted in Bhalla, A.S. (1992), *op. cit.*
6. Srinivasan, T.N. (1994): *Agriculture and Trade in China and India — Policies and Performance since 1950*, San Francisco, California.

7. Srinivasan, T.N. (1994): *Agriculture and Trade in China and India — Policies and Performance since 1950*, San Francisco, California.
8. Hook, Brian (1991): *The Cambridge Encyclopedia of China*, Cambridge University Press, pp. 52-65.
9. Mahadevan, Kuttan, Chi-Hsien Tuan et al (1994): *Society and Development in China and India*, B.R. Publising Company, Delhi.
10. Bhattacharya, B. and A. Mitra (1990): "Excess Growth of the Tertiary Sector in Indian Economy — Issues and Implications". *Eco. Pol. Weekly*, Nov. 3.
11. Gupta, S.P. (1989): *Planning and Development in India — A Critique*, Allied Publishers, New Delhi.
12. The details of his arguments have been discussed in another paper of the author. For details, see, G.K. Arora (1996): "Economic Development in China and India — Strategic Analysis", *Institute of Defence Studies and Analysis*, Feb. (XVIII, 1), pp. 1545-76.
13. Some of these are briefly discussed by Ghosh, Arun (1995): "Development Paradigms: China and India since 1949", *Eco. Pol. Weekly*, Feb. 18-25, pp. 355-60.

Index